OUTBREAKS

OUTBREAKS

The Sociology of Collective Behavior

Jerry D. Rose

94-1257

THE FREE PRESS
A Division of Macmillan Publishing Co., Inc.
NEW YORK

Collier Macmillan Publishers
LONDON

The Free Press
A Division of Macmillan Publishing Co., Inc.
866 Third Avenue, New York, N.Y. 10022

Collier Macmillan Canada, Ltd.

Library of Congress Catalog Card Number: 81–67439

Printed in the United States of America

printing number

1 2 3 4 5 6 7 8 9 10

Library of Congress Cataloging in Publication Data
Rose, Jerry D.
    Outbreaks, the sociology of collective behavior.

    Bibliography: p.
    Includes index.
    1. Collective behavior.   I. Title.
HM251.R775   302   81–67439
ISBN 0-02-926790-0   AACR2

Contents

Preface

A funny thing happened to collective behavior on the way to the 1980s. As "protest" became a household word, "disaster" a spectator sport, and "charisma" a perfume, the field that should be studying these matters, collective behavior, went into a deep sleep. College students flocked into such sociology courses as those dealing with the family, deviant behavior, ethnic groups, and social problems. Many of the colleges they attended did not even offer them courses in collective behavior.

One could speculate endlessly on the mysterious fate of a field studying matters extremely "relevant" to everyday life at just the time that college students and professional scholars were demanding such relevance for their activity. What has kept the field of collective behavior in its long period of slumber?

A possible answer to this question is that, apart from their "sex appeal," the other more popular fields of sociology have fairly well-defined paradigms that establish the basic research questions in those fields. It is easy for professors to be enthusiastic about their labors within a well-defined field, and that enthusiasm is likely to be contagious with students. Without such defining paradigms, each scholar is a self-made pioneer, and it is the rare sociologist indeed who wants to make a whole career (or even endure a whole college course) of intellectual pioneering without ever settling down into an established community of problems being studied by a community of scholars.

Another possible reason for the reluctance of sociologists to conduct research and offer courses in this field is perhaps the sense that collective behavior has studied "weird" phenomena that are somehow marginal to the main body of human social phenomena. While weirdness has recently been accepted as an avocational life style, we seem to retain enough of the Protestant ethic in our work attitudes that we want our work and ourselves as workers to be taken *seriously*. Put otherwise, we want to be where the "action" is, and sociology's action has seemed to be elsewhere than in the study of collective behavior.

The aim of this book is to treat collective behavior seriously and to put forth a paradigm that could put the field more firmly within the orbit of the central concerns of the field of sociology. The *material* for such a field of study is there, in the fruitful labors not only of sociologists but of anthropologists, psychologists, political scientists, geographers, and historians. This book ranges widely (if it doesn't always dig too deeply) into such materials. It does so from a perspective defined in the introductory chapter.

The acknowledgments that are typical at this point of a book may be fulfilled by an omnibus acknowledgment of the many, many workers who have prepared the ground in which this work is cultivated. May this book be worthy in some degree as a fruit of that cultivating labor!

Chapter 1

Introduction

COLLECTIVE BEHAVIOR AND HUMAN BEHAVIOR

A MAJOR EMPHASIS in the sociological study of human behavior is the *control* of that behavior by various social forces or influences. Human beings act as members or representatives of groups; we act to fulfill the social rules governing the behavior of people in our social statuses; we give pledges of allegiance or participate in other rituals of group solidarity. Sometimes, however, human beings act in ways that seem, in some degree, to escape the control of these social influences. To the horror of almost everybody, killers of black children and men stalked the streets of Atlanta, New York, and Buffalo in 1980. To the shame of the city of Chicago, its police force lost its professional cool in 1968 and made random attacks on people in the vicinity of the Democratic National Convention.

There is a popular tendency to dismiss such behavioral episodes by defining their perpetrators as something less than human. The behavior of the Reverend Jim Jones in leading nearly a thousand followers to suicide at Jonestown or of Adolph Hitler in leading the Holocaust extermination of millions of Jews and others—such behaviors are seen as the work of radicals, nuts, fanatics, degenerates, and paranoiacs. But sociology defines human behavior as the behavior of people and, in explaining that behavior, cannot indulge in such

1

simplification-by-exclusion. However much, as a human being with values acquired from everyday social living, the sociologist might condemn or applaud certain behaviors, he or she, as a sociologist, must practice Max Weber's famous *"value-neutrality:"* the disengagement of one's own likes and dislikes in favor of an *understanding* of such behavior.[1]

Value neutrality has not been an easy attitude to come by in the sociological study of collective behavior, and it remains a source of difficulty to today's students, including this author. In an early textbook on the subject, Lang and Lang define two varieties of attitudes toward collective behavior, which they refer to as the "progressive" and the "pathological" views.[2] In the progressive view, such collective behavioral episodes as riots, demonstrations, and religious revivals are means of improving society, providing needed goads to overcome the usual inertia of established institutions in dealing with human problems. In this vein, a contemporary social scientist, Theodore Lowi, has argued that American society, with its much-celebrated "checks and balances" political system, is beautifully designed to check *any* needed social reform, and that reforms come only when the system is pushed by the pressure of social movements.[3] Thus it has often been said that the American civil rights legislation of the 1960s occurred only because legislators were pushed by the protest demonstrations by blacks and their sympathizers in the early 1960s.[4]

The pathological view of collective behavior places a very different value judgment on this behavior. With eighteenth-and nineteenth-century mass revolutions very much in mind, such thinkers as Gustav LeBon viewed "the crowd" as something of a reversion to the bestial tendency in human nature.[5] The civilization of human behavior is swept away in the contagious excitement of behavior in crowds. Civilized members of society who would never engage in antisocial acts as individuals engage in just such acts under the cloak of anonymity provided by the crowd. Many recent critics of tendencies in the sociological study of collective behavior complain of the long shadow of LeBon that continues to fall over contemporary students of the field.[6]

The viewpoint developed in this book sees collective behavior as inherently neither "progressive" nor "pathological" in character. Rather, there is an attempt to asses the impact of various kinds of collective behavior. Whether a series of prison riots, for example, *does* have a "progressive" influence in the direction of prison reform is one possibility to be explored. But consideration must also be given to at least two other possibilities. There may be a "backlash" effect, in which an episode of collective behavior is counterproductive as regards the long-term interest of the participants. Rather than responding by correcting the grievances put forth during demonstrations, officials might simply increase their control of prisoners to make such demonstrations more difficult in the future. Another essentially conservative outcome may be that occasional outbreaks of "disorderly" behavior have a cathartic effect, providing a relatively harmless outlet for aggressions that might otherwise be directed against the established social order.

The pathological view of collective behavior, without being rejected out of hand, will be given very little attention in this book. It is questionable whether the sociologist gains much insight into a form of behavior by determining whether that behavior is more "primitive" or "civilized" in character. We are interested here in collective behavioral episodes as social facts, and we will try to heed Durkheim's insistence that "the determining cause of a social fact should be sought among the social facts preceding it and not among the states of the individual consciousness."[7] We are concerned, that is, with those social conditions that generate panics, riots, anti-Semitic pogroms, revivals, and so on and only in a secondary way with the states of consciousness of those who participate in such outbreaks (including their "good" or "bad" motives). We cannot, however, follow out the program of Durkheim's "sociologism" to its full extent, since we must understand something of the motivations involved—for example, in the decision of an individual to participate in a race riot or a feminist movement. While we must necessarily deal, then, in human motives, it is very doubtful whether applying a label of *pathological* or *normal* to such motives can much advance our understanding of this variety of human behavior.

EPISODES

After the preceding comment on the attitudes toward the subject matter that will prevail in this book, it is time to focus a bit more closely on the precise nature of this subject matter. What *is* it that we study under the heading of collective behavior? While it will require at least the reading of this entire book to answer this question, some preliminary characterization can be made by way of introduction.

We will consistently refer to collective behavior as occurring in *episodes*. The idea is to distinguish collective behavior from more routine or repetitively occurring behavior. Thus we could easily observe the difference in traffic pattern on a busy highway when traffic is "flowing" (or, on some roadways at rush hours, is predictably "crawling," as it does every workday at 7:00 A.M. and 5:00 P.M.); and the extraordinary pattern generated by a collision and a chain reaction of other collisions. The latter may constitute a kind of *disaster*, a collective behavioral form discussed in the next chapter. Likewise, it is one thing to observe the weekly ritual of a church minister inviting church attendants to come forth to make a religious commitment and quite another to see episodes in which thousands of people make a "decision for Christ" in a Billy Graham crusade or to read of multitudes of people falling into religious ecstasy during one of John Wesley's exercises in open-air preaching in seventeenth-century England.

One practical way of defining collective behavior is to suggest that it is the kind of behavior that generates *news*. Not only are collective behavior episodes largely the content of newspapers and radio and television newscasts; they are also the stuff as well of popular gossip and response in conversation to the question "what's new?" Critics of news media have decried the media's focus on the extraordinary episodes in human behavior; we read of a man who murders wife and children or rips off his employer but never of the man who kisses the dear ones goodbye each morning and goes off for a day of Bob Cratchit loyalty to his Scrooge employer. Occasional attempts to create "good news" paper with just such stories don't, of course, succeed. The public wants to hear about *unusual* events, and people will throw down a good-news paper as readily as they will shun a Pollyanna conversationalist who never seems to have any "juicy" news about unusual events.

This news value of collective behavior has two directions of special significance to the sociologist of collective behavior. In the first place, many "data" of collective behavior episodes, past and present, are recorded in the periodical archives; it is always possible, for example, to study contemporary news accounts of a given riot or disaster. The sociologist will have to recognize, of course, that such accounts are typically written under the pressure of press deadlines by reporters not trained in the methods of social scientific investigation and that such accounts must be evaluated for their sociological objectivity. Second, as we shall have many occasions to observe, the news (and informal news or rumor) reporting of events will often have an impact on the development of those events. Newspaper editors may 'sensationalize" or they may "play down" certain behaviors in their reportage, with results that make news coverage a vital part of the very episodes that sociologists are studying.

In evoking the image of the newspaper as a kind of chronicle of collective behavior, we may risk losing sight of an aspect of collective behavior that news analysis typically underemphasizes. There is a popular saying that there is nothing older than "yesterday's news," suggesting that the episodes of each "day" are more or less discontinuous with those of the day before. The sociologist, in contrast, is likely to view episodes in a bit longer time frame. While a newspaper details the events during a day of rioting (or at most recapitulates the events of several days), the sociologist tends to see a riot in the context of a "long hot summer" of similar riots. In even longer time frames a given summer of riots may be seen as part of an episode that includes several such summers; or the several riot summers may even be seen as part of a longer "episode" in which, for example, participants in a black protest movement turned from legal actions to nonviolent demonstrations to angry riots. To find such reportage in newspapers or television newscasts one would have to examine the relatively infrequent work of feature or special assignment reporters. A *New York Times* "special" on the civil rights movement on the nth anniversary of Martin Luther King's assassination would come closer than typical newspaper reportage to one kind of sociological interest in collective behavior episodes.

A final comment on collective behavior as episodic or discontinuous with routine social behavior: Without abandoning this characterization, we should note some of the ambiguity in the relationship between the episodic and the routine. Here we may refer to the perspective of sociology's master in pointing out ambiguities and ambivalences in human behavior, Georg Simmel. In his essay "The Adventurer," Simmel defines an adventure as an extraordinary episode in the individual's personal biography and then points out:

> An adventure is certainly a part of our existence, directly contiguous with other parts which precede and follow it; at the same time, however, in its deepest meaning, it occurs outside the usual continuity

of this life. Nevertheless, it is distinct from all that is accidental and alien, merely touching life's outer shell. While it falls outside the context of life, it falls, with this same movement, as it were, back into the that context again . . . it is a foreign body in our existence which is yet somehow connected with the center; the outside, if only by a long and unfamiliar detour, is formally an aspect of the inside.[8]

Simmel's image of adventure as simultaneously "inside" and "outside" normal human experience is paralleled by some typical questions about the behavior of people in episodic situations. Are a group of people participating in an outbreak of persecution of some "enemy of the people" (witches, communists, etc.) being "themselves" or are they "besides themselves" for the duration of the outbreak? The answer seems to be the same as Simmel's view of adventure: they are *both* themselves and not-themselves during these episodes. It is not necessary to resort to the mysticism of Freudian or LeBonian "group mind" to recognize that there are altered states of consciousness for the duration of an outbreak. For all the ways, for example, in which New York City residents were not themselves during a 24-hour blackout in 1977, both these people and outside observers were able to relate behavior during a "night of the animals" to some all-too-prevalent conditions of everyday life in the city.[9] Recognition of such connections between the episodic and the routine aspects of human behavior is one way of defining the sociological approach to the study of collective behavior. The definition of several such connections is our next task.

DIMENSIONS OF SOCIOLOGICAL ANALYSIS OF COLLECTIVE BEHAVIOR

We have referred very generally to the concern in this book with connections between the episodes that constitute collective behavior and the more routine behaviors occurring in established social orders. It is time to spell out the kinds of connections with which we are here concerned.

BACKGROUND

We begin with the mundane observation that some social orders—countries, cities, and so on—seem to be especially prone to generate episodes of collective behavior. Student protest occurred frequently in the 1960s but not in the 1970s; social disorganization and destruction accompanying hurricanes are usually much greater in Latin America than in the United States; and an endless number of comparisons can be made of collective behavior in different social orders or in the same social orders at different times. Why the observed differences? We come immediately to confront the difficult problem of *causation* of human social behavior. A historical explanation of, for example, student protest in the 1960s would emphasize the unique set of social forces that, in combination, produced that episode. The sociological imagination demands a different sort of explanation. The assumption here, for better or worse, is that there are general *types* of social conditions that lead to a high or low *probability* that a given type of social behavior will occur.[10] The behavior being explained may be the frequency of such individual behaviors as crime, suicide, marital infidelity, or outstanding occupational accomplishment. The behavior may also be collective episodes of any of the types discussed in this book. Is it true, for example, that the very general kind of social change called *industrialization* has spawned a kind of alienation from its technological base that is referred to as a countercultural movement? Is it the case that radical protest movements are generated by a social condition of "mass society" in which people are isolated from significant interpersonal relations? We shall be examining such questions for each of the several types of collective behavior to be analyzed in this book.

PARTICIPATION

An outbreak of collective behavior, at the height of its intensity, may give one the impression that everyone is being swept into the particular episode. In a riot it may seem that "everybody" is doing it; it may have been felt at one time that all American blacks were caught up in the civil rights movement. In fact such impressions are more or less deceptive. Sociologists require accurate quantitative estimates of the proportion of a given population that does, in fact, participate in a collective behavior episode. How many frontier Americans participated in the Great Awakening of religious consciousness in the nineteenth century? How many people in fact engage in panic during disasters or in looting during riots? What proportion of American Indians have participated in the Red Power movement? Of even greater importance to the sociologist, perhaps, is the question of what *kinds* of people participate most frequently in a collective behavioral episode. One feature of a sociological perspective on the analysis of human behavior is the tendency to see different people as occupying different *statuses*: men and women, young and old, rich and poor, and so forth. Behavioral differences are attributable to such differences in status positions for at least two reasons. First, there may be norms or standards of correct behavior that define a kind of activity as appropriate for people in one category but not in another: young and old people, for example, are expected to behave differently. Young men may be expected to be physically aggressive, while the same behavior by a mature woman would be condemned. The social world is full of such "double standards" of approved behavior for different kinds of people. If young people participate more frequently than their elders in protests against the established order, this may reflect the greater social tolerance for rebellious behavior in the young.

A second reason that collective—or any other—behavioral tendencies may vary between categories of people can be explained by analogy to a familiar explanation of differential rates of *deviant* behavior. Merton's famous essay on "social structure and anomie" describes a general social condition that features the development in people of virtually unlimited aspirations for personal success.[11] The "success theme" that pervades American and other societies exerts considerable pressure to succeed at almost any cost, including the use of deviant or cheating tactics. While *all* people in an anomic society are subject to such pressure, there is *greater* pressure on those people who have restricted opportunity to succeed legitimately (e.g., lower-class or black Americans). These people therefore tend to resort more frequently to illegitimate or criminal means of obtaining success. The validity of Merton's explanation—a matter of much controversy—is a question for the sociology of deviant behavior. The "pathological" view that pervades so much of the study of deviant behavior does not, as noted above, seem to have much relevance to the study of collective behavior. Merton's explanation is presented here as paradigm for sociological explanations of different rates of participation in collective behavioral episodes by different kinds of people. If black Americans were heavily overrepresented in the urban street riots of the 1960s, does this reflect a greater "pressure" toward collective violence arising from their relatively deprived social situation? If small-business owners are heavy participants in anti-communist outbreaks, does this reflect the insecurity of the independent entrepreneur in a social world increasingly dominated by giant corporations? With each type of collective behavior we examine, we try to determine the most factually accurate description of the kinds of people most likely to be involved in that kind of episode and to account for this behavior in terms of the social pressures or constraints operating on these kinds of people.

PROCESS

Much of sociological analysis of human behavior focuses on questions of *how* a given type of behavior originates, develops, and declines in frequency. The response of a community to a disaster episode may have a kind of "natural history" of predictable stages, as may a prison riot or a campaign to suppress the sale of pornographic literature.

Descriptions of collective behavior outbreaks as social processes are not necessarily tied to any assumption that every episode of a certain kind must follow a preordained script for that kind of action. We may observe, for example, that very repressive police action in the early stages of a riot may tend to escalate the violence engaged in by a mob. This is a process kind of generalization, telling us what phases of action tend to follow what other phases. Such generalization does not, of course, support any assumption that every riot episode must play out some cosmic drama of force and counterforce between rioters and police. Other kinds of police action are not only possible but observable. In the omniscient mind sometimes attributed to God, it may indeed be true that the world is a stage on which we play out our scripted parts and that there are no possibilities of action except the actions that we see manifested: police around the Democratic Convention in 1968 or guardsmen at Kent State in 1970 could do no other than their acts of violence against crowds. To our mortal minds, however, it will probably always appear that there are turning points at which processes may move in one direction or another. For the sociologist of collective behavior, this means that we shall probably never be able to speak with confidence of *the* riot process, *the* disaster process, or *the* process by which a successful protest is accomplished. Rather, we hope to observe such a variety of episodes that we can say with *some* confidence that a certain step, if taken, is likely to increase the probability of a next step in one of the several process patterns that we have observed. As we take our tiny human steps toward that divine omniscience, we may move toward a theory of *the* collective behavioral process (a faltering step is attempted in the last chapter of this book) and ultimately toward a more general theory of *the* social process among human beings.

CONSEQUENCES

People who participate in a collective behavior outbreak—or even those living in communities where *others* are so participating—are likely to say that their lives were "never the same" after this episode. The validity of such perceptions of major social change is a matter of great sociological concern. Actually, we have some models of the way social systems function that would tend to minimize the long-term consequences of such episodes. In this view, there may be a great deal of turmoil and apparent movement while an episode is in full swing. But once the collective excitement dies down, the episode turns out to be, in long-term historical perspective, simply an interval of "sound and fury, signifying nothing." In the fervor of a French Revolution, it may well have seemed that a permanent era of liberty, equality, and fraternity had dawned upon the earth. With the backlash of counterrevolution and with the simple dying away of revolutionary zeal, however, the "normal" human quota of coercion, inequality, and rampant bickering between people may return to support the skeptic's doubts about "permanent" revolutions.

The long-term effect—or lack of effect—of collective behavior episodes is not, in this author's opinion, a matter to be postulated in advance of our study of collective behavior. It is, as sociologists like to say, "an empirical question." We shall pose as questions of fact, with each of the types of collective behavior we examine, whether and how a given kind of outbreak affects the quality of social life that follows that kind of episode. In the final chapter we shall again try to pull together any threads that are spun in these separate investigations and shall try to have something intelligible to say about a general theory of the relationship between collective behavior and social change.

FORMS OF COLLECTIVE BEHAVIOR

The delineation of forms or types of human phenomena is one of the most crucial and also one of the most delicate and precarious tasks in the sociological enterprise. Virtually every sociologist, it seems, shares the profound insight of Max Weber on the nature of typologies in social science.[12] Any types we use are in the nature of "ideal types," exaggerations of reality that are used for specific intellectual purposes. Recognizing social "reality" as an infinitely complex matter, to classify that reality into a finite number of types is to do violence to the radical individuality of each unit of sociological analysis: each person, each group, in our case, each episode. If we are looking, then, for *the* set of types that corresponds to the delineations that exist in reality, we shall look forever in vain.

How, then, shall we judge whether we are working with an appropriate set of categories? Weber's answer is that we always approach our subject matter with a certain "interest" that will lead us to pay attention to certain similarities and differences among individuals and to ignore other ways of classifying because they are not currently of "interest" to us.[13]

At Weber's prompting, then, let us ask what it is about collective behavior that has interested sociologists. A complete and candid answer to this question would have to recognize the diversity of interests that have existed or do currently exist. To reduce this diversity of interests to contrasting *types* of interest is to run the risk of the kind of violence against diversity just mentioned. But since fools rush in where book introductions are concerned, a very simplistic typology of interests may help to locate this book and its classifications in relation to other treatises in collective behavior. The argument will be that sociology has undergone an evolution of viewpoint and interest that is reflected in an "older" as opposed to a "newer" approach to the study of collective behavior.

The founder of collective behavior as a special field of sociological study was Robert E. Park, a sociologist at the University of Chicago in the early decades of this century. When the University of Chicago Press in 1967 reprinted a collection of Park's writing, it chose a title that expressed to perfection Park's "interest" in the subject: "On Social Control and Collective Behavior."[14] As Ralph Turner says in an introduction to that volume, the master question in Park's sociology is "how does a mere collection of individuals succeed in acting in a corporate and consistent way?"[15] This very question—the problem of social control of individual behavior—is reflected in innumerable writings of American sociologists early in this century: for example in *Social Control,* by E. A. Ross, and *Human Nature and the Social Order*, by Charles H. Cooley.[16] Collective behavior is precisely that human behavior which is *problematic* for social order because it represents action by "mere" collections of individuals rather than by well-established social groups.[17]

When sociologists with such interests define the *forms* of collective behavior, the interest in social control leads to a focus on distinguishing the greater or lesser degree of social organization in different collectivities. One of the most notable of Park's followers, Herbert Blumer, distinguishes between "elementary" and "organized" forms of collective behavior.[18] The elementary forms include such phenomena as "a highly excited mob, a business panic, a state of war hysteria, or any conditions of spontaneously generated social unrest."[19] Further subclassification of the elementary forms as crowds, masses, and publics is determined by the specific mechanisms of "spontaneous generation" of unrest. People in a *crowd* stimulate one another (in what Blumer calls "circular reaction") to behave in a state of heightened emotion (fear, anger, sorrow, amusement, etc.). A *mass* is a number of people who are simultaneously influenced by such media of influence as newspapers or television broadcasts. A *public* involves a number of people interested in some area of social life who form different opinions through complex processes of public opinion formation. By contrast with these elementary forms, "organized" collective behavior is represented by what are today called *social movements:* deliberately organized attempts to bring about change in the established social order.

The underlying sociological "interest" that led to this set of collective behavior categories may lie in the preoccupation of early American sociology with the phenomenon of social disorganization. Troublesome manifestations of undesirable human behavioral tendencies—social problems—were seen as resulting from failures of social control. Durkheim had written of an anomic division of labor in conditions in which no social group was able to exercise moral authority to ensure that each person should do his or her special duty in relation to others.[20] The "Chicago school," with Park as its leader, maintained a similar interest in seeing the relationship between, poverty, racism, and so on and failures of social control resulting from massive processes of urbanization and rapid industrialization.[21] Charles H. Cooley, a University of Michigan sociologist, shared the spirit of the Chicago group in his statement that "the right is simply the rational, in the larger sense of the word," this larger sense involving the location of every thought "as part of that orderly whole which the mental instinct calls for'' and correspondingly identifies the ''wrong, the immoral'' as ''the mentally isolated, the inharmonious.''[22] When human behavior is fully rationalized or organized in terms of right principles, our social problems will tend to disappear. The ''mere collection of individuals'' will act in a ''corporate and consistent'' way. Since this rationalizing process works in different ways for crowds, masses, public, and movements, it is necessary to give separate consideration to these very forms of collective behavior.

Contemporary sociologists—and indeed contemporary people generally—are not likely to see collective action in a ''corporate and consistent'' way as a panacea for social ills. Perhaps we have had too much experience with huge corporate bodies that consistently and efficiently deprive human beings of human amenities to put this much faith in the process of social organization. We have seen modern military bureaucracies that are corporate and consistent to an extreme and completely demoralize the soldiers who work for them, not to mention the victims of their military operations. We have a welfare system that ensures that those unable to care for themselves will not have to rely on the none-too-tender (or dependable) mercies of private charity; and yet there is a feeling, at least among welfare recipients themselves, that the corporate and consistent provision of a social function lessens the human quality of the supposed beneficiaries. Modern people have come increasingly to the view that social organization is not per se a desirable *or* an undesirable human condition; it depends on the ends for which social organization is used, on the results in the betterment of the human condition. Contemporary sociologists seem to share in this process of demystification of social organization.

If there is such humanization of sociology's interest in behavior, it remains to define more clearly how there has been a shift in the understanding of ''human nature.'' Here we can take our cue from development in the academic discipline of psychology. In the older behaviorist psychology, human behavior is understood as a matter of internal responses to external stimuli. People, like rats and other animals, act in certain ways in certain situations because the response is intrinsically gratifying or because this response is associated with or conditioned by some other gratifying response. Training people to act in corporate and consistent ways is just like training a rat to push one lever rather than another. You give the rat a piece of cheese when he pushes the ''right'' lever or an electric shock when he pushes the wrong one. You give the school child a gold star for perfect attendance, a trip to the principal's office for talking back to a teacher.

A breakthrough in theorizing on human psychological nature was achieved when psychologists became interested in capacities of people and other animals as problem solvers. Looked at in a certain way, rats, just like people and other animals, are not simply bundles of response tendencies waiting to be set in motion in one direction or another by whatever variations in external stimuli happen to come along. A chimpanzee with a bunch of bananas placed outside its reach, and with such facilities available as boxes to stand on or sticks to put together, does not engage in "trial and error" behavior with random efforts to secure the bananas. It gives every indication of pausing to think about the situation and devising ways and means of achieving its purpose.[23]

The interest in human behavior as *purposive* in character is reflected in the "social action" theory associated with Talcott Parsons and a group of social scientific colleagues at Harvard.[24] One of these colleagues, Neil Smelser, made social action theory the basis of the major contemporary treatise on collective behavior.[25] Social action theory sees human behavior as purposive or goal-seeking but emphasizes that purposive behavior or social action occurs in a social situation that may facilitate or hinder the given purposes or goals. Both Parsons and Smelser tend to emphasize the normative or moral nature of the social situation. Smelser accordingly asserts that a "generalized belief" in the rightness of a course of action is at the basis of every episode of collective behavior. Just as Parsons has frequently been criticized for overemphasizing the role of *values* in human action,[26] Smelser has been brought to task for ignoring such phenomena as "issueless riots," collective violence with no very clear-cut beliefs or goals for which people are acting.[27]

The social action "package" does not, it may be argued, have to be bought wholesale to appreciate its importance in defining a direction of sociological interest in collective behavior. Without entering into the debate on the moral versus nonmoral character of collective behavior, it should be possible to develop a perspective and a typology of forms that connect collective behavior with a perspective on human behavior as purposive or goal-seeking.

The idea of social systems, as developed in Parsons' work, is probably our most extended and sophisticated viewpoint for an understanding of a *collective* level of purposive behavior. Clearly not only individuals but also groups of individuals have their purposes or goals, and it seems the unique contribution of Parsonian social systems analysis to provide a coherent picture of *how* social systems function (and how they fail to function) to achieve human purposes. Parsons calls the set of needs that must be fulfilled in all social systems the *functional imperatives*.

Since our types of collective behavior are derived from the functional imperatives, these will be described briefly here; they are outlined in the accompanying figure. To understand the several imperatives named in the figure, it is best to begin with the marginal designations: instrumental versus consummatory and external versus internal. These distinctions derived largely from Parsons' association with a Harvard psychologist, Robert F. Bales, who did extensive studies with small groups of paid research subjects brought together in the laboratory with instructions to complete a task (e.g., ''write a commercial for a new product'') as a group.[28] Observing the ''interaction process'' in these groups, Bales observed and recorded two kinds of ''phase movement'' or alternation in the content of interaction of subjects with one another. One ''movement'' was observed in a shift from *instrumental* concern with exploring the problem and generating resources for possible solution of the problem (''let's kick around some ideas about this'') to a *consummatory* concern with getting the job done (''Jesus Christ, the guy's going to be back in five minutes and we still haven't written the damned commercial''). And so it would seem to be with any social system: it must give attention both to generating resources needed by the system to accomplish its goals; and also some

FIGURE 1 Functional Imperatives and Types of Collective Behavior

	INSTRUMENTAL	CONSUMMATORY	
	Adaptation (Disasters)	Goal attainment (Protests)	EXTERNAL
	Pattern maintenance/ Tension management (Renewals)	Integration (Persecutions)	INTERNAL

ways of deciding how to apply these resources to specific problems or to allocate these resources among various goals.

The second "phase movement" observed in Bales' experimental groups was a shift from the *external* task imposed by the experimenter to an *internal* concern with the individuals who made up the group and with the quality of their relationships with one another. It was observed, for example, that before a group "got down to business," some time was spent in the internal process of getting acquainted and, after the task was accomplished, participants joked about the exercise, apologized for any offenses given while the task was being performed, and so on. Again would it appear that any social system must give attention both to the accomplishment of its goals and to the nature of its members and their relationships with one another.

By cross-cutting these two dimensions of social system problems, we arrive at the four functional imperatives as named in the figure. The functional imperatives are:

1. The *adaptive* (external-instrumental) imperative: The need of every social system to generate the resources needed to accomplish its various goals. For example, food, shelter, and clothing provisions are necessary for every social system (unless, like the non-self-sufficient community or a family "on welfare," these needs are provided by their members' inclusion in *other* social systems).

2. The *goal-attainment* (external-consummatory) imperative: The need of every social system for mechanisms for deciding how to allocate resources among various needs, goals, or demands of different members of that social system. A social club, for example, may have a constitution that requires members to vote on the allocation of funds for different activitities.

3. The *integration* (internal-consummatory) imperative: The need of every social system for mechanisms to ensure that members act in ways consistent with the established norms of that social system. Communities require, for example, police and courts to arrest and convict persons whose behavior is perceived as a threat to the lives or the well-being of other persons in the community.

4. The *pattern maintenance/tension management* imperative: This imperative calls attention to the need of every social system to develop the *human* resources required to accomplish its goals. This imperative works in two directions. In the pattern maintenance direction, a social system must ensure that it has members who are loyal, dedicated, and committed to their involvement in that system; apathy is a major prob-

lem for any system, and elaborate programs of instilling enthusiasm among members are a part of the routine of most systems. In the tension management direction, it is observed that members may become *too* emotionally involved in the social system and its tasks, and it may be necessary to maintain periodic releases of the tension if members are to continue to function effectively. Vacations, school recesses, and holiday celebrations are among the routine practices that reflect this imperative.

The functional imperatives define some respects in which social systems function *routinely*. Since the collective behavior interest is in the episodic or the extraordinary, we define types of collective behavior that refer to problems or failures of social routine in each of these areas:

Disaster represents behavior in situations of adaptive failure; when there is a sudden inability of social systems to sustain the resources required for the continuation of the system.

Protest occurs when people resort to extraordinary tactics in the area of goal attainment, using unusual or extralegal tactics in attempting to fulfill their demands for political decisions in their favor.

Persecution represents extraordinarily intense efforts to suppress persons or behaviors that are seen as dire threats to the social order. These efforts employ means that go beyond the normal operation of "law and order" forces; all persecutions represent some form of "vigilante justice."

Renewal represents extraordinarily intense episodes of pattern maintenance and/or tension management activity, typically occurring when people perceive an alarming growth of moral indifference and corruption.

All these types will be given much fuller definitions in the separate chapters that deal with each type. These preliminary definitions should return our attention to an earlier point about more modern "interest" in collective behavior. Each collective behavioral type is defined in terms of *failure* of the routine social system in some significant respect. This perspective may reflect an all-pervasive interest of contemporary people in how various "systems" work and, even more perhaps, in why they *fail* to work. As suggested above, we often see our problems not in terms of lack of system or organization in our lives but in terms of the failures of the systems we have to satisfy human needs. Our school systems seem to turn out uneducated products; our manufacturing systems shoddy products that seem quickly to self-destruct; our political system leaders who do not seem to have their fingers on the controls of government. Laurence Peter capitalizes on this mood of frustration with systems and gives us the "Peter Principle" to explain "why things always go wrong."[29] Peter is obviously using satirical license in declaring that systems always fail; none of us would be alive to read this book were this the case. But the popularity of his book does probably result from its probe at a raw nerve of contemporary mentality: "things" often do not "work" for us when we try to organize our purposive action at the collective level. Since it is our interest here to examine collective behavior as "social action," it seems quite in tune with fashions of both popular and sociological thought to classify collective behavioral episodes in terms of relevance to one of the imperatives of functioning social systems.

The treatment of certain episodes as of one type rather than another in the following analysis may seem rather aribitrary. Were the "draft riots" in New York City in the 1860s, for example, really *protests* against the draft or were they really occasions for the *persecution* of blacks? Is the contemporary "Christian crusade" really a fundamentalist revival in the *renewal* mode or is it a way of mobilizing the *persecution* of "liberals" whose views are restyled as "communist"? These episodes may "really" be all these things and more. At this point some instruction on "reality" from William James may be in order:

> We may, if we like, by our reasonings unwind things back to that black and jointless continuity of space and moving clouds of swarming atoms which science calls the only real world. But all the while the world *we* feel and live in will be that which our ancestors and we, by slowly cumulative strokes of choice, have extricated out of this, like sculptors, by simply rejecting certain portions of the given stuff. Other sculptors, other statues from the same stone! Other minds, other worlds from the same monotonous and inexpressive chaos! My world is but one in a million alike embedded, alike real to those who may abstract them. How different must be the worlds in the consciousness of ant, cuttle-fish, or crab![30]

In this book the reader will be asked to look at a "world" in terms of a perspective that, it has been argued, is consistent with current human interests in social phenomena. Though this may turn out to be a "cuttle-fish" view as we try to advance toward higher levels of understanding, the spirit of the offered paradigm is: let's try this and see how it "works." If the reader should gain some insight toward a larger understanding of the human condition, it will have worked. If perchance a sociologist should use the paradigm to organize a fruitful exploration into the "world" of collective behavior, then it will have worked in spades.

PLAN OF THE BOOK

The scheme of analysis of this book is quite simple, though it has seemed necessary to go some lengths to provide a rationale for it. The scheme involves identifying four "functional imperatives" in the Parsons paradigm; for each of these areas, we identify a corresponding form of collective behavior: episodes with a functional relevance in the designated areas. We devote a separate chapter to each of these four forms. The internal organization of each chapter is defined by the dimensions of sociological analysis outlined above. That is, we examine material on background, participation, process, and consequences for each of these four types. In the last chapter of the book we pay a visit to the realm of general theory of collective behavior; there we hope to discover a few new coherent and empirically valid points about the general role of the episodic dimension in human behavior.

Notes

1. Max Weber, *The Methodology of the Social Sciences*, trans. Edward A. Shilis and Henry A. Finch (Glencoe, Ill.: Free Press, 1949).
2. Kurt Lang and Gladys E. Lang, *Collective Dynamics* (New York: Crowell, 1961).
3. Theodore Lowi, *The Politics of Disorder* (New York: Basic Books, 1971).
4. For a study that assesses this relationship, see Paul Burstein, "Public Opinion, Demonstrations and the Passage of Antidiscrimination Legislation, "*Public Opinion Quarterly* 43 (1979): 157–72.
5. Gustav LeBon, *The Crowd* (New York: Viking, 1960). First published in 1895.
6. For example: Carl J. Couch, "Collective Behavior: An Examination of Some Stereotypes," *Social Problems* 15 (1968): 310–23.
7. Emile Durkheim, *The Rules of Sociological Method*, trans. Sarah A. Solovay

and John H. Mueller (Chicago: University of Chicago Press, 1949), p.110.

8. Georg Simmel, "The Adventurer," in Donald N. Levine, ed., *Georg Simmel on Individuality and Social Forms* (Chicago: University of Chicago Press, 1971), p. 188.

9. Robert Curvin and Bruce Porter, *Blackout Looting!New York City, July 13, 1977* (New York: Gardner Press, 1979).

10. For a general formulation of sociological explanations: that we attempt to correlate a *rate* of some kind of behavior with the *state* of a social order, see Alex Inkeles in Robert K. Merton, ed., *Sociology Today* (New York: Basic Books, 1959), pp. 249–76.

11. Robert K. Merton, *Social Theory and Social Structure* (Glencoe, Ill.: Free Press, 1956), pp. 139–57.

12. Weber, *The Methodology of the Social Sciences*.

13. Because such interests change historically, there can be no permanently valid social science, according to Weber: "The points of departure of the cultural sciences remain changeable throughout the limitless future as long as a Chinese ossification of intellectual life does not render mankind incapable of setting new questions to the eternally inexhaustible flow of life." Weber, *Methodology of the Social Sciences, p. 84.*

14. Robert E. Park, *On Social Control and Collective Behavior* (Chicago: University of Chicago Press, 1967). Also, for an explicit statement of Park's collective behavioral typology, see Robert E. Park, *The Crowd and the Public and Other Essays* (Chicago: University of Chicago Press, 1972).

15. Park, *On Social Control,* pp. xi, xii.

16. E. A. Ross, *Social Control* (New York: Macmillan, 1901); Charles H. Cooley, *Human Nature and the Social Order* (New York: Scribner's, 1902).

17. The point has been made in several studies that American sociologists were among the many turn-of-the-century intellectuals who were taken somewhat aback by the "moral evil" associated with contemporary urban life. See, for example, Jean B. Quandt, *From the Small Town to the Great Community: The Social Thought of Progressive Intellectuals* (New Brunswick, N.J.: Rutgers University Press, 1970); Herman and Julie R. Schwendinger, *The Sociologists of the Chair: A Radical Analysis of the Formative Years of North American Sociology (1883–1922)* (New York: Basic Books, 1974); and Paul Boyer, *Urban Masses and Moral Order in America, 1820–1920* (Cambridge: Harvard University Press, 1978).

18. Herbert Blumer, "Collective Behavior," in A. M. Lee, ed., *New Outline of the Principles of Sociology* (New York: Barnes and Noble, 1946).

19. Lang and Lang, *Collective Dynamics,* pp. 37, 38.

20. Emile Durkheim, *On the Division of Labor in Society,* trans. by George Simpson (New York: Macmillan, 1933).

21. For a critical treatment of this analytic tendency, see C. Wright Mills, "The Professional Ideology of the Social Pathologists," *American Journal of Sociology* 49 (1943): 165–80.

22. Cooley, *Human Nature and the Social Order*, pp. 358, 361.

23. American psychologists tended to adhere to the older stimulus-response psychology longer than did their German colleagues. "The contrast between the experimental trends among German and American psychologists led Bertrand Russell to the famous quip that rats studied by German psychologists had been observed to sit down and think and evolve the answer out of their inner consciousness while rats studied by American psychologists had been noted to rush about with great hustle and pep, finally achieving the desired result by chance." Don Martindale, *The Nature and Types of Sociological Theory*, 2d ed. (Boston: Houghton Mifflin, 1981), pp. 449, 450. Martindale's discussion of "mechanistic" versus "configurationist" perspectives in psychology is a useful summary of psychological influence on sociological functionalism.

24. Talcott Parsons and Edward A. Shils, eds., *Toward a General Theory of Action* (Cambridge: Harvard University Press, 1951).

25. Neil J. Smelser, *Theory of Collective Behavior* (New York: Free Press, 1962).

26. For example, Dennis H. Wrong, "The Oversocialized Conception of Man in Modern Sociology," *American Sociological Review* 26 (1961): 183–93.

27. Gary T. Marx, "Issueless Riots," *Annals of the American Academy of Political and Social Science* 391 (1970): 21–33.

28. Robert F. Bales, *Interaction Process Analysis* (Cambridge, Ma.: Addison-Wesley, 1950).

29. Laurence J. Peter and Raymond Hull, *The Peter Principle: Why Things Always Go Wrong* (New York: Morrow, 1969).

30. William James, *The Principles of Psychology*, vol. 1 (New York: Henry Holt, 1890), pp. 288–89.

Chapter 2

Disasters

DEFINITIONS: DISASTER AND PSEUDO DISASTER

A DISASTER IS a sudden alteration in the usable supply of facilities to accomplish human purposes.[1] Disasters occur, of course, at the level of individual life situations: a person suffers the loss of an organ or the loss of a job as a source of income. Social systems suffer disaster when they are unable to fulfill the needs for which individuals have come to depend on them. In a drought, adequate supplies of water are not available to the population; in an explosion or on a battlefield, medical facilities may be inadequate to deal with the outburst of demand for medical services.

To confine disaster to the *sudden* onset of system difficulties raises a problem. We thereby exclude those disasters with a discernible pattern of slow development. The ultimate breakdown of a transportation system because of a chronic practice of nonrepair of roadways or vehicular facilities (perhaps the way in which the crisis of American railroading developed) would not thereby be classifiable as a disaster. Closer examination even of disasters with sudden onsets may show a degree of slow buildup.[2] An explosion and an airplane crash, most assuredly "sudden" events, may be seen as the end results of a chronic ignoring of conditions of mine, factory, or air traffic safety. Although the suddenness of onset does not unambiguously define

23

disaster, it is still useful to emphasize the emergency character of disaster and of the social processes that are engendered by disaster.

By pseudo disaster, we refer to those episodes in which people imagine, without firm factual basis, that emergency conditions prevail. The barnyard animal hysteria generated by Chicken Little's imaginary belief that the sky was falling is matched by many actual episodes of people believing, for example, that the earth is being invaded by Martians or other pilots of flying saucers, that a "mad anesthetist" is spraying people with poison gas, that people are being bitten by a mysterious bug. These episodes are often analyzed under the heading of "mass hysteria." Actually there is a minitest of the utility of our analytic scheme discernible in the study of episodes of mass hysteria. The term *hysteria* has been used as well to describe outbreaks in the perception of some great danger to social order: an obsessive identification of social troubles as the work of some such "enemy" of humankind as witches, communists, purveyors of pornography, or polluters of the atmosphere. Perhaps our analysis can show that such "hysteria" is quite a different thing from the hysteria of belief in an acute life-threatening emergency. The hysteria of the pseudo disaster typically leads to fear and withdrawal from social involvement (panic). The hysteria of obsessive identification of an enemy leads to anger and to the suppression or persecution of that enemy. We deal with the hysteria of panic in this chapter, with the hysteria of persecution in Chapter 4.

PSEUDO DISASTER

The number of sociological studies of "mass hysteria" under conditions of imaginary danger is very much smaller than the vast body of studies of behavior in "real" emergencies. It will facilitate our discussion of human behavior in pseudo disaster to indicate the nature of a number of these episodes, and we shall examine these now in chronological order.

The oldest and most notorious of such episodes occurred in 1938, when the CBS radio network dramatized a fictitious invasion of the earth by Martians.[3] Millions of Americans failed, for one reason or another, to heed the reminder of the program's producer that the presentation was only a radio drama; and many indulged in various degrees and types of frightened response to the supposed Martian invasion.

There occurred in a "progressive" rural high school in Louisiana in 1943 an episode in which a number of students became ill from an epidemic of nervous twitching with no apparent physiological cause (the sort of symptoms that, 250 years earlier, might have been diagnosed as devil possession and might have instigated a witch hunt).[4]

In his wide-ranging discussion of instances of panic in human affairs, Meerloo mentions a recurring kind of incident: the erroneous belief, among one of the belligerents in a war situation, that the enemy is on the verge of total annihilation of one's own forces.[5] In 1944, as the Allied forces progressed toward the "liberation" of European countries from Nazi occupation, the Nazi occupiers were influenced by the wishful expectation of the Dutch people that their country was about to be liberated and, on one "crazy Tuesday," began a panic flight from Holland that was only stopped by Nazi troops at the German border.

Also in 1944, in the small town of Mattoon, Illinois, a number of people fell "victim" to the gas-spraying activities of a "phantom anesthetist" whose imaginary depredations occurred among townspeople for a few frightening days in September.[6]

Ten years later, another bizarre episode of collective hysteria was publicized in the United States when, during a few days' time, there was a rash of reports by residents of Seattle that their automobile windshields were being "pitted" by mysterious agents, widely thought to be the result of fallout from atomic testing in the Pacific Ocean.[7]

An episode in 1955 in Port Jervis, New York, illustrates the close affinity between "real" and "pseudo" human emergencies. The people of that town were just beginning to recover from an all-too-real severe flood when the rumor broke among the townspeople that a large dam above the town had broken, and that catastrophic inundation was imminent. On the strength of this completely false report, at least one-fourth of the residents of the town actually evacuated it.[8]

A Chinese parallel to the mad anesthetist of Mattoon appeared in Taiwan in 1956 when there was an outbreak of belief that a mysterious "slasher" was inflicting cuts on the bodies of babies and children.[9]

The next two episodes involve "hysterical illness" contagions. In 1962 a number of women in a southern textile factory complained of being "bitten" by a bug, though this insect was never located or identified.[10] In 1972 many of the women employees of a computer data center of a midwestern American university were similarly stricken by a "gas" that environmental tests of the work place indicated did not exist.[11] While one cannot say with total certainty that there were not real environmental pollutants in these cases, the most probable explanation is that these "epidemics" were the product of group hysteria.

A near-repetition of the 1938 Martian scare occurred in Sweden in 1973.[12] In order to dramatize the problem of possible radioactive leakage from nuclear power plants, the Swedish radio broadcast an eleven-minute "news bulletin" of such a leakage in 1982 of a nuclear power plant that was soon to be opened at Barsebäck. Despite assurances of the fictitious nature of the broadcast, some Swedes were frightened, though far fewer than local press reportage had suggested.

Finally, also in 1973 occurred one of the endlessly repeated scares concerning the alleged sighting of a monster: in this case not Big Foot or the Loch Ness monster but a more idiosyncratic three-legged creature that a resident of a small town in Illinois encountered at his door.[13] Press reportage of the monster sightings in the town led to a small convergence of "monster hunters" on the scene.

These few examples should serve to focus our attention on the kinds of episodes in human behavior that have been considered under the heading of mass hysteria or pseudo disasters. Each depends on an erroneous definition of facts by people at a particular time and place. If, however, we give credence to the idea of W. I. Thomas that "if men define situations as real, they are real in their consequences,"[14] then we might be prepared to see that many features of behavior in imaginary emergencies may be similar to behavior in genuine emergencies. It is for this reason alone, and not out of any desire to belabor the point that people have been "damned fools" in all times and places, that we give attention to the matter of pseudo disasters in this chapter.

BACKGROUND

We examine first the question of the general social conditions that appeared to be conducive to these outbreaks of pseudo disaster. Many students of behavior in pseudo disaster have employed the concept of Smelser and others of strain (or stress) in everyday social life as a source of behaviors that contravene the established social order.[15] Descriptions of working conditions of women employees in the southern textile factory and the midwestern university computer center are examples of such strain-oriented explanations of outbreaks of hysterical contagion. In the "June Bug" case, it was found that those women who participated in the contagion were most likely to be those who had recently worked overtime in the factory.[16] While it might be and in fact was suggested that overtime work might be connected to hysterical symptoms through the psychological effects of fatigue and heightened suggestibility associated with overtime work, a more strictly sociological explanation is offered. Working wives and mothers, especially those doing overtime work, might be suffering the strains of "role conflict" associated with possible neglect of familial responsibilities. It was found, in fact, that "affected" women (those reporting bug bites) were more likely than those not reporting bites to have large families who depended heavily on the incomes of these women.[17] There is also evidence that "strained" relations between workers and management were a factor in the outbreak. Expressing their greater alienation toward management, affected women were more likely than the non-affected to express appreciation of the value of the union, toward which management maintained a distinctly hostile attitude.[18]

This latter point is emphasized in the study of "mystery gas" victims in a university computer center.[19] Women were victims of a managerial policy of tight supervision not only of their work (which was itself repetitive and noninvolving) but also of the way they dressed, being subjected to a very unpopular dress code. The authors thus found a correlation between "job dissatisfaction" and victimization by the "gas." The idea of the outbreak as a (perhaps unconscious) revolt against a repressive management is certainly suggested in this study.

Most of the other cited studies of pseudo disasters seem to suggest another version of a social environment conducive to mass hysteria. Rather than the delusionary episode being seen as a response to a frustrating or stressful life situation of participants, the emphasis is on the lack of structure in the social situation, the presence of ambiguity, or the lack of reliable factual information in the situation.[20]

Such ambiguity will not necessarily mean that people will *accept* the faulty versions of fact to which they may be exposed. In an era of "big sell" advertising, in which it is recognized that one may be bombarded with factually incorrect propaganda, most people have erected a threshold of credibility for the various versions of the fact that they encounter. A manufacturer bent on selling me his brand of beer must *prove* and not simply assert the superiority of his product. Most of the pseudo exercises in proof in the results of "independent testing laboratories," testimonials from sports celebrities, and mass media portrayals of innocents who, blindfolded, reject a Brand X to which they were previously committed are recognized by the sophisticated as just that: phony proofs. The question—for the propagandist or for the student of mass delusion—is that of the conditions under which people let down these defenses, lower their thresholds of credibility so that they will accept as true some version of fact that they would otherwise reject as false.

Clearly there are abnormal social conditions in terms of people's credibility thresholds. The Martian invasion scare occurred in a context of "jitters" resulting from contemporary world events. Who would think, even then, that Martians might invade the earth? But then, who would have thought that an obscure house painter named Adolph Hitler would have placed all Europe on the brink of international catastrophe? The predominant feeling of many of Cantril's subjects was that "anything can happen."[21]

Jittery social atmospheres seemed to prevail in most of the other pseudo disasters, although the threshold of credibility appeared to have been more selectively lowered in most cases: not that *anything* can happen but that the very thing that is falsely believed to be happening could very well be happening. The Allies were not in fact invading Holland on "crazy Tuesday," but the Germans knew well that such an invasion could and almost certainly would happen. The dam above Port Jervis was not in fact giving way, but dams do give way under the pressure of swollen water volume, and it was certainly no fantasy of flooded townspeople that this meteorological condition existed. It is highly unlikely that fallout from hydrogen bomb testing pitted any windshields in North America, but science did not then and may perhaps never prove that it *can't* happen. In fact, one author of the Seattle study later makes the telling observation that scientific and technological development has not at all delivered us from fears of what may once have seemed unlikely catastrophes. Our science fiction and our "horror" movies depict possible traumatic realities that are certainly not ruled out by scientific development: "Science, which set out originally to 'disenchant the world' is peopling it today with more hobgoblins than were ever to be found in a medieval forest."[22] When Hadley Cantril wrote a preface to a 1965 edition of his study of the Martian invasion, he made a similar observation about the *increased*

susceptibility of people to belief in a situation that we know all too well
could happen:

> Since the Hallowe'en "Boo" of 1938 we have seen the development
> and use of atomic weapons; we know about the existence of Intercon-
> tinent Ballistic Missiles (ICBMs) and their immense destructive
> power. And we hear talk of satellites spinning about our tiny globe
> carrying warheads that could be quickly guided to any target on
> earth. Such destructive forces against which there appears to be so lit-
> tle protection can only enhance the possibility of delusions that would
> be even more plausible than the invasion of Martians.[23]

Cantril's suggestion was perhaps verified in the Barsebäck panic in
Sweden; very realistic fears (which became even more realistic a few
years later at Three Mile Island) of leakage of radioactivity from
nuclear power plants made the fictitious event "plausible" enough
that many believed it.[24]

Such realistic disaster possibilities, along with the persistent and
even increasing hazards of natural disaster (to be discussed below),
will probably mean that, while the public threshold of credibility for
delusions about Martian invaders, phantom gassers and slashers, and
mysterious bug bites has probably been permanently raised, there may
be a jittery tendency to believe false reports in these "realistic" areas.
Whether such beliefs will eventuate in panic behavior is another matter. Knowing as we do the real possibility of energy supply exhaustion
("will we freeze in the dark?"), nuclear attack, and so forth, we know
also the equally deadly danger of taking alarm without due cause:
"phony" energy crises will produce counterproductive inflation and
hoarding, and a jittery finger on the nuclear retaliation "button" cannot be permitted. Panic is not simply a function of a background of
nervousness about catastrophic possibilities. It arises also from an inability or reluctance to check authoritatively and communicate
decisively the exact degree of danger at every given moment. As we
learn to track tornadoes and ICBMs more effectively we can, perhaps,
accept the *possibility* of disaster so that we can use whatever bomb or
storm shelter we have (thus avoiding the "it can't happen here" reaction to disaster, discussed below, which has resulted in people going to
bed and to their deaths during tornado, bomb, flood, or hurricane
alerts.) At the same time, this technology of verification and warning
of danger should allow us to leave the company of Chicken Little and

sleep peacefully when our intelligence systems assure us that the sky
will not fall tonight.

PARTICIPATION

As with all other episodes in human behavior, different people will
participate to different degrees and in different ways. In outbreaks of
hysterical illness, for example, we might distinguish between those
who: (a) report themselves ill from some mysterious source; (b) believe
and give moral support to those who are ill; (c) engage actively in attempting to disabuse the ill of the reality of their victimization; (d) remain as interested (or uninterested) spectators of the whole episode.
Unfortunately, none of our studies of mass hysteria seems to make
such elementary classification of pseudo disaster behavior by clarifying
exactly who does what during one of these episodes. The studies are
limited to gross distinction between the affected and the nonaffected
(in hysterical contagion), those who do or do not report victimization
(gassing, slashing, windshield pitting), those who do or do not take action on some false report of imminent massive catastrophe (evacuating
an area about to be flooded, a battlefield about to be overcome).

The *number* of participants in a pseudo disaster has often been
grossly overestimated, both in popular perception and in less-than-
careful comments by social scientists. In the cases of both the
Barsebäck episode and the Enfield monster sightings, news coverage of
these events suggested far more widespread panic in the affected areas
than actually existed.[25] News coverage of public reaction to the
invasion-from-Mars broadcast suggested a very general panic in the
American population, while Cantril's analysis of public opinion surveys in the wake of the incident indicate that perhaps only 2 percent of
Americans were ever seriously frightened by the broadcast.[26] In this
instance even social scientists have helped to perpetuate a myth of
massive public involvement in the invasion panic, as in Rosow's statement that the broadcast "frightened half the nation" and that, as a
result, "people . . . hysterically jammed the New Jersey highways."[27]
The only pseudo disaster study cited here that suggests a level of participation remotely approaching half a population is that of the Port
Jervis dam break scare in which, as noted above, perhaps as much as
one-fourth of the population was frightened to the extent of evacuating
the town. It may be, of course, that these "objective" measures

underestimate the prevalence of panic reactions, since they are based on answers given to social scientists and people may be reluctant to admit a behavior that they think will make themselves look foolish.

In terms of *kinds* of people most active in these pseudo disasters, we shall examine differences in participation of people in different sociological categories. In this respect, three areas of investigation of differences in pseudo disaster participation have attracted attention.

1. *Social class*. The usual assumption—and sometimes the finding—of pseudo disaster research is that people of higher social status position (as measured by occupation, income, educational level, etc.) are less likely to participate in mass hysterias. Cantril found this to be the case with those who were frightened by the invasion-from-Mars broadcast (although there were some "deviate cases" of lower-class skeptics and higher-class believers.)[28] He suggests that it is the greater "critical ability" of higher-status persons (especially better educated ones) that gives them their relative immunity from being deceived. In reporting that newspaper accounts of the activity of the "phantom slasher" of Taipei were more prominent in the vernacular (Chinese-language) than in the English-language press, Jacobs suggests that the vernacular press was responding to the greater gullibility of its predominantly lower-class clientele, the English press to the sophisticated skepticism of wealthy Chinese and foreigners.[29] Johnson likewise finds that "gasser" victims in Mattoon were concentrated in the lower classes,[30] and Medalia and Larsen find more educated people among those who were "skeptics" that windshield pitting reflected any more than ordinary road damage.[31]

2. *Sex*. In Mattoon, 93 percent of all "gasser" victims were women.[32] In Seattle about the same proportion of men and women were firm "believers" in some extraordinary explanation of windshield pitting, but many more men than women were outright "skeptics," while women tended to be more "undecided."[33] Similarly, among Cantril's subjects, women tended to take a rather passive role in terms of believing or not believing in the reality of the Martian invasion. Many more women than men had someone else (presumably a man) to check *for* them on the validity or invalidity of the catastrophe.[34] As one woman described this passive or undecided female stance, "We women were nervous and just kept saying it can't be true. Finally the men came back and told us it wasn't real."[35] Both the instances of hysterical contagion in work situations (in the textile factory and the computer center) involved all-female work crews.[36] All

this evidence demonstrates the influence on female social behavior of the traditional female role of relative passivity and suggestibility as opposed to the aggressiveness and autonomy of the male social role. "Hysteria" is, indeed often considered a peculiarly "women's" disease. It is perhaps almost unnecessary to say that this sex difference in favor of greater female participation in mass hysteria may well disappear as women's liberation progresses.

3. *Officials and lay persons*. There is, finally, the interesting question of the relative involvement of rank-and-file citizens and of persons who are recognized community leaders. Two studies—the Taipei slasher episode and the Port Jervis dam break scare—make similar points about the tendency of responsible community officials to avoid participation in community scares. Police and fire officials in Port Jervis, for example, were, along with the local radio station, almost exclusively involved in efforts to calm the citizenry and to assure them that the danger was only a rumor.[37] Likewise, Taipei police held frequent news conferences to assure the public that all reports of slashings were being investigated and to indicate when each report was found to be spurious.[38] There may, however, have been inadvertent official contributions to the scare in both cases. Officials queried about the reality of the danger in Port Jervis did not at first deny the rumor; they only indicated it was unsubstantiated and was being checked out. For some nervous persons this may have been tantamount to a confirmation of their fear. A more blatant example of official reinforcement of popular fear is noted for a New Jersey woman who heard the Martian invasion broadcast and "I immediately called up the Maplewood police and asked if there was anything wrong. They answered, 'We know as much as you do. Keep your radio tuned in and follow the announcer's advice.' Naturally after that I was more scared than ever."[39] In the Taipei case, the police conscientiously did its job of checking out each "slasher" case and, while all verbal police statements to the public were reassuring, to some citizens "the unusual interest [of the police] was to some degree self-defeating, as it only incited the imagination of the uninformed that something was up to which they were not privy."[40]

A followup study of the Seattle windshield-pitting episode by Medalia puts a rather different light on the matter of involvement of "responsible" persons in collective delusions.[41] Medalia found that those who reported windshield pittings fell into two categories, those who reported that their own windshields were damaged, and those who reported that the windshields of many others in their vicinity were damaged. The latter reporters were perhaps more contributory to the buildup of the delusion, and Medalia found—surprisingly, perhaps—that people of higher income and education were overrepresented in this group. This finding led Medalia to a questioning of some prevailing assumptions in the pseudo disaster literature about the behavior of people during such episodes:

> When the wolf-crying process is taken out of the theoretical context of individual hysteria, and placed into that of social role and structure analysis, we are led to the hypothesis that persons who are oriented by status to community responsibility and leadership will play a more significant role in alerting their fellow citizens to the threat of disaster *and* of pseudo disaster than will persons of the class traditionally labeled as "highly suggestible."[42]

This emphasis on the *responsibilities* of officials in pseudo disasters is probably a useful corrective to prior assumptions that such responsibility was limited to controlling the effects of public panic. What is a "real" disaster and what is a false "scare" is, after all, something that can sometimes be known only after the time for effective warning (an official responsibility) has passed. Many police officials in Port Jervis and elsewhere must have felt themselves in the dilemma described by a radio operator in that town who was not able immediately to reach the dam site to confirm or reject the rumor.[43] Although she "responsibly" made the decision not to sound the alarm until the danger was authenticated, she had grave misgivings that perhaps her caution would deny citizens a few precious minutes to take precautionary action against an impending deluge.

PROCESS

Pseudo disasters, like all other forms of collective behavior to be discussed in this book, can be examined in terms of their origin, the process of their spread, and their ultimate decline or extinction.

The *origin* of pseudo disasters seems, at this stage of our knowledge, to be a rather random or idiosyncratic matter. Individual delusions about traumatic events probably occur hundreds of times for every one such delusion that becomes the subject of a pseudo disaster. Often no more is known about the origin of an outbreak than was known in the case of the Port Jervis dam break scare: that a "stranger" walked into a diner outside the town and sounded the alarm.[44] We may speculate—the studies do not support nor refute this—that pseudo disasters have their origin in the influence of persons who are the episodal equivalent of the *charismatic* leader; they are, that is, persons who are believable even about unbelievable matters. Others respond to them "in spite of themselves" and their better judgments. As indicated, there is not sufficient evidence in the literature to show whether this is simply speculation. Two cases in which the origin is clearly known are those of the Martian invasion and the Barsebäck panic: radio broadcasts of fictitious emergencies were the stimulus to public panic. In both cases, the dramatic quality of the presentation (the "we take you to the scene" style of reportage, the use of sirens and other sound effects to simulate emergency) was sufficient to make the broadcast "convincing" in the way that a charismatic individual is convincing. Even people who *knew* that the Martian invasion was a "Hallowe'en Boo" were given goose bumps in the realistic style of the presentation. Other originators of pseudo disasters may have more or less of this dramatic flair.

The *spread* of pseudo disaster participation, as an unfounded fear affects more people, is a much more studied matter. News that a dam has broken or that a mad killer is on the streets can travel in either one or a combination of two modes of communication: the *interpersonal* mode, as individual people tell individual other people; or the *mass media mode,* by which one agency (newspaper, TV station, loudspeaker operator, etc.) informs (or misinforms) a large number of people.

The influence of the mass media in encouraging participation in pseudo disaster is well documented. The local newspaper in Mattoon, on the basis of one case of gassing followed by the alleged sighting of a prowler, informed the Mattoon citizenry with the headline "Anesthetic Prowler on Loose.[45] In Seattle, the newspapers were the major agency through which information about windshield pitting came to the public.[46] The authors found that radio and television were much less powerful sources of information in this situation and suggest that this will be the case wherever the idea of a crisis is built up over a longer period of time. The prominent role of the newspapers in the Taipei slasher episode illustrates this point.[47] The electronic media would presumably be more influential in spreading panic related to an instantaneous emergency such as a tornado, fire, or dam break. In the case of the Port Jervis dam break, the one radio station was off the air for the night and, as we shall see below, went back on the air for the precise purpose of *denying* the rumored catastrophe. The closest thing to a "mass media" agency in spreading the Port Jervis rumor was the instance of one emergency vehicle driving through the streets with siren blasting while the driver "warned" residents.[48] This was apparently a potent incident in the buildup of the dam break scare.

In other pseudo disasters, the direct influence of people on one another was apparently the more powerful communication mode for the spread of participation in the episode. In the June bug case, local news agencies were quick to inform audiences that a mysterious insect was believed to be afflicting people in the textile plant; and early reports of this kind may have influenced the later "victims."[49] But the authors found a pattern of sociometric ties (friendship, acquaintance, car pooling, etc.) among victims that strongly suggested a "group influence" explanation of the spread of the contagion. A similar finding in the case of the "mystery gas" victims in a university computer center leads the authors to describe their study as a replication of the June bug findings.[50]

This view of the nature of the process of spread of hysterical contagion has been severely critized by Gehlen, who believes that the studies just cited have given inadequate attention to the "positive" aspects of illness from the perspective of the victims.[51] Many sociologists have referred to a "sick role," which, like all roles, has its privations and obligations (one can't play in a ball game if one has a fever, a patient must follow doctor's orders) but also its privileges (a person may literally "get away with murder" upon demonstration of mental illness). Gehlen's idea is that perhaps hysterical illness follows, in its development, more a "craze-model" that a "panic-model" of collective behavior. The panic model is based on the old LeBon notion of "emotional contagion," the tendency of people to be influenced by others' emotional expressions. The June bug authors give a "group influence" modification to the contagion process, suggesting the *selective* influence of emotional expression by significant others. A craze model would presumably incorporate more of the viewpoint of human behavior as purposive or goal-seeking. A craze is a temporarily very popular item of human behavior or possession: the crazes of the Fonz and Farah Fawcett are recent instances that come to mind. It is really doubtful that wearing a tee-shirt depicting one of these TV stars is clustered into particular sociometric circles. Bobbie wears his Fonz shirt, not because friend Frankie does so, but because Bobbie and

Frankie are both competitors for status in the same market of pre-teenage Americans. The tee-shirt is a gain for Bobbie in this market, and he doesn't need the example of Frankie to "suggest" this gain to his mind; the example of any popular pre-teenager would do it as well, although Frankie's personal example may be a powerful reinforcing factor.

Adaptations of the craze model to the pseudo disaster process could explain certain facts in our studies. In the Louisiana high school outbreak, the first "victim" of body twitching was a popular girl who undoubtedly influenced others but pointedly *not* her own friends, none of whom were among the victims.[52] Her seizure *did*, however, give her a legitimate excuse not to attend social dancing classes, recently made compulsory, and there is some suggestion that her illness may have helped to rekindle the interest of a straying boyfriend. Many other students with similar problems may have used her example of how to make the most of her "illness." In this connection, there is a very interesting finding in the June bug study. Women in the study were asked whether they thought it wrong for a worker to stay home when the worker was not sick but simply felt the need for a rest. More of the "affected" than of the nonaffected expressed disapproval of work absence in this circumstance.[53] These women were also shown to have a "greater inclination to adopt the sick role."[54] It is tempting to suggest that hysterical illness is a product of strain (discussed above) and of the inability to cope with strain in any other way than illness.

Similar considerations may be involved in pseudo disasters of mass victimization by human agents: gassers, slashers, and the rest. People sometimes find that reported victimization is the "easiest way out" of a difficult situation: one's money or one's virginity is lost, and a charge of theft or rape may be raised to cover the loss. When a victimizing delusion is in full swing, these "victim role" gains may be relatively easy to come by. Taipei police, as noted above, carefully investigated all "slasher" reports and found that several were of the cover-up variety.[55] A child might know very well the cause of a cut, but if it was sustained while the child was playing in a forbidden area or while engaging in a fight, it might be best to feign ignorance, leading parents to believe in a mysterious origin for the cut. The Taipei police also found instances of victim role motivations that must exist in other pseudo disasters. Given the publicity to the slasher's work being given by the local press, a "cheap" way to ensure getting one's name in the newspaper must have appealed to some publicity seekers. Other alleged personal "gains" may be based on the simple enjoyment or sport of participating. A boy in Enfield who claimed to have sighted a "monster" later admitted that he made up the story to tease his neighbor (the original monster sighter) and to "have some fun with an out of town newsman."[56]

The *termination* of pseudo disaster always occurs, since, as in all "episodes," that which peaks at one time will ultimately decline in frequency and intensity. In order to understand termination processes more closely, it will be useful to refer to an observation by Medalia and Larsen on the "extinction" of the Seattle windshield pitting episode.[57] They indicate that, in that episode, most people ultimately lost *interest* in the matter, although many continued in their *belief* that windshields had been pitted by extraordinary agencies. Similarly, Kerckhoff and Back found that, two months after the June bug epidemic had subsided, women in the plant still subscribed to the belief that an insect, not "hysteria," had caused the illnesses.[58] In other pseudo disasters, extinction may be more related to the decline of false beliefs. This was clearly the case with the Martian invasion scare as well as the panic associated with the rumored dam break at Port Jervis. We shall, therefore, give separate attention to the matters of decline of interest and belief in pseudo disaster episodes.

INTEREST DECLINE.

The human ability to sustain interest in any subject matter may be limited. If variety is indeed the "spice" of life, then even a "spicy" story of victimization by a mad slasher or gasser may lose its tang after a certain number of repetitions. Also, whatever the "gains" for the assumption of a victim role may be (public attention to oneself, exemption from social responsibility, etc.), these gains tend ultimately to diminish. While the tenth victim may gain from the legitimation of his or her behavior from that of predecessors and also the publicity value of public interest in an "epidemic," the fiftieth victim in the same episode may have to face a situation in which this legitimacy is beginning to be questioned and/or in which the news value of new victim cases has declined. The evolution of news media interest in an episode will illustrate these possibilities. The Mattoon newspaper, an early agent in spreading fear of the phantom anesthetist, shortly began to refer to the episode as a matter of "hysteria," and finally reported gasser-related news with a "comical twist": reporting "two false alarms which turned out to be a black cat and a doctor trying to break into his own office after he had forgotten his keys."[59]

In the Seattle windshield-pitting episode, individual "gains" from victimization were not prominent, and Medalia and Larsen suggest other reasons for extinction of interest in the pittings. First, since the H-bomb testing that generated fallout anxiety was a transient event, the interest in the fallout effects could similarly be episodic. As we note in the case of "real" disasters, the flurry of concern about the hazard of further floods, fires, and so on during an actual crisis easily breaks down as time elapses from the last round of actual disaster. Second, the authors suggest, the belief in windshield pitting from fallout may have been a relatively harmless focusing of diffuse anxiety about all kinds of possible fallout effects (dangerous radioactivity, for example). The feeling of many after the episode was: "Something was bound to happen to *us* as a result of the H-bomb tests. Windshields became pitted—it's happened. Now *that* threat is over."[60] The belief in the pittings is thus seen as having introduced an element of "magical control," which reduced anxiety. Similarly, in the "mystery gas" episode, a factor of extinction of interest in the epidemic was apparently the action of officials in telling employees that their illnesses were probably caused by an "environmental inversion."[61] While the explanation was probably false, it seemed to provide, in parallel to the windshield-pitting extinction, a psychological sequence: there *has* to be an explanation—an explanation has been offered—now *that's* over.[62]

BELIEF DECLINE.

In the cases of the Martian invasion, the Barsebäck panic, and the Port Jervis dam break scare, probably no sane person continued to believe in these disasters for more than a few hours after they were first believed to occur; yet *interest* in at least the Martian episode has been quite durable. These studies, then, are useful in isolating the factor of belief decline and provide examples of some of the processes by which people have their erroneous beliefs about life-threatening disasters corrected by new and accurate information. These cases illustrate Shibutani's point about the nature of the rumor process: that people go through more or less *deliberative* processes of comparing rumors they hear against other information they already have or can generate.[63] They also illustrate how difficult it may be to arrest a panic through deliberative processes once the panic is in full swing.

People who heard and were frightened by the fictitious invasion from Mars tended to *check* the validity of the invasion by some combination of what Cantril calls internal and external checks.[64] Internal checks consist in comparing a version of reality against what one already knows. Some listeners found it impossible to believe, for example, that military units could arrive at the scene of a "disaster" as rapidly as they were reported as doing. Similarly, internal checks were apparently made by listeners to the fictitious nuclear disaster at Barsebäck.[65] People who knew that the power plant in question had not yet opened were much less likely to be frightened than were those who did not have this information. External checks involve turning to other sources of information: calling friends, police, radio stations; or consulting a radio log in a newspaper to discover that "War of the Worlds" was scheduled for broadcast on this station at this hour. Some of these checks failed to allay anxiety. People who called friends may have found them as misinformed as themselves. Those who called police officials may have found them reluctant to make a categorical denial of the invasion.

In Port Jervis, people made such external checks (internal checks were probably not effective in allaying aniexty because people knew that a dam break *could* happen), but the study's authors found that many evacuated upon receiving only one or two warning messages—understandable perhaps in terms of the imminence of the feared disaster.[66] The study focuses on the efforts of public officials, once they had clearly disconfirmed the rumor, to correctly inform the public. They found that citizens typically required many more "denial" messages to calm them than they had required warning messages to panic them. The local radio station, off the air for the night, went back on to make repeated denials, and these, along with the fact that the disaster simply did not occur as expected, restored public order.

CONSEQUENCES

The consequences of pseudo disaster have been given little attention, perhaps because there is typically little physical or human damage that survives such episodes. One aftermath effect of pseudo disasters—a dangerous effect from the standpoint of disaster problems—is that the episode may immunize the public against acceptance of danger warnings. In Mattoon, Johnson suggests, the wave of suggestion leading to popular belief in a criminal prowler led to a wave of "contra-suggestibility," in which people were reluctant to report suspected prowlers whom they would have reported before the episode.[67] Experiences with air raid or fire warnings done as drills, pranks, or accidents may lead people to ignore warnings in real disasters.[68]

Another likely consequence of a pseudo disaster, as of a disaster, is a heightened level of hostility directed toward those persons deemed "responsible" for the episode. Considering the large role of the press in many popular scares, it is understandable if much of the public comes to distrust newspapers, radio, and television—again, with dangerous consequences if these media are depended on as agencies of warning in genuine disasters. There may even be acute expressions of hostility against the media. When a radio station in Quito, Ecuador, attempted in 1949 a repeat of the invasion-from-Mars broadcast in that city, frightened people driven into the street by the scare turned angry when they discovered the hoax and vented their rage by destroying the building that housed the radio station.[69]

DISASTER

Disaster, as opposed to pseudo disaster, has stimulated an immense amount of sociological investigation. Some impetus to disaster research in the 1950s developed from governmental interest in predicting and, as far as possible, controlling the effects on civilian populations of massive military attacks. A committee of social scientists associated with the National Academy of Sciences carried out numerous disaster researches in the 1950s, many of which are cited below. Beginning in the 1960s, a so-called Disaster Research Group at Ohio State University has carried on the tradition of "instant research" on community disasters. The volume of these and other research efforts has necessitated periodic inventories of findings, which will be found in successive volumes by Barton,[70] Dynes,[71] and Mileti, Drabek, and Haas.[72] Since 1975 the journal *Mass Emergencies* has published studies of disasters throughout the world, including many contributions by members of the Disaster Research Group.

BACKGROUND

In a sense, it might be argued that "background" of disaster is of little sociological interest since, from the human standpoint, disasters such as floods, explosions, plane crashes, and droughts happen without human agency and are, indeed, often characterized as "acts of God." One critic of disaster research has complained of such a "bolt from the blue" attitude in much of this research: a focus entirely on what follows from disaster without much concern with what precedes it.[73] Yet we need only observe the frequent demand following disasters for investigations of "why it happened" to know that human beings themselves recognize the human element in disaster development. We may note that much of the interest in disaster backgrounds derives from the work of professional geographers which, unfortunately, has apparently not penetrated into the consciousness of sociologists who conduct disaster research.

To open this discussion of the human element in disaster development, we can note an observation of a leading figure in this geographical school, Gilbert White, that floods would constitute no great human disaster unless human beings insisted on living and working in areas susceptible to period flooding.[74] The question then becomes that of the reasons that people develop an "adjustment to hazard" of various sorts that will allow them to continue to subject themselves to such hazards.

One such adjustment to hazard is simply for people to deny to themselves that the hazard exists. Although, in a sense, all American communities are at some risk of tornado strikes, there is likely to be a wishful belief that "it can't happen here." This attitude was found to be common in the cities of Vicksburg, Mississippi, and Worcester, Massachusetts, where damaging tornadoes did in fact occur.[75] Even in Topeka, Kansas, located in an area known for its tornadoes, residents believed until the devastating tornado of 1966 that a hill outside the city provided immunity from tornadoes.[76] Some of this false security may arise from an overestimation of the value of protective devices. Thus, many of the residents of the English town of Shrewsbury believed that a recently constructed dam would give them flood immunity, when in fact the dam was too far upstream from the town to have this effect.[77] Finally, and ironically, the very experience of a given community with a particular disaster may lead to a belief that further hazard of that sort of disaster is minimal. Some people operate with a "lightning never strikes twice" view, believing that each community has its quota of hardships that, once the quota is fulfilled, will never occur again.[78] Prior experience may lead to false security as "was illustrated recently in Rapid City, South Dakota, where the flood of recent memory prior to 1972 had been a 'moderate' one. After the impact of the devastating 'big one' on the night of June 9, 1972, the response within the community was slow and faltering. Many persons apparently couldn't conceive of the magnitude of the event because their prior flood experience gave them a less than adequate view of what a 'flood' could produce."[79] In some cases prior experiences may lead to uncertainty of the magnitude of local hazard at its next activation. Residents of the Mount St. Helen's area of Washington in 1980 could not predict whether a given volcanic eruption would be the last of a series or would be followed by further eruptions. In 1800 there had been only a single eruption; the eruptions beginning in 1831 had inaugurated 25 years of turbulence.[80] Given the wishful thinking tendency, it is easy to understand that local people would apply the 1800 model or would at least hope that the latest in the series of eruptions that actually occurred in 1980 would be the last.

A second kind of "hazard adjustment" is a kind of fatalistic resignation to the inevitable—not "it can't happen here" but "it's going to happen anyway, so why bother with preventive activity?" There were British citizens who, in the midst of massive German bombings during World War II, took the attitude that if one's "name is on a bomb," one will die whether or not one takes shelter, and refused therefore to take shelter.[81] Such resigned attitudes have been found to be more characteristic of Latin American than of North American residents. Puerto Ricans were found to be more passive in response to hurricane hazard than were the residents of Gulf coastal towns in Texas, Louisiana, and Mississippi,[82] and a comparison of American and Mexican towns on two sides of the Rio Grande River found such fatalistic attitudes toward flood hazard more characteristic of the Mexican town.[83]

Such fatalistic acceptance is facilitated if people define their living environments as very favorable except for the hazard and are willing to accept the hazard as the "price" one pays for an otherwise favorable environment. Many Californians are able to accept the earthquake hazard along the San Andreas fault on this basis. It is thus reported that a California geological engineer, a major proponent of earthquake safety practices, "lives high in Bel Air in Los Angeles, in a home precariously perched on a steep hillside. From his house he can, at times, actually look *down* on the smog. At night there is nothing but the stars and a pervasive quiet. 'In a good strong shake,' he says, leaning over to look down at his very own precipice, 'I guess this whole lot could wind up in our neighbor's pool down there someplace. We'd never move. We love the house and we love the area.'"[84] While admitting that many Californians thus attain a "healthy denial" that allows them to go about their daily lives without immobilization by fear, Fried argues that this adjustment to hazard becomes dysfunctional when they "go to the extreme of denying the need for safer schools, safer buildings and safer land use.[85]

As a third kind of hazard adjustment, it may be noted that concern with impending disaster may be minimized if there is anticipation of outside assistance in the aftermath of the disaster. Thus, residents of areas subjected to recurring cyclones may be reluctant to leave the area if they perceive that disaster relief efforts will follow any cyclone.[86]

Finally, in this inventory of hazard "adjustment," it must be noted that many disasters are the culmination of a series of errors in relation to safety conditions.[87] Apart from the simple fallibility of the human capacity to anticipate trouble, it may be noted that there are sometimes patterns of chronic negligence that, subsequent to a disaster, may become the subject of criminal investigation.[88] Some of these failures illustrate a chronic human tendency to ignore remote dangers if attention to them involves immediate inconvenience to oneself. At the level of individual accident, it is sometimes noted retrospectively that, if only an individual had taken a moment to fasten an easily available automobile seat belt, serious injury in a crash might not have occurred. Similarly, in the aftermath of an explosion that killed 89 persons at the Coliseum of the Indiana State Fairgrounds in 1966, it was found that the likely cause was a bottle of compressed (LP) gas used by a concessionaire for heating popcorn.[89] The use of LP gas containers in enclosed buildings was clearly against the state law and clearly official fire inspectors should have refused the usage that led to the disaster. Yet, "the sports promoter who had leased the Coliseum from the State indicated that he did not have permits for the bottled gas tanks used in heating popcorn. He further declared that such tanks had been openly used for 10 years, during which time no one had said anything to him about a permit."[90] The local fire chief reported that understaffing of his department, largely in response to public demand for the curtailment of government expenditures, made it impossible for all fire hazards to be checked. The predisaster situation in Indianapolis was probably similar to that in most other communities. With limited time, energy, money, and interest to deal with a seemingly limitless number of human concerns, it may be understandable if individuals or public officials take the attitude that they are "too busy" to fasten a seat belt, conduct a safety inspection, or look to the repair of a faulty dam or a chaotic system of air flight control.[91] As we shall note under the heading of disaster consequences, it may require an actual disaster to focus attention on a given kind of hazard.

Lest our hazard-adjustment discussions suggest a tendency to engage in a "blaming the victim" explanation of disaster damage, we might observe that people are sometimes precipitated into hazard situations quite apart from their will or knowledge. People who bought homes in the Love Canal section of Niagara Falls, New York, were apparently for the most part unaware of the chemical contamination in the area until they had already committed themselves to investments in home ownership, and, far from being reluctant to leave a cherished area, they demanded state, federal, and/or Hooker Chemical purchase of their homes so they could afford to move elsewhere.[92] On a broader scale an anthropological insight into disaster hazard is that many preliterate people had made hazard adjustments that were actually functional to their ability to withstand disasters and that the European colonization of their areas destroyed these adjustments and left them more vulnerable to disaster.[93] Thus, people in areas subject to drought had developed nomadic patterns of ranging into new territories when rainfall deficiencies occurred in their accustomed habitats. The colonizers' introduction of settled agriculture and industrial cities severely disrupted these functional precolonial adjustments to hazard.

PARTICIPATION

The idea of "participation" in a disaster may seem somewhat ambiguous. People typically *choose* their behavioral participation, but in an earthquake, fire, drought, or explosion there is typically no question of choice of whether or not to be affected. Explosion debris, like the rain, falls on the believer and the nonbeliever. Any meaningful application of the participation dimension to disaster must, then, deal with those parts of the disaster process in which there *is* some choice exercised by people in a disaster-affected area. Two such areas will be discussed here: participation in the *precautionary* activity that typically precedes a disaster ("instantaneous" disasters such as explosions being the exception), and participation in the *rescue* activity that typically occurs at the onset of a disaster. Precautionary behavior would include such activities as (1) evacuating an area about to be bombed, flooded, or wind-stricken; (2) taking shelter or other protective action, such as climbing to avoid flood waters; (3) participating in such emergency damage-preventive measures as sandbagging against flooding and securing property against wind damage; and (4) passing along warnings of an imminent disaster danger. Rescue activities involve assistance to people in a disaster area to (1) prevent their imminent death or injury and/or (b) facilitate medical attention for those who have been injured.

Both precautionary activity and rescue activity typically demand participation by a *mass* of people in the disaster area. It can be assumed, however, that not all people in the area will so participate and that some *categories* of people will be more active than others. Although the disaster studies tend to be weak in informing us of these category differentials, we shall review below the rather sparse findings on participation as related to sex, age, and social class, the only variables that have been given any degree of attention.

SEX

The beginning of precautionary activity may be a perception of hazard of a particular sort.[94] If so, a study by Kates, finding no sex difference in hazard perception,[95] would suggest a lack of general sex difference in precautionary activity. There is, perhaps, a differentiation of sex roles among the several dimensions of precautionary activity mentioned above. Given their greater rescue involvement, shown below, we might expect that men would also be more involved in emergency damage-preventive activity such as sandbagging and also, perhaps, in the warning network. (The latter point is far more problematic. In some communities and with some kinds of disasters, the greater involvement of women in telephone-conversational networks and daytime television watching may give them a greater role in warning systems. Apparently, none of our disaster studies has investigated this matter.) When it comes to evacuation or shelter-taking, women may be somewhat more active participants, men more often taking the "courageous" attitude of indifference to possible personal harm. Women were somewhat more likely than men to evacuate in anticipation of hurricane Carla on the Gulf coast in 1961.[96] However, since most evacuation, here as elsewhere, occurs in family groups,[97] the degree of sex difference in evacuation is usually very slight.

Rescue activity is a predominantly male activity in most disasters. Immediately after disaster impact, when most rescue activity is devoted to family members and immediate neighbors, men and women are about equally involved. However, as rescue proceeds and more attention is directed to rescue of more distant persons, men become more involved than women. In the Flint, Michigan tornado of 1953, for example, once immediate family members had been rescued, "the women tended to withdraw from active rescue and turned to their traditional tasks of caring for children and providing supportive functions for the men still at work."[98] The sex-role determination of these behaviors is indicated in data from an Arkansas tornado in 1952.[99] Men with dependents were especially active in rescue operations (reflecting a general role of protector for the male "head of household"), while, for women, having dependents tended to *reduce* their rescue activity. (It seems that "women's place is in the home" even in a disaster.) Whether these sex differences remain in recent disasters, as the rigidity of sex-role differentiation in everyday life declines, is perhaps a little doubtful.[100]

AGE

Age, like sex, does not seem to correlate with hazard perception. There is a popular stereotype of the elderly person refusing to leave his or her home in spite of rising flood waters. Research support for this notion seems to be lacking. There is an implication that older people will be *more* prone to evacuation in the finding that this propensity is positively related to prior experience with disaster (which, of course, older people are more likely to have had).[101]

In the study of the Flint tornado, the interesting question was raised of the participation of adolescents in rescue activity.[102] The "normal" social situation of adolescents—the constraints against their playing responsible adult roles—might presumably be altered under the less structured conditions of a disaster. In fact, Form and Nosow found that a group of adolescent boys, unencumbered by other responsibilities and quite willing and able to do rescue work, showed a striking lack of initiative and self-determination in the rescue situation.

Here, as elsewhere, the roles of people in routine social life tend to be carried over into a collective behavioral episode.

SOCIAL CLASS

The less literate residents of three Gulf coast communities (Galveston, Texas; Pass Christian, Mississippi; and Tallahassee, Florida) tended to be more fatalistic about the possibility of activity to minimize hurricane damage.[103] On the other hand, there is some evidence that lower-class people are more likely to evacuate their homes in anticipation of a disaster.[104] This may reflect to some extent the greater tendency of lower-class homes to be located in disaster-prone areas, so that we are dealing with a "greater stress" rather than a "role" explanation of participation differentials.

Class differences in rescue activity have not been too clearly defined. The greater involvement of "skilled" than "unskilled" workers in the Arkansas tornado would suggest some positive correlation between class position and rescue activity.[105] The discussion by Taylor, Zurcher, and Key of the activity of an upper-middle-class woman in a "helper" role after the Topeka tornado illustrates the influence of a kind of "noblesse oblige" responsibility for helping the "unfortunate" that may be built into the role of the higher classes.[106] Since, however, most rescue activity is carried out by people in the immediate vicinity of a disaster, it seems altogether likely that the class composition of rescuers will closely reflect the class composition of the disaster-stricken area.

PROCESS

Several attempts have been made to define the various "stages" of the disaster process.[107] For our purposes it will be sufficient to define 3 such stages: (1) a period or warning or threat immediately preceding the disaster onset; (2) the arrival of the disaster (impact) and the period of "isolation" immediately following, when people in a disaster area are engaged in rescue efforts before outside help arrives; and (3) a "relief and rehabilitation" period, when outside resources are brought to bear to assist in recovery from the impact of the disaster.

WARNING AND THREAT

The ultimate destructiveness of a disaster is clearly related to the possibility that people, duly warned, may take action to prevent loss of life and property. This point is well illustrated in the immense destructiveness of hurricane Audrey in 1957, when 400 lives were lost, [108] as opposed to the much lesser damage of hurricane Carla in 1961, after hurricane warning systems were better developed.[109] It has been noted in the case of tornadoes, however, that only a very brief forewarning may be worse than no warning at all, since people may expose themselves to damage in the process of seeking shelter.[110] In other disasters, even extremely brief warnings have been effective in minimizing damage. During the atomic bombing of Hiroshima, even the brief interval between the bomb flash and the destructive impact was a highly functional warning interval for those people who reacted to the flash as a warning and took some kind of available shelter.[111]

Sociological studies of disaster have appropriately focused on the failure of warning systems in many disasters. This is sometimes the result of a failure by authoritative persons to convey information about impending disaster to endangered populations. The English town of Kimbark received the full impact of a flood without warning in 1953, although the likelihood of floods could have been predicted from floods occurring earlier to the north.[112] But the traditional structure of responsibilities for flood control—the existence of separate "River Boards" for each river—had produced a situation in which each board looked after its own river without feeling responsible for any other. There was a similar lack of information passed from one region to another that contributed to the lack of preparation of the residents of Worcester, Massachusetts, for a tornado that struck that city in 1953.[113]

Even when local officials are aware of an impending local emergency, they may be reluctant to alert the public. Some of this reluctance may be based on a lingering uncertainty that the impending disaster is real and an awareness of public hostility against those officials who have "cried wolf" in pseudo disasters. In the English case, "Kimbark's constable went from one dyke to the other trying to decide the degree of danger and whether he should alert the community. By the time he had decided that the flood was going to be disastrous he was isolated by the water himself and was unable to warn anyone."[114] Military intelligence agents at Pearl Harbor in December, 1941, were much criticized for failure to convey what, in hindsight, were clear signals of Japanese intention of a bombing attack. However, these officials were accustomed to having to deal with a flood of simultaneous signals—"noise"—including some Japanese efforts to send out decoy signals.[115] Thus their caution against sounding an alert in what might turn out to be merely another bit of warning noise.

Sometimes, too, the failure of officials to alert the public is based on a fear of panic by people upon learning of the threat.[116] (This is apparently a misperception of panic likelihood in disaster, as we shall see below.) We noted in the pseudo disaster section the duality of official responsibility with reference to community danger: to alert the public and to allay false public fears. We saw there that the alert responsibility sometimes interfered with the allaying one; and the reverse difficulty in genuine disasters is now being suggested.

Even when officials believe they are delivering clear warnings, response to these warnings by citizens may minimize their impact. People in the Australian city of Darwin were given authoritative warning of an impending cyclone.[117] However, the infrequency of cyclones in the area and the lack of a cyclone a few weeks earlier following an alert produced an attitude of "it can't happen here" that led many to ignore the warning.[118] Sometimes the lack of response results from unclear *interpretations* of warning systems by people. In Hawaii, a siren sounded to warn people of an impending tidal wave, but many failed to evacuate because they took the siren as only a preliminary signal and maintained a "wait and see" attitude when officials had in fact given their final warnings.[119]

IMPACT AND ISOLATION

How do people behave in the immediate situation of being bombed, flooded, hurricane-stricken, and so on? A popular stereotype that is finally dying as disaster research accumulates is that *panic* or irrational flight is the typical disaster reaction.[120] In the rare instances of disaster panic, it seems to be the case, according to Fritz and Marks, that: "1. the individual believes himself to be in a situation involving *immediate threat* of personal destruction, and 2. the individual believes escape is possible at the moment but may become impossible in the immediate future—i.e., that unless one gets away, one will be trapped."[121] In fact, few disaster victims seem to display such patterns, even though many report extreme fright.[122] The rush to exits during a fire in an enclosed space is perhaps the most common instance of disaster-related panic.[123]

A more controversial idea about victim behavior in disaster is represented in Wallace's concept of a "disaster syndrome."[124] This behavioral pattern, at its first stage, is marked by a "dazed" reaction in which people are essentially immobilized by the shock of the situation. People may wander about aimlessly in the rubble of physical destruction, with little outward show of emotion or sense of direction. People pass easily from this stage to one of passive dependency on others as "helpers" and express gratitude for any help received. Many victims of the Topeka tornado exhibited this behavioral pattern.[125] In the Flint tornado it was shown that people displaying such "dysfunctional" reactions tended to be those alone or separated from their families.[126]

Other disaster researchers have challenged this notion of a "dazed" and "dependent" reaction to disaster impact. Quarantelli argues that such "withdrawal behavior" in disasters rarely occurs: "disaster victims react in an active manner, not passively as implied in the dependency image. They do not just wait around for offers of aid by organizations. They act on their own."[127] Drabek found Quarantelli's characterization to be accurate for the victims of the Indianapolis explosion.[128]

The daze and dependency in the early stages of disaster reaction tend to be replaced, according to Wallace, with a "euphoric" reaction of survivors. Many observers have noted the sense of comradeship in common victimization and a common struggle to survive. A "therapeutic community" is thus created[129] in which, in one description, "differences of class, race, rank and age dissolve as they work side by side to clear debris and rescue the injured."[130] In Topeka after the tornado, it was reported as "not uncommon" for people to hold parties in the midst of the debris, these events being described as acts of "solidarity and of symbolic renewal in the face of devastation."[131] Residents of Buffalo, New York, "celebrate" their notorious "Blizzard of '77" by holding an annual "Blizzard Ball" to commemorate the event.

The "euphoric" stage of community solidarity is not reported in all disaster studies. The community solidarity engendered by the electrical blackout in New York City in 1965 was not repeated in 1977, when many thousands of residents used the disaster as an occasion for looting and other antisocial acts.[132] In Cameron Parish, Louisiana, after hurricane Audrey in 1957, there was much more self-seeking and antisocial behavior in the immediate aftermath than other studies have suggested.[133] Bates indicates that this finding may have resulted because researchers in this study spent more time with subjects and developed more rapport with them so that subjects would more readily "wash dirty linens" about behaviors that occured after impact. He also suggests that the totality of destruction of the community may have been a factor. Erikson makes the same point in observing the lack of a euphoric stage for victims of the flood in the Buffalo Creek area of West Virginia in 1972:

> It may very well be that the emergence of a stage of euphoria depends upon the continuance of most of the larger community, so that survivors, digging out from under the masses of debris, can discover that most of the body is still intact and is mobilizing its remaining resources to dress the wound on its flank. In Buffalo Creek this was simply not the case. Most of the work of rescue was done by outsiders following plans and initiatives issued from distant headquarters. They were strangers, many of them in uniform, and they cleaned up wreckage without consulting the owners, sealed off the residents from their own homes, and generally acted more like an army of occupation than a local disaster team.[134]

COMMUNITY RESPONSE: RESCUE AND REHABILITATION

When disaster strikes, there tends to be a mobilization of resources from the wider social system to rescue the victims, provide for their immediate life-preserving needs, and assist them in eventually "getting back on their feet" after the disaster. There is thus developed what Barton calls the "emergency social system."[135] There are two major points to be made here about such systems: (1) their *emergent* quality; and (2) the *functional exigencies* of such systems, their problems in accomplishing their goals.

Emergent groups.

Most communities have some set of officials with formal responsibility in the event of disaster: Red Cross, civil defense, police, fire departments, and so on; and these often have a more or less detailed contingency plan to be activated in emergency conditions. Yet, for some reasons to be discussed below, these formal organizational plans may be insufficient to deal with the situation. To mention an additional factor now: bureaucracies are always organized to deal with routine matters; predictable problems are the precondition of established organization. It is the very unpredictability in disaster situations which guarantees that there will have to be, at minimum, a modification of established bureaucratic procedure. Thus, even these established organizations tend to become "debureaucratized" for the duration of an emergency.[136] Some person without formal authority to do a given task finds that it needs to be done and simply directs traffic, organizes a relief crew, or requisitions food and medical supplies. The study of community response to the Topeka tornado is richly detailed on the development of such "ephemeral roles." For example:

> We started down the street, and it finally came upon me that I was an official of the Shawnee County Chapter of the Red Cross. So I told my wife I had better go down to the Chapter House. . . . But when I got there I was overwhelmed. . . . The captain of the guard ran up to me. I certainly was frightened for a minute as he addressed me as somebody who knew what to do under these circumstances. Up there everybody was trying to find anything they could do to help. . . . Finally there was a fellow—and I don't know his name—he was one of these take-charge men, and he pretty well took charge and started directing us around.[137]

Not only individuals but also ad hoc groups of individuals "emerge" for rescue activity during disasters. Zurcher thus describes the origin and evolution of a "volunteer work crew" of men who spontaneously united their rescue efforts in the aftermath of the Topeka tornado.[138] Likewise Ross shows how, in several tornado-stricken communities, religious leaders organized "interfaith" efforts to participate in the various aspects of disaster relief.[139] As with "volunteers" of all sorts, these groups were ultimately obliged to seek "recognition" for the legitimacy of their efforts by the established disaster relief organizations in their areas.

Another indication of emergence in the emergency social system is the playing by some agent of a larger role in disaster relief than one might anticipate on the basis of routine social structure. The role of the military in disaster situations provides an illustration.[140] In the United States, with its pattern of "civilian control," military authorities can act only in a "support" role when so requested by local officials. When local officials, for any reason, are unable to handle the situation, there may emerge a pattern of de facto military control of the relief operation, although the fiction of military subordination to civilian authority must be carefully maintained. This seems to have been the situation in Waco, Texas, following a devastating tornado there in 1953.[141] When there *are* civilian officials ready and willing to perform disaster relief, there may be resentment of any attempted military involvement. Thus officials in several European countries reacted quite negatively to initiatives from the NATO military command that seemed to suggest military usurpation of what were seen as civilian responsibilities.[142]

Functional exigencies.

We are treating disasters in this book as breakdowns in social systems and we can similarly observe that *emergency* social systems instituted to repair such breakdowns have, in turn, *their* problems, which threaten their functioning as goal-achieving systems. Several of the major problems for emergency social systems will now be reviewed.

Convergence. We must note, in the first place, that disasters typically generate what is called "convergence behavior." Contrary to popular imagery of people leaving a disaster scene in panic flight, there is usually a great convergence of persons *toward* a disaster site. Fritz and Mathewson classify convergers as falling into five main types: (1) *returnees,* residents who fled the disaster and who return looking for survivors or their homes; (2) the *anxious,* people from outside who are looking for friends or relatives; (3) *helpers,* those who participate in the emergency social system; (4) the *curious,* those who want a sightseer's look at the disaster scene; and (5) *exploiters,* those who see the area as an opportunity to loot, sell goods and services, and so forth.[143]

Where *helpers* are concerned, Wallace refers to the *cornucopia* of surplus supplies and personnel that one may find at a disaster scene.[144] With reference to Halifax, Nova Scotia, in the wake of a munitions ship explosion in the harbor in 1917 that killed 2,000 people and destroyed much of the city, Prince writes:

> To a very considerable extent the material losses were replaced by communities and countries which not only supplied the city with the material of recuperation but with men and means as well. Were her own workmen killed and injured? Glaziers, drivers, repair men and carpenters came by trainloads bringing their tools, their food and their wages with them. The city's population was increased by thirty-five hundred workmen, twenty-three hundred of whom were registered with the committee at one time. Was her glass destroyed? Eighty acres of transparences came for the temporary repairs and had been placed by January the twenty-first. Were her buildings gone?

Seven million, five hundred thousand feet of lumber were soon available to house the homeless. Were her people destitute? Food and clothing were soon stacked high.[145]

This convergence of helpers and others tends to create a major problem of social control for the emergency social system. Traffic jams impede the movement of relief vehicles into the area and the movement of the injured to medical facilities.

An interesting feature of the convergence process is the contribution of officials themselves to the inundation of people. In the Indianapolis explosion, would-be helpers called the police, who were unsure of the relief needs at the Coliseum, and gave callers such messages as "we need all the help we can get," resulting in numerous unneeded wreckers and other service vehicles arriving on the scene to augment the traffic jam.[146] The chief of police of Topeka expressed another reason for official failure to discourage convergence:

> It is difficult to hold back anyone who is searching for his daughter. I don't think they've ever passed laws that say what you can do with human behavior in the time of disaster. We have been asking people to come to the aid of their fellow men for many many years now. I don't think it was any time for us to tell people we didn't need their services.[147]

Convergence is likely to stimulate "victim" resentment at the presence of most or all of the various kinds of convergers. The curious are resented for their giving a fishbowl quality to the disaster region. In Topeka, angry residents erected signs saying "Gawk You Bastards" and "Free Tour of the Tornado Area.[148] Some victims find it hard to accept the fact of being "helped," though some are able to maintain their sense of humor about the matter:

> He had to laugh about some of the things which happened. The helpers were so anxious to help and yet they made for difficulties. The men who were trying to salvage the things came from a farm background and had different values than his. They would pull out some half-destroyed article and tell him, "if you take a hammer to that you can fix it up okay."—and then they would put it on the truck. The informant didn't want to discourage them because they were being so helpful, but was quite sure he would never fix up the article. So, surreptitiously, after the helpers had put it in the truck he would sneak up behind them and throw it away again.[149]

Lack of relief facilities. The "cornucopia" of surplus personnel and equipment seen in some disasters is far from the reality of other disasters. Prince, who noted the good fortune of Halifax in receiving outside assistance, observes as well the plight of victims of "lesser" disasters who may not receive any of this outpouring of outside relief effort.[150] He cites an instance from the United States of the Red Cross, with a surplus of facilities for relief for the dramatic Triangle Shirt-waist fire in New York City, diverting some of the cornucopia to the relief of victims of less dramatically visible disasters. In a more recent case, the failure of international relief for famine victims in the Sahel desert region of Africa is attributed to the lack of interest of other countries in this essentially forgotten region.[151] The inadequacy of relief effort by the United States was related to the country's tendency to concentrate its African attention on countries with more "development" potential or those with a history of friendly diplomatic relations with the United States.

Mobilization problems. While the resources of some communities are more or less adequate "on paper" to deal with disasters, it is still necessary to mobilize those resources as people assume their disaster-related responsibilities. In fact, crucial portions of the disaster-relief system may not be informed of the disaster, as was the case in the Indianapolis explosion, when hospital mobilization was delayed by the fact that none of the area's hospitals were informed until victim cases began to arrive.[152] In the Flint tornado, local fire departments, police, and Red Cross agencies did not share a common communications net, so that mobilizing information available to one agency could not be quickly disseminated to the others.[153]

Mobilization delay has also been reported to result from the highly centralized decision-making structure of some organizations.[154] Local officials in the English town of Kimbark did not care to "stick their necks out" by taking initiatives that might be disapproved by higher authorities.[155] This was also found to be a factor in the very slow mobilization of disaster relief work after the 1972 earthquake in Managua, Nicaragua.[156] On the other hand, one disaster organization with a highly centralized command structure, the Salvation Army, is widely praised for its effectiveness in disaster mobilization.[157] This may be the result primarily, however, not of this military-like authority structure but of the strong degree of cohesiveness, mutual aid and community service orientation of the organization.

A great deal of attention has been given to the idea of "role con-flict" as a source of difficulty in mobilizing disaster rescue and relief forces. Killian's study suggests that, in a disaster, faced with a conflict between responsibility for the safety of one's family and for that of peo-ple at large, most people—even those with emergency social system responsibilities—will opt to take care of familial responsibility.[158] Only those who are sufficiently ensured of their own family's safety tend to mobilize for the community's rescue efforts. As a firemen in a tornado-stricken town said: "All the rest of the firemen had relatives that were hurt, and they stayed with them. Naturally they looked after them. If it hadn't been that my wife was all right, this town would probably have burned up. It's hard to say, but I kind of believe I would have been looking after my family, too.[159] Official behavior in the Waco, Texas, and Flint, Michigan, tornado disasters was found to show this same tendency to place private over public obligations.[160] In addition, people may have felt conflict between their roles in a specific disaster-related job and their roles as human beings responsible to fellow human beings. In Flint, for example:

> Only one-quarter of the firemen interviewed indicated that they went to the station *before* they did anything in the field. Most of them did something else because they defined the disaster as one which they, as firemen, could not deal with in a traditional and expected way. Even when attempting to proceed to the fire station, the demands of the situation were too much for them. They began for-tuitously to administer first aid, direct traffic, dig into the debris, load the injured into vehicles, and improvise according to what they, as in-dividuals (not firemen), felt was necessary in the situation.[161]

These role conflicts have not been found relevant to disaster mobilization in all cases. In a mine collapse disaster in Halifax in 1958, it was found that untrapped miners rushed quickly to the scene of disaster operations, and considerations of family responsibility acted as no deterrent.[162] Interviews with miners' wives revealed that they supported the primacy of their husbands' responsibility to fellow miners in a disaster situation:

> The wives had relatives, friends, and husbands of friends trapped in the mine, and the wives had to live in a community in which behavior was judged in part by the males' conformity to the code. In no interview could any reservation concerning a husband's decision on the part of the miners' wives be found. Rather than conflicting

group norms, Minetown rescue behavior illustrated the reinforcement
of common values shared by multiple groups.[163]

A major criticism of the role conflict explanation of mobilization
difficulties was presented by Meda Miller White in an unpublished
study.[164] Interviewing people in disaster-related organizations in the
Waco, Flint, and Worcester tornadoes, she found many discrepancies
between an official's knowledge of his family's safety and his performance or nonperformance of official duty. She suggests that people in
a disaster tend to take whatever is the "first certain solution" to the
problem of role conflict; "put in more familiar terms, the individual
will jump at the first chance to do something to help."[165] Those officials "on the job" when disaster strikes will do their disaster-related
jobs in spite of fears for family safety. Those at home will tend to delay
their mobilization for disaster duties until they have secured the safety
of their own families. Her findings, if confirmed, would suggest the
disaster-mobilization utility of keeping a cadre of officials "on duty"
rather than depending entirely on a mobilization in which people are
summoned from their homes in the event of an emergency.

The observation has also been made that mobilization problems
may center not on the *number* of workers who respond to the call for
duty but on the efficient distribution of those workers who do report.
In a study of hospital personnel in an emergency room, it was shown
that a substantial number of off-duty personnel requested to report to
medical facilities did not do so; still an adequate number of personnel
were mobilized but not very effectively mobilized to points of greatest
need.[166] Similarly, in the New York blackout of 1977, there was
tremendous need for off-duty police to report for antilooting patrols.[167]
However, these people were directed to report to the police stations
nearest their homes rather than their duty stations. The result was unfortunate in two respects. First there was an overabundance of police
at stations in Queens, the North Bronx, and other areas where there
was little looting activity and a dearth of police in Brooklyn and the
South Bronx, the major looting scenes. Second, police reported to stations that did not have on hand their personal riot gear or, in some
cases, even their uniforms. One police official complained that when a
contingent of reinforcements finally arrived at the point of need, they
"looked like a tennis team."

Coordination problems. Finally, given the complexity of rescue
operations and the variety of people getting into "the act" during

helping convergence, it is understandable if simple coordination of the separate efforts of rescuers is a major problem for the emergency social system. Most disaster-related activity may be carried out in an atmosphere similar to that which Moore describes for the Waco tornado:

> Because of the lack of a single top headquarters or directing authority, chaotic conditions resulted during the first hours following the tornado. The National Guard commander, surveying the scene later, said, "There were thousands of persons milling around. It looked like the storming of the French Bastille". . . . As an official later reported: "Little coordination between the many headquarters existed at first. Red Cross and other representatives, seeking someone in command, found nowhere to report." Or, as the Chief of Police put it more graphically: "For the first twenty-four hours, we went around in circles in one direction, for the next twenty-four, we went around in circles in the other direction."[168]

Extreme lack of organization of the rescue effort is also observed in the emergency social system following hurricane Audrey in southern Louisiana:

> So disorganized was the situation that the new parish civil defense administrator was unaware of the fact that state civil defense officials were maintaining an office upstairs in the courthouse. Outside workers by the hundreds were being hired by this office with no supervision whatsoever, and equipment and supplies were being purchased and brought into the disaster area by almost anyone who wished to do so.[169]

CONSEQUENCES

An immediate aftermath effect of disaster is likely to be a decline in the community cohesiveness that may have prevailed in the period of maximum community disaster mobilization. When the smoke clears or the dust settles, the euphoria of the one united community is likely to give way to divisiveness and bitterness. People begin to look for villains or scapegoats upon whom to blame the disaster.[170] Survivors of a devastating flood produced by the collapse of a dam that had impounded waste products from a coal mine rejected angrily the claim of mine officials that the flood was an "act of God" and entered a large and ultimately successful damage suit against the mine company.[171] A grand jury in Indianapolis indicted a number of public officials for negligence in the Coliseum explosion.[172] Another jury in Yuba City California, issued a "blistering fifty-two page criticism" of officials for their negligence in the flood that hit the city.[173] In the aftermath of destructive air raids, it is sometimes argued, people feel more hostility toward their own officials who "allowed it to happen" than toward the enemy nation that inflicted the bombing. A review by Janis, however, suggested greater hostility toward *both* one's own political leaders and toward the enemy country.[174]

Much of this new hostility may be based on resentment at the way disaster relief is being administrated. There was much public dissatisfaction with the rather indiscriminate distribution of "food stamps" to Buffalo, New York, area residents in the aftermath of the "Blizzard of '77" snowstorm. The Red Cross is a frequently criticized relief agency, apparently because the organization refuses to relax its ordinary standards of careful investigation of relief eligibility; and this persistence of bureaucratic rules in the midst of disaster strikes some observers as "heartless."[175] Rural Louisiana residents who were unfortunate enough to find themselves on "relief committees" to distribute rehabilitation funds to local residents after hurricane Audrey in 1957 were targets of hostility by citizens who resented the way the funds were distributed.[176] The change from euphoric to hostile social relations as disaster subsides is perhaps best expressed in a description of the changed community atmosphere in Anchorage, Alaska, shortly after the 1964 earthquake. Anchorage citizens had prided themselves on their "self-reliance" and their "frontier spirit" and had accepted outside assistance reluctantly if gratefully. However:

> After the first emergency problems are under control and aid from outside the community becomes available, it is normal to see an accelerating shift from accepting help to expecting it and almost demanding it. Firms which offered supplies, personnel or equipment "free for the duration" begin to expect to be reimbursed. Individuals remember long hours of overtime and ask payment. So it goes. Altruism and a communal orientation begin to be dispersed in a plethora of private interests.[177]

Another predictable immediate consequence of a disaster is an enhanced public concern with preventing future disasters and/or the community's difficulty in coping with the disaster. Warning systems are sharpened, flood-control projects are accelerated, and evacuation drills are instituted. In the case of Indianapolis, local hospitals developed a system of intercommunication among themselves that made it possible for better coordination of their efforts in future emergencies.[178]

Some skepticism about long-range improvement in disaster preparedness following a disaster may be in order. As the memory of the disaster recedes, so may public concern with prevention of that kind of disaster. Public indifference may be reinforced by outright hostility to disaster preparedness if, for example, earthquake prediction would negatively affect business and property values in an area or if it is believed that programs designed to prevent hail damage might also produce a diminishment of needed rainfall.[179] It has also been suggested that after a disaster a community prepares itself for its most recent disaster and not necessarily its *next* one:

> If a relatively new city in California is hit by a flash flood there may be a period of several years thereafter where most of the attention and all of the available "hazards component" of the city budget are invested in the development of a comprehensive flash flood warning system. The city may therefore, have a significant increase in level of preparedness for flash flood, but be quite mis-prepared for an earthquake. Monies which could have been used to hire building inspectors to check on the seismic resistance of buildings was used instead to pay for the flash flood warning system.[180]

Some possible longer-range consequences of disaster may now be considered. One generalization would have it that disaster tends to *accelerate* whatever changes are already occurring in a society. The movement from a *gemeinschaft* social order, based on relations of family and other ascriptive ties, toward a *gesellschaft* growth of impersonal or bureaucratic organization, already under way in rural Louisiana in 1957, may have been accelerated by the massive organizational imperatives of disaster relief after hurricane Audrey.[181] The "modernization" of a community, long delayed by the inertia of past vested interest, is accelerated by the necessity of "starting from scratch" in the rebuilding of a destroyed community. The modernization of Halifax was much accelerated in this way after the 1917 explosion,[182] and, in the aftermath of the destruction in the Buffalo Creek area of West Virginia in 1972, a long-planned highway through the area was initiated as any semblance of local community opposition to it collapsed.[183] Trends toward decentralization of population and activities (suburbanization) and the segregation of specialized activities into "natural areas" were greatly accelerated by the San Francisco earthquake of 1906 and that of Managua, Nicaragua, in 1972.[184] The Peruvian earthquake of 1970 had the effect of forcing many peasants into the labor economy of the emerging industrial society.[185] An aftermath effect of an Italian earthquake was that it helped to undermine the strength of the patriarchal extended family, which had been typical of Italian peasant society.[186]

Another and very different long-range consequence of disaster has been suggested. Working from Wallace's idea of "revitalization" movements as stemming from situations of cultural privation,[187] Barkun suggests that disasters may be a major source of those outbreaks of millennial religious enthusiasm that we shall be discussing in Chapter 5.[188] Millennialism involves the belief in the imminent destruction of the world, and Barkun thus suggests the connection between disaster and millennialism:

> Men cleave to hopes of imminent worldly salvation only when the hammerblows of disaster destroy the world they have known and render them susceptible to ideas which they would earlier have cast aside. . . Disaster, by removing the familiar environment, removes precisely those frames of reference by which we normally evaluate statements, ideas and beliefs. Belief systems which under non-disaster conditions might be dismissed, now receive a sympathetic consideration. The disaster victim is not "mentally ill," and millennarianism is not a form of collective psychopathology. Rather, disaster victims constitute a population among whom many show the functional analogues of mental illness, transient conditions induced by sudden environmental instability. It is small wonder that among persons so situated doctrines of imminent salvation find such ready acceptance.[189]

This is a provocative notion about the origins of millennialism[190] that we shall be examining in Chapter 5 under the heading of "Background for Renewal Episodes."

Notes

1. "Disaster . . . may be defined as a condition in which the established social life of a community or other type of social organization abruptly ceases to operate." William H. Form and Sigmund Nosow, *Community in Disaster* (New York: Harper, 1958), p. 11. Except for the implication in the Form and Nosow definition that disaster involves a *total* cessation of social system functioning, our definition could be considered as identical with theirs.

2. B. A. Turner, "The Development of Disasters: A Sequence Model for the Analysis of the Origins of Disaster," *Sociological Review* 24 (1976): 753–74.

3. Hadley Cantril, *The Invasion from Mars* (Princeton University Press, 1940).

4. Edgar A. Schuler and Vernon J. Parenton, "A Recent Epidemic of Hysteria in a Louisiana High School," *Journal of Social Psychology* 17 (1943): 221–35.

5. Joost A. M. Meerloo, *Patterns of Panic* (Westport, Conn.: Greenwood Press, 1974), p. 9

6. Donald M. Johnson, "The 'Phantom Anesthetist' of Mattoon: A Field Study of Mass Hysteria," *Journal of Abnormal and Social Psychology* 40 (1945): 175–86.

7. Nahum Z. Medalia and Otto N. Larsen, "Diffusion and Belief in a Collective Delusion: the Seattle Windshield Pitting Epidemic," *American Sociological Review* 23 (1958): 180–86.

8. Elliott R. Danzig, Paul W. Thayer, and Lila R. Galanter, *The Effects of a Threatening Rumor on a Disaster-Stricken Community* (Washington, D.C.: National Academy of Sciences—National Research Council, 1958).

9. Norman Jacobs, "The Phantom Slasher of Taipei: Mass Hysteria in a Non-Western Society," *Social Problems* 12 (1965): 318–28.

10. Alan C. Kerckhoff, Kurt W. Back, and Norman Miller, "Sociometric Patterns in Hysterical Contagion," *Sociometry* 28 (1965): 2–15. Also see Alan C. Kerckhoff and Kurt W. Back, *The June Bug: A Study of Hysterical Contagion* (New York: Appleton-Century-Crofts, 1968).

11. Sidney M. Stahl and Morty Lebedun, "Mystery Gas: an Analysis of Mass Hysteria," *Journal of Health and Social Behavior* 15 (1974): 44–50.

12. Karl E. Rosengren, Peter Arvidson, and Dahn Sturesson, "The Barsebäck 'Panic': A Radio Programme as a Negative Summary Event," *Acta Sociologica* 57 (1975): 309–14.

13. David L. Miller, Kenneth J. Mietus, and Richard A. Mathers, "A Critical Examination of the Social Contagion Image of Collective Behavior: The Case of the Enfield Monster," *Sociological Quarterly* 19 (1978): 129–40.

14. See Robert K. Merton, "The Self-Fulfilling Prophecy," in *Social Theory and Social Structure* (New York: Free Press, 1957), pp. 421–36.

15. Neil J. Smelser, *Theory of Collective Behavior* (New York: Free Press, 1963), chap. 3. On the "stress" concept, see J. Eugene Haas and Thomas E. Drabek, "Community Disaster and System Stress: A Sociological Perspective," in Joseph E. McGrath, ed., *Social and Psychological Factors in Stress* (New York: Holt, Rinehart and Winston, 1970), pp. 264–86.

16. Kerckhoff and Back, *June Bug*, p. 62.

17. Ibid., p. 72.

18. Ibid., p. 70.

19. Stahl and Lebedun, "Mystery Gas."

20. The major social-psychological treatises on rumor similarly treat the tendency of people to "improvise" information about important situations when reliable "news" is not available in highly ambiguous situations. Gordon W. Allport and Leo Postman, *The Psychology of Rumor* (New York: Holt, 1947); Tamotsu Shibutani, *Improvised News* (Indianapolis: Bobbs-Merrill, 1966).

21. Cantril, *Invasion from Mars.*

22. Nahum Z. Medalia, "Who Cries Wolf? The Reporters of Damage to Police in Pseudo-Disasters," *Social Problems* 7 (1959-60): 223-40.

23. Hadley Cantril, *Invasion from Mars* (New York: Harper & Row, 1965), pp. vi, vii.

24. Rosengren, Arvidson, and Sturesson, "Barsebäck 'Panic.'"

25. Miller, Mietus, and Mathers, "A Critical Examination of the Social Contagion Image of Collective Behavior." Rosengren, Arvidson, and Sturesson, "Barsebäck 'Panic.'"

26. Cantril, *Invasion from Mars,* pp. 57, 58.

27. Irving Rosow, "The Social Context of the Aging Self," *Gerontologist* 1 (1973): 82-87

28. Cantril, *Invasion from Mars*, chaps. 5, 6.

29. Jacobs, "Phantom Slasher of Taipei."

30. Johnson, "Phantom Anesthetist of Mattoon."

31. Medalia and Larsen, "Diffusion and Belief in a Collective Delusion."

32. Johnson, "Phantom Anesthetist of Mattoon."

33. Medalia and Larsen, "Diffusion and Belief in a Collective Delusion."

34. Cantril, *Invasion from Mars* (1965), p. 148.

35. Cantril, *Invasion from Mars* (1965), p. 143.

36. Kerckhoff and Back, *June Bug;* Stahl and Lebedun, "Mystery Gas."

37. Danzig, Thayer, and Galanter, *Effects of a Threatening Rumor.*

38. Jacobs, "Phantom Slasher of Taipei."

39. Cantril, *Invasion from Mars* (1965), p. 95

40. Jacobs, "Phantom Slasher of Taipei," p. 328

41. Medalia, "Who Cries Wolf?"

42. Ibid., p. 239

43. Danzig, Thayer and Galanter, *Effects of a Threatening Rumor.*

44. Ibid.

45. Johnson, "Phantom Anesthetist of Mattoon."
46. Medalia and Larsen, "Diffusion and Belief in a Collective Delusion."
47. Jacobs, "Phantom Slasher of Taipei."
48. Danzig, Thayer, and Galanter, *Effects of a Threatening Rumor.*
49. Kerckhoff and Back, *June Bug*, pp. 3, 4.
50. Stahl and Lebedun, "Mystery Gas."
51. Freda L. Gehlen, "Toward a Revised Theory of Hysterical Contagion," *Journal of Health and Social Behavior* 18 (1977): 27–35.
52. Schuler and Parenton, "A Recent Epidemic of Hysteria in a Louisiana High School." Likewise in the "mystery gas" episode, the first "victim" was a highly popular woman whose disturbance undoubtedly was highly visible to other workers. Stahl and Lebedun, "Mystery Gas."
53. Kerckhoff and Back, *The June Bug*, p. 78.
54. Ibid., p. 88.
55. Jacobs, "Phantom Slasher of Taipei."
56. Miller, Mietus, and Mathers, "A Critical Examination of the Social Contagion Image of Collective Behavior," p. 136.
57. Medalia and Larsen, "Diffusion and Belief in a Collective Delusion."
58. Kerckhoff and Back, *June Bug*, pp. 7–12.
59. Johnson, "Phantom Anesthetist of Mattoon," p. 181
60. Medalia and Larsen, "Diffusion and Belief in a Collective Delusion," p. 186.
61. Stahl and Lebedun, "Mystery Gas."
62. While people may indeed "love a mystery," a mystery that is never "cleared up" is a continuing source of interest and anxiety: e.g., unexplained disappearances in the Bermuda Triangle, the difficulty of health officials in providing a definitive explanation of the "Legionnaire's disease."
63. Shibutani, *Improvised News.*
64. Cantril, *Invasion from Mars* (1965), chap. 4.
65. Rosengren, Arvidson, and Sturesson, "Barsebäck 'Panic.'"
66. Danzig, Thayer, and Galanter, *Effects of a Threatening Rumor.*
67. Johnson, "Phantom Anesthetist of Mattoon."
68. On the lack of public responsiveness to air raid sirens accidentally set off in Oshkosh, Wisconsin, see Robert E. Forman, "Resignation as a Collective Behavior Response," *American Journal of Sociology* 69 (1963): 285–90.
69. Meerloo, *Patterns of Panic*, p. 13.
70. Allen H. Barton, *Social Organization Under Stress: A Sociological Review of Disaster Studies* (Washington, D.C.: National Academy of Sciences—

National Research Council, 1963). See also Allen H. Barton, *Communities in Disaster: A Sociological Analysis of Collective Stress Situations* (Garden City, N.Y.: Doubleday, 1969).

71. Russell R. Dynes, *Organized Behavior in Disaster* (Lexington, Mass.: D.C. Heath, 1970).

72. Dennis S. Mileti, Thomas E. Drabek, and J. Eugene Haas, *Human Systems in Extreme Environments: A Sociological Perspective* (Boulder, Colo.: Institute of Behavioral Science, University of Colorado, 1975).

73. Turner, "Development of Disasters."

74. Gilbert F. White, ed., *Natural Hazards: Local, National, Global* (New York: Oxford University Press, 1974), p. 3.

75. Steward E. Perry, Earle Silber, and Donald A. Black, *The Child and His Family in Disaster: A Study of the 1953 Vicksburg Tornado* (Washington, D.C.: National Academy of Sciences—National Research Council, 1956); Anthony F. C. Wallace, *Tornado in Worcester* (Washington, D.C.: National Academy of Sciences—National Research Council, 1956).

76. James B. Taylor, Louis A. Zurcher, and William H. Key, *Tornado: A Community Responds to Disaster* (Seattle: University of Washington Press, 1970).

77. Donald M. Harding and Dennis J. Parker, "Flood Hazard at Shrewsbury, United Kingdom," in White, *Natural Hazards*, pp. 43–52.

78. Thus, White reports the belief by flood plain residents that the area will not be flooded again for many years after the last flood. Gilbert F. White, *Changes in Urban Occupance of Flood Plains in the United States* (Chicago: University of Chicago Department of Geography Research Paper #57, 1958). A common attitude among residents of Atlantic coastal areas of the United States after the devastating storm of 1962 was "We get storms once in ninety years; we're not due for another." Ian Burton, Robert W. Kates, and Rodman E. Snead, *The Human Ecology of Coastal Flood Hazard in Megalopolis* (Chicago: University of Chicago Department of Geography Research Paper #115, 1969), p. 160.

79. Miletti, Drabek, and Haas, *Human Behavior in Extreme Environments*, p.20.

80. *New York Times,* 25 July 1980, p. 24

81. Irving L. Janis, *Air War and Emotional Stress* (New York: McGraw-Hill, 1951), pp. 165, 166.

82. Duane D. Baumann and John H. Sims, "Human Response to the Hurricane," in White, *Natural Hazards*, pp. 25–30.

83. Roy A. Clifford, *The Rio Grande Flood: A Comparative Study of Border Communities* (Washington, D.C.: National Academy of Sciences—National Research Council, 1956).

84. John J. Fried, *Life Along the San Andreas Fault* (New York: Saturday Review Press, 1973), p. 209.

85. Ibid., p. 210.

86. M. Aminul Islam, "Tropical Cyclones: Coastal Bangladesh," in White, *Natural Hazards,* p. 22

87. Turner ("Development of Disasters") reports a total of 191 "human errors" associated with three British mining disasters.

88. These investigations of British disasters are the basis of the analysis in Turner, "Development of Disasters."

89. Thomas E. Drabek, *Disaster in Aisle 13* (Columbus: College of Administrative Science, Ohio State University, 1968).

90. Ibid., p. 113.

91. When people in natural hazard areas are asked about the "disadvantages" of the areas in which they live, they are more likely to mention such "social hazards" as traffic, crime, and lack of entertainment rather than showing any major preoccupation with natural hazards. See, for example Harding and Parker, "Flood Hazard at Shrewsbury, United Kingdom," p. 48.

92. *New York Times,* 18 May 1980, p. 1

93. W. I. Torry, "Anthropological Studies in Hazardous Environments: Past Trends and New Horizons," *Current Anthropology* 20 (1979): 517-40.

94. Earl J. Baker, "Predicting Response to Hurricane Warnings: A Reanalysis of Data From Four Studies," *Mass Emergencies* 4 (1979): 9-24.

95. Robert W. Kates, "Natural Hazards in Human Ecological Perspective: Hypotheses and Models," *Economic Geography* 47 (1971): 438-51.

96. Harry E. Moore et al., *Before the Wind: A Study of Response to Hurricane Carla* (Washington, D.C.: National Academy of Sciences—National Research Council, 1963).

97. This was found to be true, for example, in the evacuation of persons in the Port Jervis "pseudo disaster." Danzig, Thayer, and Galanter, *Effects of a Threatening Rumor.* It is shown in another study that people are very reluctant to evacuate a disaster area unless all members of the family are present and accounted for. Ronald W. Perry, "Evacuation Decision-Making in Natural Disasters," *Mass Emergencies* 4 (1979): 25-38.

98. Form and Nosow, *Community in Disaster,* p. 70.

99. Barton, *Communities in Disaster,* pp. 76-87.

100. The persistent tendency of all-male volunteer fire companies and

emergency rescue squads to refuse to admit women as members suggests that these conceptions of the woman's "place" are still prevalent.

101. Kates, "Natural Hazard in Human Ecological Perspective"; Fred C. Ikle and Harry V. Kincaid, *Social Aspects of Wartime Evacuation* of *American Cities* (Washington, D.C.: National Academy of Sciences—National Research Council, 1956).

102. Form and Nosow, *Community in Disaster*, pp. 40–47.

103. Earl J. Baker and Donald J. Patton, "Attitudes Toward Hurricane Hazards on the Gulf Coast," in White, *Natural Hazards*, pp. 30–36.

104. Moore, *Before the Wind*.

105. Barton, *Communities in Disaster*, p. 74.

106. Taylor, Zurcher, and Key, *Tornado*, pp. 55–60.

107. The most notable of these is contained in Wallace, *Tornado in Worcester*.

108. Bates, *Social and Psychological Consequences of a Natural Disaster*.

109. Moore, *Before the Wind*.

110. Charles E. Fritz and Eli S. Marks, "The NORC Studies of Human Behavior in Disaster," *Journal of Social Issues* 10 (1954): 26–41.

111. Janis, *Air War and Emotional Stress*, p. 13. That many Americans might not have taken this flash as a signal of a dropped atomic bomb is suggested in a study by Killian of people's interpretation of a Houston explosion in a fireworks factory which some people thought was an atomic explosion; however, in their "checking" the facts, almost none of them gave any consideration to whether there had been the characteristic atomic bomb flash. Lewis M. Killian, *A Study of Response to the Houston, Texas Fireworks Explosion* (Washington, D.C.: National Academy of Sciences—National Research Council, 1956).

112. John P. Spiegel, "The English Flood of 1953," *Human Organization* 16 (1957): 3–5.

113. Wallace, *Tornado in Worcester*.

114. Spiegel, "English Flood of 1953," p. 4.

115. Roberta Wohlstetter, *Pearl Harbor: Warning and Decision* (Stanford, Cal.: Stanford University Press, 1962).

116. Henry B. Williams, "Human Factors in Warning-and-Response Systems," in George H. Grosser, Henry Wechsler, and Milton Greenblatt, eds. *The Threat of Impending Disaster* (Cambridge: M.I.T. Press, 1964), pp. 87–89: Hirotada Hirose, "Volcanic Eruption and Local Politics in Japan: A Case Study," *Mass Emergencies* 4 (1979): 53–62.

117. D. L. Webber, "Darwin Cyclone: An Exploration of Disaster Behavior," *Australian Journal of Social Issues* 11 (1976): 54–63.

118. In contrast, the people of Cameron parish, Louisiana, so reluctant to evacuate before hurricane Audrey in 1957, were extremely cooperative at the time of hurricane Carla in 1961. This was undoubtedly related to the traumatic experience with the earlier hurricane. Bates, *Social and Psychological Consequences of a Natural Disaster*, pp. 148, 149.

119. Roy Lachman, Maurice Tatsuoka, and William J. Bonk, "Human Behavior During the Tsunami of May, 1960," *Science* 133 (5 May 1961): 1405-9.

120. On the persistence of the "panic" and other stereotypes of disaster behavior in a nondisaster population (New Castle, Delaware), see Dennis E. Wenger, James D. Dykes, Thomas D. Sebok, and Joan N. Gurney, "It's a Matter of Myths: An Empirical Examination of Individual Insight into Disaster Response," *Mass Emergencies* 1 (1975): 33-66.

121. Fritz and Marks, "The NORC Studies of Human Behavior in Disaster."

122. "Nowhere in the research literature can one find confirmation that panic is a common reaction to disaster situations." Dynes, *Organized Behavior in Disaster*, p. 71. See also Enrico L. Quarantelli, "The Nature and Conditions of Panic," *American Journal of Sociology* 60 (1954): 267-76.

123. For graphic descriptions of, among others, the panics associated with the Chicago fire of 1871 and the Cocoanut Grove (a Boston night club) fire of 1942, see Douglas Newton, *Disaster, Disaster, Disaster* (New York: Franklin Watts, 1961).

124. Wallace, *Tornado in Worcester*.

125. Taylor, Zurcher, and Key, *Tornado*, pp. 32-34.

126. Form and Nosow, *Community in Disaster*, p. 87.

127. E. L. Quarantelli, "Images of Withdrawal Behavior in Disasters: Some Basic Misconceptions," *Social Problems* 9 (1960): 68-79.

128. Drabek, *Disaster in Aisle 13*.

129. Barton, *Communities in Disaster*, chap. 5.

130. E. L. Quarantelli and Russell R. Dynes, "When Disaster Strikes (It Isn't Much Like What You've Heard and Read About)." *Psychology Today* 5 (February 1972): 69.

131. Taylor, Zurcher, and Key, *Tornado*, pp. 48, 49.

132. Robert Curvin and Bruce Porter, *Blackout Looting! New York City, July 13, 1977* (New York: Gardner Press, 1979).

133. Bates, *Social and Psychological Consequences of a Natural Disaster*.

134. Kai T. Erikson, *Everything in Its Path: Destruction of Community in the Buffalo Creek Flood* (New York: Simon & Schuster, 1976).

135. Barton, *Communities in Disaster*.

136. John R. Brouillette and E. L. Quarantelli, "Types of Pattern Variation in Bureaucratic Adaptations to Organizational Stress," *Sociological Inquiry* 41 (Winter 1971): 36–46.

137. Taylor, Zurcher, and Key, *Tornado*, p. 63.

138. Louis A. Zurcher, "Social-Psychological Functions of Ephemeral Roles: A Disaster Work Crew," *Human Organization* 27 (1968): 281–97.

139. G. Alexander Ross, "The Emergence of Organization Sets in Three Ecumenical Disaster Recovery Organizations: An Empirical and Theoretical Exploration," *Human Relations* 33 (1980): 23–39.

140. William A. Anderson, "Social Structure and the Role of the Military in Natural Disaster," *Sociology and Social Research* 53 (1969): 242–53.

141. Harry E. Moore, *Tornadoes Over Texas* (Austin: University of Texas Press, 1958).

142. John Gange, "NATO's Approach to Natural Disaster Relief," *Mass Emergencies* 1 (1975): 11–19.

143. Charles E. Fritz and J. H. Mathewson, *Convergence Behavior in Disasters* (Washington, D.C.: National Academy of Sciences—National Research Council, 1957).

144. Wallace, *Tornado in Worcester*.

145. Samuel H. Prince, *Catastrophe and Social Change* (New York: Columbia University Press, 1920), pp. 113, 114.

146. Drabek, *Disaster in Aisle 13*.

147. Taylor, Zurcher, and Key, *Tornado*, p. 13.

148. Ibid., p. 44.

149. Ibid., pp. 41, 42.

150. Prince, *Catastrophe and Social Change*, p. 115.

151. Hal Sheets and Roger Morris, "Disaster in the Desert," in Michael H. Glantz, ed., *The Politics of Natural Disaster: The Case of the Sahel Drought* (New York: Praegar, 1976), pp. 25–76.

152. Drabek, *Disaster in Aisle 13*

153. Irving Rosow, *Public Authorities in Two Tornadoes* (Washington, D.C.: National Academy of Sciences—National Research Council, 1954).

154. Mileti, Drabek, and Haas, *Human Systems in Extreme Environments*, p. 53. One study shows that, while centralization does inhibit disaster relief mobilization in Italy, it does not do so in Japan, which combines high political centralization with considerable official flexibility. Benjamin F. McLuckie, "Centralization and Natural Disaster Response: A Preliminary Hypothesis and Interpretations," *Mass Emergencies* 1 (1975): 1–9.

155. Spiegel, "English Flood of 1953."

156. Robert W. Kates, "Human Impact of the Managua Earthquake," *Science* 182 (December 1973): 981–90; Alcira Kreimer, "Post-Disaster Reconstruction Planning: the Case of Nicaragua and Guatemala," *Mass Emergencies* 3 (1978): 23–40.

157. Form and Nosow, *Community in Disaster*, chap. 11.

158. Lewis Killian, "The Significance of Multiple Group Membership in Disaster," *American Journal of Sociology* 57 (1952): 309–14

159. Ibid., p. 312.

160. Moore, *Tornadoes Over Texas*; Form and Nosow, *Community in Disaster.*

161. Form and Nosow, *Community in Disaster*, p. 162.

162. H. D. Beach and R. A. Lucas, *Individual and Group Behavior in a Coal Mine Disaster* (Washington, D.C.: National Academy of Sciences—National Research Council, 1960). See also Rex A. Lucas, *Men in Crisis* (New York: Basic Books, 1969).

163. Beach and Lucas, *Individual and Group Behavior in a Coal Mine Disaster*, p. 19.

164. This study is reviewed in Barton, *Communities in Disaster*, pp. 114–21.

165. Barton, *Communities in Disaster,* p. 116.

166. Robert A. Stallings, "Differential Response of Hospital Personnel to a Disaster," *Mass Emergencies* 1 (1975): 47–54.

167. Curvin and Porter, *Blackout Looting!*

168. Moore, *Tornadoes Over Texas*, p. 11.

169. Bates, *Social and Psychological Consequences of a Natural Disaster*, pp. 29, 30.

170. E. L. Quarantelli and Russell R. Dynes, "Community Conflict: Its Absence and Its Presence in Natural Disasters," *Mass Emergencies* 1 (1976): 139–52; Rue Bucher, "Blame and Hostility in Disaster," *American Journal of Sociology* 62 (1957): 467–75; Thomas E. Drabek and Enrico L. Quarantelli, "Scapegoats, Villains and Disasters," *Transaction* 4 (March 1967): 12–17.

171. Gerald W. Stern, *The Buffalo Creek Disaster: The Story of the Survivors' Unprecedented Law Suit* (New York: Random House, 1976).

172. Drabek, *Disaster in Aisle 13.*

173. William W. Stiles, "How a Community Met a Disaster: Yuba City Flood, December, 1955," *Annals of the American Academy of Political and Social Science* 309 (1957): 160–69.

174. Janis, *Air War and Emotional Stress*, p. 133.

175. Moore, *Tornadoes Over Texas*; Taylor, Zurcher and Key, *Tornado.*

176. Bates, *Social and Psychological Consequences of a Natural Disaster.*

177. Daniel Yutzky, *Community Priorities in the Anchorage, Alaska Earthquake,*

1964 (Columbus: Disaster Research Group, Ohio State University, 1969), p. 159.

178. Drabek, *Disaster in Aisle 13.*

179. Barbara C. Farhar, "Hail as Sudden Disaster: Public Response to Hail Suppressive Activity," *Mass Emergencies* 1 (1976): 313-21.

180. Mileti, Drabek, and Haas, *Human Systems in Extreme Environments*, p. 19.

181. Bates, *Social and Psychological Consequences of a Natural Disaster.*

182. Prince, *Catastrophe and Social Change.*

183. Erikson, *Everything in Its Path.*

184. J. Eugene Haas, Robert W. Kates, and Martyn J. Bowden, eds., *Reconstruction Following Disaster* (Cambridge: M.I.T. Press, 1977).

185. Jorge P. Osterling, "The 1970 Peruvian Disaster and the Spontaneous Relocation of Some of Its Victims: Ancashino Peasant Migrants in Huayopampa," *Mass Emergencies* 4 (1979): 117-20.

186. Guido Barbina, "The Friuli Earthquake as an Agent of Social Change in a Rural Area," *Mass Emergencies* 4 (1979): 145-49.

187. Anthony F. C. Wallace, "Revitalization Movements," *American Anthropologist* 58 (1956): 264-81.

188. Michael Barkun, *Disaster and the Millennium*, (New Haven: Yale University Press, 1974).

189. Ibid., pp. 1, 56, 57.

190. Barkun admits that there are several "exceptions" to the disaster-millennialism connection: areas like upstate New York that spawned millennial movements without disaster and disasters like the Irish potato famine that did not generate millennialism.

Chapter 3

Protests

THE STUDY OF collective behavior throughout its history, from LeBon's preoccupation with "the crowd" until the present time, has been overwhelmingly concerned with the form of *protest*. Several social scientists have argued, quite persuasively, that protest actions by masses of aggrieved individuals have had profound effects on the outcomes of a number of major political struggles.[1] The sociological study of protests—their backgrounds, their participants, the process of their development and decline, their ultimate social consequences—is the subject of this chapter. Before beginning this analysis, we must give some attention to definition of protest as a field of study.

THE NATURE OF PROTEST

To define our field of study, we need a rather involved statement of the nature of protest. Each major element in this definition is italicized, and the italicized words and phrases are defined in the discussion that follows:

Protest is a *collective action* using *extraordinary means* in which the protesters attempt to secure *responses* to their *demands* by constituted *authorities*.

By *collective action* is meant that a protest involves the more or less simultaneous and coordinated demands by a number of people. One person's protest against authority is not a protest in the collective behavioral sense unless either: (1) many other people support his/her protest; for example, many people on a street helping a criminal suspect in resisting arrest; or (2) many other people are protesting in the same way at the same time; for example, many people refusing to pay rent or obey an order.

Authorities, those persons toward whom protests are directed, are those in legitimate control of the power to make the demanded responses. These are typically public officials (presidents, governors, zoning boards, etc.), but they may also be officials of more or less private organizations: heads of churches, labor unions, political parties, private schools, and so on. Whether their power is public or private, these persons have the right to make the very decisions that are demanded by the protesters.

In framing the purpose of protest in terms of *demand* and *response,* we aim to relate protest to the political process generally. Protesters demand responses in the form of political decisions. Typically demands are for (1) changes in laws, (e.g., in a law prohibiting racial discrimination in employment); (2) changes in general administrative practices (e.g., an end to "police brutality" or to "snooping" by social workers into the private lives of welfare recipients); (3) revision of some exercise of administrative "discretion" by authorities (e.g., protests against the arrest, conviction, or execution of a prisoner, the hiring or firing of an official—Douglas MacArthur, Archibald Cox, Julius and Ethel Rosenberg, etc.).

The *extraordinary means* involved in protest refers to the tactics employed in putting forth demands. In a sense, these means are defined negatively: anything other than ordinary political tactics. Ordinary tactics would include proposing and lobbying for legislative changes, filing grievance complaints, campaigning for or against the election of an official. Typical protest tactics include: (1) *strikes,* the withholding of ordinary activity in support of the established system (e.g., students refusing to attend classes until demands are met); (2) *demonstrations,* mass gatherings in rallies or marches, often with some dramatic or symbolic display of demands; (3) *disruptions* of ordinary activity (e.g., sit-ins in buildings, traffic tie-ups); and (4) *coercion,* the threatening of dire consequences if demands are not met (e.g., the holding of hostages in a prison riot while demands are being negotiated). Common to all protest tactics is the bringing to bear of *pressure* on authorities. This pressure goes beyond the ordinary strains of office, beyond the routine concerns with whether one will be reelected or fired, whether one will be able to leave office with a good reputation.

Protest of the sort we are defining is a ubiquitous feature of contemporary life. If one adds reports of disaster to those of protest, it might almost be said that our news media are largely daily chronicles of collective behavioral episodes. With such an amorphous field from which to take examples, sociological analysis has necessarily slighted certain kinds of protest at the expense of others. Without any particular rationale, it happens that there is considerable sociological interest in several kinds of protest. Three of these are covered in Skolnick's *The Politics of Protest,* reflecting the kinds of "violence" that were predominant in public consciousness in 1969.[2] These are: (1) student protest, the extraordinary series of strikes and disruptions on campuses around the world; (2) "black militancy," the civil rights protest movement and the "riots" and other radical protests that are the arguable concomitants of that movement; and (3) the antiwar protests focused on American military involvement in Vietnam. In addition to these, we will give considerable attention to several other kinds of protest, including prison riots and the protest activities of "the poor" as reflected, for example, in rent strikes and the welfare rights movement. Of these several kinds of protest, the study of "black militancy" has gotten the most sociological attention, and what follows will accordingly be somewhat shaded toward problems raised specifically by this form of protest.

Any useful definition *excludes* certain phenomena from consideration, and our protest definition excludes some episodes that are popularly called protests. Two of these will be mentioned. First, we exclude protests directed not against authority but against a party with which the protesters are in a direct conflict relation. When consumers boycott the purchase of coffee, gasoline, or other products because of alleged overpricing or poor quality, their boycott typically aims to bring extraordinary pressure on the producers and/or distributors of these products. These marketplace-oriented revolts are quite prevalent today and are frequently called protests, but they will not be considered here because they do not usually demand that "authorities" take any specified action. Also certain "riots" are excluded for essentially the same reason. Anti-Semitic pogroms and vigilante lynching mobs are riotous acts, but they are not protests in our sense; their appeal is not to authority—rather, they aim directly to coerce their victims. This type of collective behavioral episode is covered in detail in the following chapter. We also exclude such episodes as the holding of hostages at the Iranian embassy; while this event has often been described as an anti-American "protest," the demands of the captors are again not directed toward any higher authority over that of the sovereign nations involved.

A second exclusion concerns the kind of outbreak of political protest involved in the phenomenon of *revolution*. Revolutions are not protests as here defined because they involve an extraordinary effort to overthrow or remove a set of authorities from power rather than to "pressure" those authroities into specific political decisions. Revolution and protest are closely related, if for no other reason than the fact that revolution may be the outgrowth of protest failures. Unable to satisfy their political demands of a given set of authorities by "ordinary" political means or by protest, people may reach the conclusion that only through revolution can their political demands be satisfied. While revolution is outside the scope of analysis of this chapter, it is an important phenomenon that may be better understood as our understanding of protest develops.

BACKGROUND

The social conditions that facilitate or lead up to an outbreak of protest are matters of great concern both popularly and in sociological analysis. At the popular level, this concern is reflected in a seemingly inevitable aftermath effect of any major episode of riotous protest: the appointment of "riot commissions" of prominent citizens to investigate, among other things, the "causes" of such protest episodes as student demonstrations or race or prison riots.[3] Based on the findings of such commissions and from much other sociological research, we may formulate the following general statement of the conditions leading to a protest outbreak:

Protest occurs when (1) a large number of people harbor grievances against conditions in the established social order; and (2) when their discontent can be mobilized into collective forms of protest; and (3) when authorities are unresponsive to political demands made in other than protest terms.

The rest of this section is an elaboration and discussion of this very general statement.

GRIEVANCES

People who resort to extraordinary protest tactics are those who, in the first place, are likely to nourish more or less longstanding grievances about conditions in the established social order. The concept of *relative deprivation* can probably be used to cover all such grievances, provided that we are clear on the scope of coverage of the term.

Relative deprivation exists when people feel deprived as a result of comparing reality against some standard of what they feel that reality *should* be. There are two important questions here: what does it mean to be *deprived*? and to *what* is one's deprivation being compared in *relative* deprivation?

On the first question—the meaning of deprivation—most users of the concept have emphasized a *status* meaning of deprivation. People look at how well they—or those of their own kind—are doing in terms of possession of the "good things" of life (material goods, secure homes, good reputations, etc.) and judge themselves as privileged or as deprived. If the judgment is one of status deprivation—especially "relatively" in any of the ways described below—the deprived are likely to demand authoritative responses to help them improve their status. Protest has been call the "politics of the powerless,"[4] and we should certainly expect protest to emanate from deprived rather than more privileged groups.

This expectation is not always fulfilled, however, as we find, for example, youth revolts among the children of very affluent and indulgent parents and an antiwar protest movement from a predominantly middle-class constituency. In their critique of the relative deprivation perspective, Feagin and Hahn quite correctly point out that sometimes a person protests "because the situation violates his 'learned standards of justice and right,' not because of frustration in the sense of blockage of his own goal-directed activity."[5] In his study of the youth revolt, Feuer emphasizes, with some alarm, just such an idealistic rejection by youth of the "corrupt" world of their elders.[6] However, youth and other idealists *do* experience deprivation in the sense that reality is not judged to be what it *ought* to be.[7] We deal here simply with a *moral* (as opposed to a status) dimension of deprivation.

There is another sense, too, in which privileged persons may engage in protests against deprivation, even deprivation of the *status* sort. Studies of activists in the civil rights movement have shown that such activism is greatest among blacks who are the *least* personally deprived, among black college students in the South, for example.[8] Likewise, women activists in the women's liberation movement tend not to be the downtrodden "barefoot and pregnant in the kitchen" housewives whose liberation is being promoted; but rather they are relatively well-employed working women with relatively liberated personal domestic situations.[9] Along this same line, Abeles finds black militancy correlated with "fraternal relative deprivation," the belief that *blacks in general* are relatively deprived.[10] This "fraternalism" on behalf of a deprived brethren or sisterhood may represent a midpoint between protest based on purely personal status deprivation and the indifference to status and the idealism of the youth movement.[11]

The question "relative to *what*?" must now be raised. Poor or otherwise deprived persons may not *feel* status-deprived; and where nonstatus or idealistic protests are concerned, people are sometimes notorious for tolerating morally corrupt conditions that others might define as intolerable. Some comparison between reality and a standard of judgment is always involved in relative deprivation.

One type of comparison is indicated in the concept of *reference group*. In one of its meanings, a reference group is "a group which the person uses in making evaluations of himself and others."[12] Personal satisfaction depends to a large extent on the groups with which one compares oneself. If a woman, for example, compares her personal status with that of other *women*, she may be satisfied to be the third assistant vice-president if she is the only woman employed in an executive position. She may, on the other hand, compare her company status with that of *men* who are higher in rank and no more competent than herself and accordingly feel relatively deprived. Wherever, as in traditional India, a *caste* system of stratification exists, persons are vigorously discouraged from making any cross-caste comparisons, and status revolts are supposedly minimized in such systems. It might be added, in the light of our mention above of moral or nonstatus protests, that dissatisfactions may arise from negative comparisons of moral conditions in one's own social environment with the "better" conditions known to exist elsewhere. The knowledge that there *are* societies that do not allow militaristic considerations to dominate foreign or domestic policy increases the frustration of pacifist critics of militarism in their own societies. The problem of concern for a reference group analysis of protest is this: under what conditions do people experience deprivation (status, fraternal, or moral) by making such comparisons? We return to this question below, particularly with reference to the ghetto riots of the 1960s.

A rather different comparison standard is a judgment based on the discrepancy between perceived reality on the one hand and aspiration or expectation on the other. Though people may perceive themselves "in the same boat" with others with whom they compare themselves, they may perceive this "boat" to be leaky or otherwise to fall short of what it could and should be.

It is very important to observe, with reference to this expectation/reality discrepancy, that it may grow wider even while the absolute level of deprivation is being reduced. Even though people (and their comparison others) may be improving their status and/or the moral quality of their social environment, their expectations may in fact be rising more rapidly than their accomplishments. In fact, a line of sociological analysis suggests that this is often the case. Durkheim observed that suicide rates (presumably a measure of personal dissatisfaction) tend to rise in times of extreme prosperity.[13] Status improvements tend to generate escalated levels of aspiration for further improvement that may be impossible to fulfill. Thus it was suggested that the Attica prison riot came at a time when there had recently been major improvements of conditions within the prison.[14]

A slight variation on this theme of protest being generated by rising expectation is James Davies' "J-curve" theory of protest-generating conditions.[15] Using several notable revolutions as examples (Dorr's rebellion in the United States in 1842, the Russian revolution of 1917, and the Egyptian revolution of 1952), Davies shows that each revolution followed a long period of improved social conditions and a short-run reversal in the form of massive misfortunes immediately before the revolution. The reasoning seems to be that when people become accustomed to ever-improving conditions, they are especially frustrated by events that suggest deterioration rather than improvement.[16] One study of protests in Japanese-American relocation camps, Nazi concentration camps, Soviet forced labor camps, and American military and civilian prisons suggests the validity of the J-curve perspective.[17]

From the analytic perspective just developed, we turn now to a specific look at the ghetto riots in the United States in the 1960s.[18] A very large amount of research and controversy has centered on the question of the applicability of relative deprivation as an explanation of the "long hot summers" in American race relations between about 1964 and 1969.[19] We review some of the evidence on relative deprivation in the next section in examining the matter of participation in the riots. Here we deal with comparisons at the level of different communities: some American cities had no riots or riots of only slight duration or destructiveness, and many sociologists have wondered whether conditions of black deprivation were "worse" in the communities experiencing such destructiveness. The *timing* of these riots has also come under consideration; did blacks feel *especially* deprived in the period of 1964–69 as compared with lesser deprivation in the years before and after this time?

We consider first studies of whether riots occurred in the relatively most-deprived sectors of black America. A model for such studies was the comparison by Lieberson and Silverman of riot and nonriot cities for the period of 1913–63, with their concern for the "underlying conditions" that may have made some cities prone to riot.[20] Their findings were largely negative in the sense that by various measures of black income, employment, and so on blacks were no more deprived in those cities with disturbances than in those cities without them. However, their data covered a period when American "race riots" were, as often as not, instances of violence of threatened whites against "upstart" blacks (this type of riot is treated in the next chapter) and not the familiar black "protest" riots of 1964–69. Studies of riots in the latter period are more germane to our present concern. Downes shows, for example, that racial disturbances in this period were correlated with such deprivation variables as the unemployment rates of blacks, their family incomes, and their degree of home ownership.[21] In contrast, Spilerman's studies show a notable lack of any such correlations, whether one is referring to the occurrence or nonoccurrence of disturbance in cities,[22] or whether one considers the intensity of such disturbances.[23] In fact, the only significant correlations are between riot occurrence/severity and (1) the number of blacks in a given city; and (2) whether the city in question is located in the South or outside it (most riots occurred in nonsouthern cities). Spilerman's counterevidence to the deprivation hypothesis has been interpreted by suggesting that, by the 1960s, riot as a mode of political protest had become legitimated in all black communities (outside the South) as a "riot ideology."[24] The argument seems to be that *all* black Americans are deprived and that it requires only a sufficient demographic concentration of blacks in a nonsouthern area to produce a riot-prone situation. A variant on this interpretation is the argument that, by the 1960s, grievances in the black communities everywhere had crossed a "threshold" beyond which differentiations in deprivation were irrelevant to the likelihood of protest.[25] (If 3 units of grievance are sufficient to generate protest, one should not predict any difference between the protest-generating capacities of 3 and 4 units.)

A less-developed line of analysis would examine the question whether riots may have occurred in especially deprived local areas within cities. As we shall note below, rioters were not a cross-section of all urban blacks, and this may be partly because rioting was concentrated in the "worst" parts of the black ghetto, while black grievances elsewhere had not crossed the protest-generating threshold. Thus, Adams shows that riots in five midwestern American cities (Detroit, Cincinnati, Cleveland, Kansas City, and Milwaukee) occurred in areas of particularly severe housing shortages, areas "midway between the ancient, emptying ghetto cores and youthful, prosperous, advancing ghetto margins."[26]

A detailed analysis of the Hough section of Cleveland shows this "crisis ghetto" was characterized by low and deteriorating socio-economic conditions in the years 1960–65 as compared to the substantial gains being made by Cleveland blacks *outside* the ghetto area.[27] Such analyses suggest that some social scientists may have been hasty in relegating a sense of black deprivation relative to whites to a negligible role as a factor in determining riot occurrence and/or severity.

When we turn to the other meaning of relative deprivation-—relative to expectation—the relative deprivation model comes to the fore as a powerful explanatory concept. The problem of the timing of the riots now becomes more understandable. Many white (and some black) Americans were shocked that blacks were resorting to violent protest at the very time—the mid-sixties—when significant civil rights legislation had been passed and when, after a decade of white resistance to court-ordered desegregation, massive desegregation was occurring, especially in the South. But clearly the turn toward "militancy" among American blacks was related to escalated expectations for rapid improvement in their status.[28]

Whether there was anything like a J-curve of long-term improvement followed by short-term deterioration of the social condition of

American blacks is a much-debated point. Davies, the originator of the J-curve theory, believed that the explanation did fit to some extent the "contained rebellion" of the 1960s street riots.[29] As one indication, Davies computed the ratio of black income to number of years of schooling of blacks, apparently reasoning that black "satisfaction" would be measured by an increasing tendency for blacks to achieve income rewards commensurate with their educational preparation. (We consider below this idea that an income/education discrepancy may have been common among riot participants.) Davies found that this ratio had, indeed, increased into the early 1950s but then made a precipitous decline. The riots of the 1960s were characterized as a delayed reaction, coming when the example of white violence against blacks (e.g., police brutality in breaking up peaceable demonstrations) galvanized retaliatory black violence against whites.

Further study of the J-curve interpretation of riot background for the 1960s disturbances casts much doubt on the validity of this interpretation. Using opinion survey data on American blacks between 1956 and 1968, Miller and his colleagues show that there was *no* consistent direction of increasing or decreasing frustration or optimism about the future on the part of American blacks.[30] They found, instead, rapid fluctuations of black dissatisfaction/optimism from year to year. They suggest that this finding throws a different light on the peculiarity of the state of black morale in the background of the riots. The real frustration for blacks may have been the *uncertainty* of what they might expect in treatment by whites. They observe, for example, that "the inconsistent fluctuation between responsiveness and nonresponsiveness to black needs by the government produced alienation, fear and anger."[31] Aaron Wildavsky has put the same point a bit more graphically in his "recipe for violence" that he feels was being followed by white Americans at the time of the riots:

> Promise a lot; deliver a little. Lead people to believe they will be much better off, but let there be no dramatic improvement. Try a variety of small programs, each interesting but marginal in impact and severely underfinanced. Avoid any attempted solution remotely comparable in size to the dimension of the problem you are trying to solve. . . . Get some poor people involved in local decision-making, only to discover that there is not enough at stake to be worth bothering about. Feel guilty about what has happened to black people; tell them you are surprised that they have not revolted before; express shock and dismay when they follow your advice. Go in for a little

force, just enough to anger, not to discourage. Feel guilty again; say you are surprised that worse has not happened. Alternate with a little suppression. Mix well, apply a match, and run.[32]

It might be added about this bitter "recipe" that not only "government" officials but black leaders themselves participated in the concoction of the recipe. The expectation of freedom *now* was held out in full knowledge of the likelihood of a long-term struggle, and "moderate" black leaders alternated between shock at black violence and "surprise" that it had not happened before.

MOBILIZATION OF DISCONTENT

As critiques of the relative deprivation perspective point out, no collective action occurs simply because a number of people are similarly aggrieved in a certain way. Just as, on the individual level, a person may "put up with" an errant spouse or a degrading job for years on end, so may prisoners chronically bitch about prison food or students complain about a meaningless curriculum without any collective action being launched to change these conditions. In this section we examine background conditions that either facilitate or hinder the mobilization of widespread discontent into mass action.

REMOVAL OF RESTRAINTS

Many communities operate in terms of a "political culture" that defines as illegitimate any resort to protest tactics. This culture may evolve over a period of many years. Britain, a country once notable for the tendency of masses to take things into their own hands in riotous protest, gradually "settled down" into her present state as a country in which all the cultural presumptions are against extreme political action.[33] The United States, given its own lesser-known history of violent protest, is also a country in which presumptions in favor of "order" are very strong, as we shall see in examining public responses to protest. The problem, then, is an understanding of conditions that lead to a breach in the ability of a society to restrain its members from extraordinary collective action.[34]

One large generalization is that lessened restraints against extreme political action are associated with so-called *mass society* social conditions. In this perspective, people are ordinarily restrained by their involvement in a network of group memberships—primary groups, such as family, friends, and neighbors, and secondary groups, such as unions and fraternal organizations—that reinforce the political culture of order and that, perhaps, provide satisfying outlets as substitutes for fanaticism in the wider society.[35] These groups serve as buffers against mobilization into mass protest movements. Whole societies may be characterized by mass politics,[36] or particular categories of people may have the mass characteristic of being available for mobilization; thus the relatively high "propensity to strike" among miners, longshoremen, and seamen has been explained by noting the relative isolation from "normal" social contacts of people engaged in these occupations.[37] Young people, especially students, have more or less left home communities and families of orientation yet have not "settled in" with new networks of social involvement. Recent immigrants—for example, recent black migrants to American cities—are socially "marginal" and therefore available for protest mobilization.

An adaptation of the mass society view has characterized some explanations of ghetto revolts. Ransford found social "isolation" to be a frequent characteristic of Los Angeles rioters, and Geschwender and Singer similarly note that Detroit rioters tended to be those who lived alone or were otherwise socially isolated.[38]

Vigorous attacks on the "mass society" perspective with reference to the ghetto riots are developed both in the Kerner Commission report on the 1967 riots and in a special study of the Los Angeles riot of 1965.[39] Riot participants were not recent migrants to the city; they tended much more than nonparticipants in the riot area to be natives to the city. This does not quite mean, however, that participants were not relatively isolated individuals. Warren also found that most of his sample of Detroit rioters were Detroit-born, but they were much more likely than nonrioters to be recent migrants to the neighborhood.[40] This supports his finding that neighborhoods with relatively transient populations and with few formal or informal neighborhood interactions were likely to contribute riot participants in disproportionate numbers. In their zeal to correct the popular stereotype of the rioter as the "fearsome stranger,"[41] sociologists may have missed the grain of likely truth in the mass society perspective.

The concentration of riot participation among northern-born blacks raises another dimension of the "removal of restraints" explanation of protest propensity. Blacks socialized in the South were reared in a political culture that emphasized the necessity of restraining any protest against discrimination by whites.[42] The political subculture of the northern-born black was quite different. As early as the 1930s, Johnson was observing that northern blacks were being encouraged not to "take anything off" whites, some blacks even going out of their way to precipitate confrontations with whites.[43] Accordingly, the mere demographic factor of movement of blacks from a southern to a northern political culture may account for much of the racial explosiveness of the 1960s. This effect may be exaggerated if, as Sears and McConahay suggest, there is a *resocialization* of young southern blacks into the greater militance of the popular subculture of the northern "new ghetto man."[44]

In a similar way, prison officials have in recent years encountered a "new prison man" with ideas about inmate-guard relations quite at odds with that of the "old prisoner." The traditional political culture of the prison bears some resemblance to the traditional race relations in the American South. As Sykes describes a maximum security prison of a few years ago, the normatively approved guard-prisoner relation is one essentially of silent hostility.[45] The approved prisoner, from the prisoner (and probably from the guard) perspective, is the "real man" who does his time stoically with minimum involvement with officials. The prisoner who "sucks up" to guards by feigning his interest in his rehabilitation is condemned; but so is the "ball buster" type of troublemaker who protests and thereby encourages repressive action for which all must pay. The "new ghetto man" in prison, as he so often is, may be just this type of ball buster, and militant prisoners demanding their *rights* from their captors are a recent part of the prison scene.[46]

A related point about removal of restraints is made by Fogelson,[47] He observes the extreme hazard of personal injury and/or arrest for participation in riots and the expectation that these dangers will deter most people from riot participation. These restraints are less operative on ghetto blacks for two reasons: (1) "the concern for personal safety is not very effective mainly because many of them have been hardened to the point of indifference by the continuous and haphazard violence of ghetto life . . . the level of crime, and especially violent crime, is much higher here than anywhere else in urban America."[48] and (2) "the fear of arrest is not very effective mainly because the great majority of them, or at least of the men, have already been arrested (if not convicted.) According to the arrest sheets of the rioters, 39% had previous records in Buffalo, 53% in Detroit, 64% in New Haven, 67% in Atlanta, and 91% in Dayton,"[49] Similar considerations would explain lack of restraints against prison protests: prisoners already have "records," and the daily life of the typical prison is notoriously violent.

CRITICAL MASS

A large number of relatively aggrieved and unrestrained individuals may be a necessary condition for protest activity, but these conditions are hardly sufficient to explain such outbreaks. In addition, protest is facilitated if these individuals are in close communicative contact with one another. Borrowing an analogy from physics, we might suggest that there is a "critical mass," a certain number of similarly disposed people who must be in a given area before protest will occur in that area.

We have already seen above, from Spilerman's studies, that the *number of blacks* in a given city was a predictor of whether a ghetto riot occurred in that area. When one controls, as does Spilerman, for certain "deprivation" variables and still finds that cities with more blacks were more riot-prone, the critical mass interpretation seems to gain some support. Likewise, the student protests on American college campuses of 1964–70 occurred most frequently on the *largest* campuses, a finding that holds up after account is taken of the fact that protests occurred more frequently on private than on public campuses, on four-year than on two-year campuses.[50] A small campus might simply not have had enough students to supply the critical mass needed to conduct a protest.[51]

The *timing* of protest outbreaks also tends to support the critical mass influence. The ghetto riots occurred very predominantly in the hottest summer months.[52] While it has been suggested that the physical discomfort and irritability accompanying hot and humid weather may be the explanation,[53] the Kerner commission and others have suggested a different interpretation. Hot weather in the city tends to send people out of their homes in search of relief, contributing to the formation of a critical mass of people on the street and immediately available for mobilization to a protest action. Failing to realize the importance of this factor, police in Kent, Ohio, may have made a serious mistake in attempting to control disturbances at Kent State in 1970. On one violent evening the police, apparently believing that bars inflamed the situation either by promoting drunkenness or by furnishing places for protest conspiracies, closed the bars early.[54] They thus put people on the street who were potential participants in the riotous events of that evening.

PREPROTEST ORGANIZATION

There is another perspective on background conditions facilitating protest mobilization that is highly critical of the "mass society" perspective discussed above. The small-scale groups that have the allegedly *restraining* influence on protest mentioned above may, in fact, provide the very experience and leadership in organized social activity that is a vital resource for anyone interested in organizing a protest.[55] To cite one example: black Americans have been subject to the "communal deprivation" of inability to develop their own network of small-scale groups.[56] There is a great exception, however, to the nondevelopment of autonomous black institutions: the black *church*, which was long the mainstay of black social organization in America.[57] The relation of the black churches to protest activity is rather controversial, a question of whether the religion of blacks served more as "opiate" or as "inspiration" to black militancy.[58] But to some degree the evidence is unequivocal: certain black churches and clergymen were in the forefront of the civil rights protest of blacks.

We shall have other occasions, in the chapters that follow, to note that a given kind of collective behavioral episode may develop out of a prehistory of much organizational work among those who ultimately are involved in extraordinary episodes. Perhaps, as the mass society perspective suggests, many or even most protest participants are the relatively isolated who have little to "lose" by protest activity. Even so, organized protest does not grow out of totally unorganized masses, and the state of such preprotest organization of aggrieved individuals is an extremely important consideration.

PROTEST IDEOLOGY

Finally, an important "resource" that may be vital in the mobilization of protest is a set of ideas that justify or legitimate the protest. Not only Marx but many other sociologists have emphasized how people in positions of power use that power to dominate the stock of ideas available to people: to Marx the "ruling ideas" at any time are the "ideas of the ruling class."[59]

For protest to be mobilized, it may be necessary that this monopoly of ideas by the "ruling class" be broken; that, in the words of Mannheim, there be not only *ideologies* that justify the social status quo but also *utopias* that challenge the legitimacy of the established social order.[60] Highlighting this factor in his study of the closely related phenomenon of revolution, Crane Brinton notes that, before a number of major revolutions, there was a "desertion of the intellectuals" from the side of ideological support for the ruling classes to sympathy with and promotion of revolution.[61]

The importance of ideological support in mobilizing protest can be shown in several different respects. As concerns intellectuals per se (professors, writers, artists, etc.), such persons may spark the only glimmer of protest opposition to be seen in a totalitarian community, as in the Soviet Union, where a few writers maintain their "dissident" status in spite of severe governmental repression. Intellectuals seem to be more attracted to certain kinds of protest than to others, for example, protest against such alleged miscarriages of justice as occurred in the Dreyfus case in France, and the Sacco-Vanzetti and Rosenberg cases in the United States. The behavior of intellectuals in the Sacco-Vanzetti case is perhaps typical.[62] There was much expressed sympathy among intellectuals for these victims who were (perhaps) not guilty of the murders for which they were executed but only of being "radicals" at a time after World War I when, as we note in the next chapter, there was much fear of radicals. However, intellectuals only "discovered" the case in its later stages, and this, plus their tendency to idealize the victims and politicize the struggle, made their support of rather doubtful help in protesting the executions. Similarly, as we also note in the next chapter, intellectuals often become involved in protests against persecutions of such victims as witches or communists, but this protest support may again come very late in the process of persecution.

At another level, the support of "popular" leaders of all sorts may be a key factor in mobilizing protest. We might note, for example, the shifting content of popular music during the protest decade of the 1960s.[63] While earlier popular music was almost exclusively focused on "romantic" themes, the music of this era began to have a more decided theme of social protest. It is difficult to measure the value of Bob Dylan, Joan Baez, or Pete Seeger as a protest "resource," but one might hazard the guess that the influence of one of these popular singers must have represented a social force equal to at least a half-battalion of armed troops. Protest music of this sort is part of a broader category of "symbols" that protesters may use very effectively in mobilizing support for themselves.[64] Included in this category are the slogans of a movement ("Freedom now," "Hell, no, we won't go") that epitomize the aims and the sentiments of protesters.

Finally, protest ideology may include ideas among a potential group of protesters that legitimate the use of protest tactics. The riots of the 1960s severely polarized black and white attitudes about the legitimacy of riots as a mode of protest. In a Los Angeles sample, for example, 75 percent of whites but only 24 percent of Watts-area blacks (and only 9 percent of black arrestees in the riot) said they believed that the black cause had been "hurt" by the Watts riot.[65]

LACK OF OFFICIAL RESPONSIVENESS

If protest represents demands made by extraordinary means, it should be clear that a factor in the resort to protest is the inability to satisfy these demands through routine means. As Etzioni puts it, "When people have institutionalized channels to express themselves and channels which are effective, why should they take to the street?"[66] Some difficulties in the way of maintenance of such channels will now be reviewed.

FAILURES OF PLURALISM

According to one frequently articulated view of American government, the United States has a *pluralistic* political system responsive to the demands of any reasonably large and well-organized interest group.[67] In this model, there is "something for everyone," since elected officials must satisfy the demands of a wide range of members of a supporting coalition. On the national level, with two great pluralistic parties more or less evenly matched in electoral strength, neither party can afford to offend any major voting bloc, whether it be the poor in Appalachia, the Poles in Milwaukee, or the gays in San Francisco.

The trouble with the pluralistic system is that it does not always work this way. It may in fact be necessary to be *nonresponsive* to one part of the constituency in order to appeal to another part. Thus the Republican party largely "wrote off" any hope of black electoral support in order to pursue its "southern strategy" in 1968 (although, with federal money in its pocket to entice support, it did launch a "minority responsiveness program" for the 1972 election and many ethnic minorities did support the Party[68]). The Democratic party similarly wrote off any attempt to appeal to the interests of far right constituents.

As if such writeoffs were not problem enough, some groups find that even their votes for a successful candidate will not always lead to expected payoffs in fulfillment of their demands. John Lindsay was elected mayor of New York with heavy black support, but he was unable to overcome middle-class white opposition to several programs designed to help this black constituency.[69] More vexing still, perhaps, when Gary, Indiana, became in 1967 the first large American city to elect a black mayor, Richard Hatcher, the new mayor found that he was unable to fulfill certain demands of his supporters.[70] He was unable, for example, to bring many blacks into his administration as officials, and his followers had to be satisfied with what Hatcher and his mostly white government could "do for" Gary (which was a great deal). American voters have almost come to recognize the promises to help after election as so much campaign rhetoric. The presidential candidate who promises to be the president of *all* the people is understandably going to be *more* the president of a big campaign contributor than of those citizens whose demands are not backed by the power of money.

SOCIAL AND CULTURAL DISTANCE

One reason for nonresponsiveness of authorities and their powerful supporters to relatively weak groups may be a sense of cultural and social superiority to those making demands. Social welfare agencies operating in slum areas believe they have a professional expertise to know what is "best" for the poor. Accordingly, as Cloward and Elman observe, "there are few institutionalized safeguards against the potentially unjust exercise of power by governmental 'poor agencies' and virtually no place where low-income people can turn for assistance in availing themselves of the channels of redress that do exist."[71]

Other instances of communication difficulties between officials and those subject to their authority may be cited. Police officials resist demands for civilian review boards to investigate charges of police brutality as intrusions on professional integrity. When citizens complain to the police about the police, they are likely to find *themselves* being discredited or shamed for making the complaint.[72] A hospital patient who demands his or her rights too vociferously may be defined as a "problem patient" to be gotten rid of.[73] Students who demanded inclusion in a one-person–one-vote system of deciding on academic matters outraged their "liberal" professors, who were aghast at the thought of professors being outvoted by students.[74] Slightly aging professors in the 1960s found to their surprise that this "new student" was so much harder to deal with than was that "apathetic" student of the 1950s that they complained about so often. The "new ghetto man"—blacks and Puerto Ricans from Buffalo, New York City, and other cities—made up most of the prisoners at Attica State prison, and the guards from this small town in western New York were unable to understand this new breed of prisoners.[75] The protests on the campuses, in the prisons, and in the streets were related to this inability of authoritative people to "understand" students, prisoners, blacks, or poor people.

Related to this distance—as cause or as effect?—is the relative invisibility of some relatively powerless groups of people. Since "we" law-abiding citizens do not understand the criminal, we place him or her behind bars and out of sight. We do not have to look at conditions therein unless some muckraking journalist does an "expose" for us, but even then we can look the other way. Any ethnically segregated community is relatively invisible to outsiders. Watts in Los Angeles represents perhaps the extreme of an invisibility tendency for black ghettos.[76] In the great urban sprawl called Los Angeles, whites had no occasion even to pass *through* Watts; as someone said, you go in or out of Watts, you never go through it. (Harlem in New York is similar in this way.) Students live in segregated on-campus housing or sometimes in youth ghettos off campus,[77] and most middle-income people "know all about" poverty because they have seen or read *The Grapes of Wrath* or have given money to send a ghetto kid to a summer camp.

LACK OF CAPACITY TO RESPOND

Even the most sympathetic authorities may be unable to respond to all the demands placed on them by various interest groups. Two reasons may be mentioned.

First, the structure of political power may place it beyond the capacity of given officials to yield to demands. Parents demanding a school curriculum change may be truthfully told by a local school board that such a change would jeopardize the school's standing with an accrediting agency or a state or national office of education. With no effective electoral or other power at that higher level, any demand is simply at the mercy of that authority. "Community control" is thus demanded to make such local pressure effective, but this may fly in the face of another great tendency of "mass society": the tendency to centralize decision-making structures.[78] Two of the most tumultuous campus confrontations of the 1960s were in the California system of higher education, at the University of California at Berkeley in 1964, and at San Francisco State College in 1968-69.[79] In both cases, local presidents and faculties were favorable to many student demands, but local campus decisions could be and were overturned by the Board of Regents for the University (in the case of Berkeley) and the Chancellor and the Board of Trustees for State Colleges (in the case of San Francisco). Similarly, the warden at Attica state prison could not grant prison reforms without the approval of the State Commissioner of Corrections (who would in turn require the Governor's approval).[80]

Second, even with adequate authority to respond to demands, the established grievance machinery may be unable to respond to an overload of demands. In a city like New York in which, as Lipsky claims, millions of people live in buildings that had already been condemned in 1900, a housing authority cannot respond to all housing complaints, and one official admits that the agency deals only with "crisis cases" forced to their attention, perhaps by dramatic protests.[81] As civil rights legislation developed, various "human rights commissions" were set up by states and local communities to investigate charges of discrimination. These commissions are limited in what they can accomplish for grievants by the long and arduous process typically involved in prosecuting a case before one of these commissions.[82] Their effectiveness has further been reduced in recent years with many additions to their workloads, as women and members of miscellaneous other groups (homosexuals, the handicapped, etc.) are now processing complaints through the same agencies, which have not seen any expansion of staff.[83] As more poor people were encouraged to participate in poverty programs, a similar overtaxation of official resources occurred. As Bell and Heald put it, "The very fact that there is an increase in the number of claimants leads, inevitably, to lengthier consultation and mediation, and, more importantly, to a situation wherein thousands of different organizations, each wanting diverse and contradictory things, simply check each other in their demands."[84]

PARTICIPATION

The questions *who?* and *how many?* dominate most discussions of protest participation. Before we can attempt any intelligible answers to these questions, we must consider the meaning of protest participation.

NATURE OF PROTEST PARTICIPATION

In the area of political participation generally, Milbrath has referred to the distinction between political *gladiators* and *spectators*.[85] While some people—the gladiators—run for office or manage campaigns, others limit their political activity to something less intense: voting, wearing a campaign button, reading about an election campaign in a newspaper. The gladiator-spectator distinction is applicable to the politics of protest as well. Lewis has observed a pattern during the Kent State protests that he believes is typical of other episodes: (1) a *core* of the most active (throwing rocks, shouting, burning, looting, etc.); (b) a *cheerleader* group of people encouraging and applauding this action ("right on," "burn baby burn"); and (c) a more passive and perhaps ambivalent group of *spectators*.[86] Most of the participation studies mentioned below refer to active core participants, but these distinctions might help refine our future participation studies.

The method of determining *who?* and *how many?* participate in a protest is a matter of some difficulty. People typically do not stand still to be counted in a mass crowd and are hard to count if action is dispersed in many places simultaneously (as in many riots).[87] Objective observers are seldom on the scene anyway. If one depends on estimates by supporters or opponents of the protest, one typically finds estimates that under- or overestimate participation, depending on the wishes of the estimators.[88] Like Joseph McCarthy with his dwindling list of "known communists in the State Department" as he was called on to document his numbers, the leader of a rent strike in New York in 1963–64, Jesse Gray, claimed many more buildings were on strike than he was ever able to prove to reporters.[89] Likewise, when black leaders called for a 1980 Christmas buying boycott in downtown Buffalo in order to pressure local merchants to pressure the district attorney for a more effective investigation of the "22 caliber killings" of blacks by a white man, these leaders claimed wide participation in the boycott even as the local news media observed the failure of the boycott, basing their assessment (somewhat illogically) on interviews with blacks who *were* shopping in downtown Buffalo.

Two major after-the-fact counts are employed in most sociological studies: (1) studies of people arrested for allegedly illegal protest activity (such counts will not, of course, tell us how many or what kinds of people participated and were *not* arrested, especially where activities that are not illegal are concerned, and there is also the serious possibility of false arrest of those not actually participating); (2) self-reports of having participated in a given protest (such reports may again not be totally accurate, since people do sometimes forget or misrepresent their activity even in routine actions such as voting or going to church and presumably will be at least as unreliable about their participation in extraordinary behavior). Virtually all sociologists are sophisticated about such methodological problems, and the "findings" we report here are based on honest efforts to deal with such problems of data bias.

PERSPECTIVES ON PROTEST PARTICIPATION

The quantitative and qualitative questions about protest participation can be dealt with together by examining several prominent views about the nature of the participation in protests. Though our discussion is mostly derived from reports of ghetto riot participation, we shall be able as well to bring in material on participation in other types of protest.

THE RIFFRAFF VIEW

A popular interpretation of protest is that it is participated in by those *few* people who represent the lowest status elements of a community: its criminals, chronically unemployed, and perhaps "agitators" who use the disturbance for some politically subversive purpose. Two studies by Rude suggest the historical persistence of this popular image of the protester and show the factual inaccuracy of the image.[90] In neither the food riots of eighteenth-century England and France nor in the protests of prisoners in the British penal colony in Australia is the "riffraff" view consistent with evidence of participation by relatively respectable elements of the respective populations.

Many Americans, including some highly authoritative ones,[91] have held similar beliefs about the ghetto rioters of the 1960s. In fact there is apparently no support in sociological studies for the riffraff view of ghetto riot participation. The National Advisory Commission on Civil Disorders (the "Kerner Commission") was very anxious to determine the validity of this view.[92] Its social science staff, using arrest data from riot cities, arrived at the following conclusions, all contradictory to the riffraff theory:

First, it was *not* the case that only 1 or 2 percent of ghetto residents were active participants, a view frequently stated; a larger percentage than that were *arrested* in the riot cities and clearly there were many other participants for each arrestee (as is true of most kinds of "crime"). Depending on how participation is measured, best estimates of active core participation fall somewhere around 15 percent of the total ghetto population of Watts and and 11 percent of Detroit's ghetto population.[93] These are really low estimates of participation, since they are based on the total ghetto population. If one considers only that age and sex group most prone to participation—males from 15 to 35 years of age—it is shown in Newark, for example, that probably fully 45 percent of the young ghetto males participated in that riot.[94]

Second, it is also not true that the riot participants were predominantly "hoodlums and agitators." Although, as noted above, a very large percentage of riot arrestees had prior arrest records, this merely reflects the almost universal experience of young ghetto males of being arrested at some time, often just on suspicion. Bayard Rustin, an eminently respectable middle-class black, in commenting on the Mc-Cone Commission's report, which gives an authoritative stamp to the riffraff interpretation of the Watts rioters, says: "I myself have been arrested twice in Harlem on charges that had no basis in fact: once for trying to stop a police officer from arresting the wrong man; the second time for asking an officer who was throwing several young men in a paddy wagon what they had done wrong."[95]

As far as agitators are concerned, the Kerner Commission, which was specifically directed to investigate the question, "concludes that the urban disorders of the summer of 1967 were not caused by, nor were they the consequences of, any organized plan or 'conspiracy.'"[96]

Likewise the commission to study the New Jersey disorders states: "Clearly, the evidence that witnesses or interviewees were able or willing to provide to the Commission would not support a conclusion that there was a conspiracy or plan to organize the disorders."[97] Probably the nearest thing to a "conspiracy" conclusion in commission reports is the 1970 statement of the Scranton Commission on student unrest: "Most student protestors are neither violent nor extremist. But a small minority of politically extreme students and faculty members and a small group of dedicated agitators are bent on destruction of the university through violence in order to gain their own political ends."[98] The agitating activities of Mark Rudd at Columbia or of Mario Savio at Berkeley might almost fit this decription, except that it is extremely doubtful that either was "bent on the destruction" of his university.[99]

Third, there is counterevidence to the alleged lack of sympathy of the general population in ghetto black communities for the rioters. On this point, Fogelson asked rhetorically, "Is it conceivable that several hundred riots could have erupted in nearly every black ghetto in the United States over the past five years against the opposition of 98 or 99 per cent of the black community?"[100] Not only is this proposition "inconceivable," it has been proven false, in the research of Fogelson and others. To cite one survey finding, blacks in 15 cities with riots covered by the Kerner report were interviewed and 54% expressed sympathy with the riots.[101] Similarly, in the matter of the campus demonstrations it is true, as the Scranton Commission indicates, that "the majority of the students are not tactical extremists."[102] It is also true, as the Commission reports, that the great majority of students did, at the height of the period of confrontation, believe that such tactics might be necessary to achieve desired social changes.[103]

THE UNDERCLASS VIEW

A given protest may be concentrated in a large, relatively deprived group of people. The ghetto riots, if clearly not "riffraff"-dominated, were clearly protest by and on behalf of lower-class blacks with some degree of involvement of poor urban whites. Rent strikes and protest against welfare abuses are "poor people's" protests almost by definition.

With reference to the ghetto riots, a couple of reservations to the under-class formula for participation should be indicated. First, not all lower-class blacks in American cities—even in the ghetto areas—were equally represented as participants. The activists in these protests were very predominantly young males with relatively few participants among women or older members of the black underclass.[104] Second, there is some question whether the participants were the most relatively deprived in *all* dimensions of status. Various studies of riot participation and/or attitudinal "militancy" among ghetto blacks have suggested that in one dimension of status, that of educational level, participants may in fact have been better educated than nonparticipants.[105] In another dimension, that of occupational status, some studies have indicated that participant blacks were more likely to be unemployed or in unsatisfying lines of employment.[106] A promising interpretation of these facts is the possibility that riot participation, like other forms of "radical" political behavior, may be related to a lack of consistency of status in different dimensions, a low level of *status crystallization*.[107] One of the more striking improvements of black conditions in America has been a recent expansion of educational opportunity, but this has not been accompanied by corresponding improvements of occupational opportunities (and accompanying better incomes), leading to the increasing frustration of well-educated but underemployed blacks.[108] It is thus shown that blacks in the Watts area were much more likely to have participated in the riot if they indicated a large discrepancy between the jobs they held and the jobs they would like to hold.[109]

PROTESTERS AS REPRESENTATIVE

Another interpretation of protest participation in some instances is that protest enlists the support of a representative cross-section of the protesting group. In noting this tendency among black ghetto residents, Moinat et al. observe that "anyone living under the conditions prevalent in the ghetto may be predisposed to riot."[110]

Protests may in fact *become* broadly representative at one stage of a development process. They may originate with an "underclass" or some other particular population element and then add support at later phases of development. Observers of street riots have noted that, in the early phases of violence, the action is dominated by youngsters who, for example, break store windows, but that as full-scale looting develops, older people may move into the action.[111] Other protests may originate with an elite and later become more popular and representative in the character of their participants. The student movement, originally sparked by activists who were the children of middle-class and intellectual parents,[112] came to attract the support of an increasing number of students on "nonelite" campuses and from lower-class origin.[113] Similarly, the antiwar demonstrations, originally dominated by a small group of ideological pacifists, gained support from a broader representation of the American public. This happened partly because the movement attracted the support of many prominent clergymen and influential black leaders such as Martin Luther King. Also, as the Vietnam war went on, increasing numbers of people who called themselves "hawks" became antiwar critics; not because, as for the "doves," they questioned the moral propriety of American military involvement, but because of indignation at the war's drain on American resources and/or frustation that we were not "winning" the war.[114]

PROCESS

We turn now to the dynamic side of protest episodes, the study of some of the processes by which protests grow or diminish in size and also in their qualitative natures. Any protest episode has its points of initiation, development, and termination. There are growths and declines in the number of protest participants and also changes in the nature of protest activities: student petitions at one time, sit-ins at another time, and so on. The ebb and flow of protest activity may strike one as being as chaotically unpredictable as are gusts of wind. Skeptics may, indeed, suggest that the answers to sociological questions about these proceses are "blowing in the wind." In the perpetual wind tunnel that sociological analysis inhabits, we should perhaps be able to say a few coherent things about the nature of such processes.

A PERSPECTIVE

As we examine protest process, we shall note some unique sociological perspectives that will influence the direction of analysis. "Social process" tends to be examined, by sociologists, from two perspectives.

First, there is an emphasis on the *communication* process. The actions of human beings influence one another in essentially *symbolic* ways: through the use of language but also through such nonlinguistic devices as meaningful gestures (an upraised fist, for example) or the presentation of an object with a symbolic meaning (mounting a flag, wearing an armband, etc.) The distinction between interpersonal and mass media modes of communication, mentioned in the last chapter, will again be important to the analysis here, as will be the distinction between official (news) and unofficial (rumor) sources of information about a protest episode.

In the second—and perhaps less obvious—place, the analysis will emphasize the importance to the development of protest episodes of the *interaction* between the protesters and those agents of social control who attempt to suppress or contain the protest. The common-sense view of protest seems to be that a protest develops and *then* police and other agents of social control attempt, with more or less success, to bring the protest under control.[115] In fact, as study after study of protest episodes has shown, the actions of police, other public officials, influential opinion leaders, and, indeed, of "public opinion" generally will have profound effects on the qualitative and quantitative development of a protest. The "societal response" to protest is, in a word, an integral part of the process by which protest develops.[116]

PHASES

INITIATION

Protests typically begin with some precipitating incident. The nature of the precipitant depends, of course, on the nature of the protest. In the violent American street riots of the 1960s, the usual precipitant was the use of force by police against black civilians in a public setting.[117] Typical precipitants: (1) the arrest of a black motorist and an ensuing argument on a Los Angeles street before the Watts riot of 1965;[118] (2) a police raid on an after-hours speakeasy with a black clientele before the 1967 Detroit riot;[119] and (3) the shooting of a black youth by an off-duty policeman on a New York street before the 1964 riots in Harlem and Bedford-Stuyvesant;[120] A frequent observation about such precipitants is that, in many cases, the incidents were not especially unusual events in their social settings; black ghetto residents were accustomed to just such acts.[121] It was the *symbolic* character of these incidents that gave them their protest-generating power. The repetition of "police brutality" in the ghetto had apparently generated a level of smoldering resentment in the black community, ready to be "set off" by a single incident that could symbolically evoke the whole pattern of police maltreatment.[122]

Some protests, in contrast, seem to result from mass objections to policy decisions made and implemented at higher levels of authority than that of the police patrolman. In this case, too, relatively routine decisions may precipitate more diffuse resentments by their power to serve as symbols of more general grievances. President Nixon's announcement of a Cambodian invasion in 1970 set off a wave of protest against the Indochina war, even though this decision was not so different than many other "escalating" decisions by the Pentagon during the war. The Free Speech Movement in Berkeley in 1964 was precipitated by the relatively trivial decision by university officials to deny students the use of university property for political activity.[123] A wave of strikes against cooperation with the Nazi occupation government in Holland was precipitated by an announced call-up of civilians for forced labor service, again not so unusual an action in that repressive context.[124] A 1980 riot in Miami followed the acquittal of several white police officers charged with the illegal murder of a civilian, again an all-too-familiar example of southern "justice."[125] In each of these cases, the "trivial" or routine official act symbolized more general resentments: against the Indochina war itself, against overly conservative university administration, against the indignity of the Dutch in having to collaborate with the Nazis, against the perceived lack of protection against police violence in the black community.

In addition to understanding the symbolic quality of precipitating incidents, we must attempt to understand why some such incidents and not other similar ones precipitate protests. A direction for a partial explanation is that the precipitating power of certain incidents is enhanced by the exaggerations generated by the rumor process. In both the Los Angeles riot of 1965 and the Philadelphia riot of 1966, the false rumor circulated among blacks that the police had beaten a pregnant woman in the course of the precipitating incident.[126] One reason for the violent Dutch reaction to the Nazi labor call-up in 1943 was that there was published a version of the scope of the call-up that was a large exaggeration of the facts.[127]

Rumor may also serve to generate an expectation of a protest episode, and the expectation may be realized through a self-fulfilling prophecy. After a typical precipitating incident in Richmond, California (white police pursuing black civilians in a stolen car), witnesses at the scene were reported as calling friends to "tell them to bring their shit because it's going to happen in North Richmond tonight."[128] These anticipations may also emanate from public officials who anticipate disturbances and perhaps help generate them by their nervous reactions to otherwise "minor" incidents. Police in Cambridge, Maryland, in 1967, believing that an "inflammatory" speech by H. Rap Brown had precipitated a riot, mobilized their riot control forces in a way that helped set the riot in motion.[129] Police forces throughout the nation anticipated riots following the April 1968 assassination of Martin Luther King; and the tremendous mobilization of police force in anticipation of these riots may have been a force in the fulfillment of their expectations.

BUILDUP AND QUALITATIVE CHANGE

The "escalation" of an incident into a full-scale mass protest may occur in a more or less predictable series of stages. Studies at the Lemberg Center for the Study of Violence at Brandeis University suggest that, following the precipitating incident, there are three such stages of development that *may* follow, depending on what happens at each stage.[130] These stages, discussed below, are: confrontation, Roman holiday, and war or siege.

Confrontation

Many protests involve public acts of defiance of constituted authority. Rocks, bottles or other missiles are hurled at police officers, obscene epithets are pronounced, draft cards are burned, and so on. These are acts that ordinarily either do not occur or else occur "behind the backs" of constituted authorities. The *symbolic* character of these defiant acts should be emphasized. To call a police officer a "motherfucker" or to hold a police car captive (as did students at Berkeley in 1964) are not in themselves acts that are intrinsically threatening to social order. Rather, in Zinner's words, such acts tend to have a "symbolic meaning as a point of no return in resolving the differences" between protesters and authorities.[131] These "point of no return" actions tend also to occur from the side of the authorities: for example, the "disperse or else" order to a crowd, the action of

University of California officials giving suspension notices to students refusing to obey official orders.

At perhaps a somewhat more advanced stage of confrontation, protesters often articulate *demands,* the fulfillment of which is a condition for ending the protest. Prisoners at Attica quickly organized a committee of spokesmen to list their demands for prison reform.[132] In another typical episode, students and professors in Budapest in 1956 worked out "sixteen points" in their demands for the lightening of Soviet domination of Hungary.[133] In many cases these demands include the granting of "amnesty" for protesters, the promise of nonreprisal for any illegal protest acts.

Sometimes, as in the cited cases, these demands are "nonnegotiable," in that protesters will not compromise, and they are also demands that it is understood that officials cannot or will not accept. In this situation, the articulation of demands represents simply a way for protesters to mobilize support by the symbolic rejection of their demands by authorities: the intransigence of authorities "proves" that the protesters are correct, especially if they are complaining about lack of official responsiveness to their everyday demands. From their side, officials may reject negotiation under pressure, even if the demands of protesters are "reasonable" from the perspective of officials. Their message to protesters is likely to be: "go home (to your cells, your classes, etc.) and *then* we will talk about your grievances." This stance may be adopted because of its *symbolic* value: if we yield, even on small and reasonable grounds, to demands made in this way, we shall later have to yield in larger and less reasonable ways. When protesters and authorities behave with such an eye to the symbolic value of their actions—to mobilize support or to protect their authority—the likelihood of a resolution of demands at this stage is obviously very slight, and the further stages of protest development may be anticipated.

A protest need not, however, move beyond the confrontation stage if either of two conditions is satisfied. On the one hand, protesters may indeed "go home" with their demands unfulfilled. Resolute police action may force prisoners to their cells, but there may be more subtle forces leading protesters to relinquish their demands. Officials at the University of Chicago in 1966 learned a lesson from the Berkeley disturbance by avoiding "point of no return" repressive acts against campus demonstrators.[134] Even though officially maintaining the line of not negotiating under pressure—and thereby maintaining their "authority"—many university officials in an *informal* way expressed sympathy with the demonstrators and encouraged students to expect a favorable response to their demands. Under these conditions the protesters were increasingly isolated as "extremists," and their protest collapsed.

Second, a protest may end after the confrontation stage if officials choose for whatever reason to yield to demands. Piven and Cloward summarize their findings on "poor people's protests" with several instances:

> Political leaders will offer concessions, or press elites in the private sector to offer concessions, to remedy some of the immediate grievances, both symbolic and tangible, of the disruptive group. Thus mobs of unemployed workers were granted relief in the 1930s; striking industrial workers won higher pay and shorter hours; and angry civil rights demonstrators were granted the right to desegregated public accommodations in the 1960s.[135]

The motive for such official responsiveness to demands may be the need of political elites for the electoral support of members of "disruptive groups." Even without such electoral power, protesters may prevail. When, in 1944, employees of the Dutch national railroads refused to collaborate further with the war effort of the occupying regime, the Nazis were impotent to resist this mass action.[136] Even the threat to starve the population by refusing rail service for domestic needs as well ultimately failed, because the Allied invasion of Holland had been the "signal" for the uprising, and the Germans did not want Dutch food rioters at their backs as they fought the Allies at the front. These are a few instances of successful "politics of the powerless," a theme to which we shall later return.

Roman Holiday

Some protests escalate to a stage in which there is a rather thorough breakdown of constituted authority and protesters "conquer the street" for a time.[137] Along with this enlargement of control of the protesters, there is likely to be a *euphoric* state of intense pleasure at this sudden display of mass power. There may be a feeling among protesters very similar to that in the euphoric stage of the "disaster syndrome"—the feeling that the protest is a *community* event: "We're all

in this together.'' There may also be a sense of collective accomplishment through the dramatic impact of the protest—the feeling, for example, that "we put Watts on the map."[138]

These euphoric feelings are typically expressed in behavior that
suggests that protest actions become a kind of sport or game. As Conant describes the behavior at this stage, the protesters "displaying an
angry intoxication indistinguishable from glee . . . may hurl rocks,
bricks and bottles at white-owned stores and at cars containing whites
or police, wildly cheering every 'hit.' They taunt law-enforcement officers, risk capture, and generally act out routine scenarios featuring
the sortie, the ambush and the escape."[139] In this same spirit, it was
observed "in Newark some youths did not want to stop the riot
because the score in deaths stood '25–2' with the police and Guardsmen leading."[140]

The danger to protesters in this sporting relation to police authority
(a danger that is, of course, part of the attraction) is indicated in the
observation about the sportlike quality of interaction between Kent
State students and National Guardsmen in the minutes before the killing of four students by the guardsmen. To Lewis this interaction
seemed "almost choreographed, and one had the feeling that a sporting event was in progress."[141] The "police riots" by which a number
of street demonstrations have been terminated are sufficient evidence
of the danger of protesters "playing" with such lethal force.

War

A condition of the Roman holiday stage is that the protesters have
"conquered the street" or at least have had enough street power to
carry out acts of defiance rather promiscuously. No public authority
worthy of the name will permit its monopoly on the use of violence to
be challenged for long. After a protest against the anti-Semitic
persecutions in Amsterdam, the residents of that city got a "one-day
vacation" from Nazi occupation rule in 1941.[142] Students at Columbia
University effectively controlled administrative offices for several days
in 1968;[143] and Attica prisoners "held" the prison, along with several
hostages, for several days in 1971.[144] Each of these protests ended in
the deployment of whatever police force was necessary to reestablish
official control of protester-occupied territories. For some time—
whether a few minutes or a few days or weeks—the issue of territorial

control was in doubt, and the protest had entered the stage of war or siege for this interval of indetermination. The euphoria of uncontested street control by protesters is replaced, at this stage, by the grim process of protesters attempting to "hold out" against capitulation to the repressive efforts of authorities.

TERMINATION

The termination of protest episodes has been given much less explicit sociological attention than either their initiation or their development. At the risk of stating a truism, it might be said that protests terminate as a result of a combination of internal and external forces. As an example of internal forces: protests may end when protesters feel that "we've made our point," having gotten concessions to their demands or at the least having dramatized their grievances. In saying "protesters" have this feeling we are, of course, overgeneralizing. Diehard protesters may decry the half loaves they are being offered, but many others may gladly settle for what is in any case more than they had ever hoped to gain. Thus a militant student organization, Students for a Democratic Society, was far from satisfied with the results of student protests, but SDS found itself unable to mobilize continued student protest against rapidly liberalizing universities.[145]

Some protests terminate when officials decide to bite the bullet and take coercive action to repress protest. Governor Rockefeller in 1971 finally resolved to send state troopers with adequate weaponry into Attica prison to regain control from rioting prisoners. The "one-day vacation" that the Dutch took against Nazi rule ended as soon as the Germans could reestablish their control of the streets, and Russian tanks terminated the several days of the Hungarian revolt.

In a complex combination of internal and external factors, protests may terminate in the weariness and disillusionment of protesters. A psychiatrist who worked closely with participants in the southern civil rights movement describes a clinical pattern of "weariness" among activists who found ultimately that the struggle was not worth the effort.[146] Coles attributes much of this weariness to the very "success" of the movement: its growth in membership and, with this, the growth of tiring organizational work. Enthusiasm for a protest may also wane as protesters become aware of the futility or even the counterproductivity of their activity. Students at UCLA in the early 1970s were observed by Turner to be no less dissatisfied with their academic conditions than students of a few years earlier; but they had seen how little change had resulted from all the previous turmoil and were disillusioned with protest as an instrument of change.[147] Indeed, so Cohen argues, college students were beginning to see how public reaction against student demonstrations was undermining public support for the university, making further protest against the university only self-defeating.[148] At a more personal level of negative consequences of protest activism, many students at Florida State University in 1973 cited a "fear of sanctions" as one of the reasons for the decline of the student movement.[149]

FACILITATING PROCESSES

Underlying the protest phases analyzed above are some social processes that, when they occur, tend to facilitate various types of protest action. These processes, like the actions of "agents," to be discussed below, do not occur in any obvious sequential order but seem to be involved at all phases of the protest action.

KEYNOTING

There is, first, the observation that any more or less unified action of a group of protesters—shouting slogans, looting, presenting demands or whatever—depends on some sort of process of focusing collective action in that particular direction. This process of setting directions for collective action has been called *keynoting*.[150] Given the variety of inclinations toward action or inaction of persons who are potential protesters, the importance of a *suggested* line of action by an influential person or persons is an obvious matter. The problem is that of *how* protest action is keynoted.

One perspective emphasizes the rather unpredictable character of protest keynoting, just as some analysts would emphasize the unpredictability of those who take leadership roles in disaster relief. People with no particular previous history of social leadership may emerge in the exigencies of an extraordinary situation. At Berkeley in 1964 a shy girl (with a famous father), Bettina Apthteker, rose to speak compellingly at a campus demonstration and a campus unknown (to a lesser extent, however) named Mario Savio emerged rapidly as an instigator of the campus revolt.[151]

Other studies sugget, in contrast, more continuity in leadership between protest keynoters and those prominent in routine community affairs. In his study of the riots in several American cities in 1966 and 1967, Hundley found that riot leaders tended to be people well known and informally influential in their communities.[152] There may, in fact, be a significant difference in the character of keynoters at the more and less escalated levels of protest. Officials of CORE, an established black civil rights organization, planned and executed protest rallies that first galvanized black protest against the police shooting in New York of a black boy in 1964,[153] and Stokeley Carmichael keynoted early protest in Washington, D.C. against the assassination of Martin Luther King by taking a band of followers from store to store, demanding that these stores close out of respect for Dr. King.[154] In both cases, these demonstrations quickly escalated into riots, against the wishes and efforts of the established leaders who initiated the first protest action. Perhaps at the escalated phases, keynoting passed into the hands of people with less established leadership roles.

Careful study of protest episodes is likely to show that keynoting is not engaged in by a single individual or organization, even at a given stage. Different individuals with different ideas about what should be done about some situation are likely to compete for influence with one another. A carefully documented instance is the study by Heirich at the Berkeley campus in 1964.[155] After students "captured" a police car and surrounded it for many hours, the car was used as a kind of soapbox for speaker after speaker to mount and to exhort the crowd to take one action or another. In particular, a group of "counterdemonstrators" composed of campus fraternity men made vigorous efforts to dissuade the crowd from continuing the confrontation.

A final observation about the keynoting process is that it also operates among officials trying to arrive at actions to "handle" a protest episode.[156] Since we often think of officials as operating in a highly "rational" way in deciding how to deal with protesters, we are often unprepared to learn of "muddling through"—for example, in the San Francisco police handling of a gay protest in 1979 against the light sentence handed out to a man who had murdered a prominent homosexual official.[157] The agonizing debates that often occur on the question of whether and when to request federal troops or National Guardsmen to supplement the local police force provide many opportunities to observe keynoting in the decision-making process.[158] Various public officials as well as numerous interested and influential outside "observers" similarly debated among themselves the merits of various ways of dealing with the Attica prison uprising.[159] Also, at the level of police action by individuals in direct confrontations with protesters, this action sometimes deteriorates to the level of a "police riot" against protesters, as happened in Chicago in 1968.[160] The keynoting processes by which such violent action is "suggested" to a group of law enforcement officials have not been much studied but are worthy of close consideration.

EMERGENT NORM FORMATION

Another process that may occur during protests is the emergence of a set of norms to govern the behavior of protesters during this unusual episode. The popular image of a race riot, for example, as a "rampage" of antisocial behavior would hardly suggest that riot behavior is normatively regulated. But true to the sociological tradition of trying to determine whether "deviant" behavior is actually conforming to an alternative set of norms, collective behavior theorists have postulated that such special norms *do* emerge during protest episodes.[161]

These emergent norms, in some respects, are simply the reverse side of routine norms: if respect for the police officer, the schoolteacher, the flag are norms of everyday behavior, *disrespectful* treatment of these objects becomes the normative order of the day during a period of defiance of authority. When rioters loot stores they may see their acts not as deviant acts but as consistent with a redefinition of property rights ("this stuff belongs to the people")[162] or as a symbolic attack on the prevailing system of property rights.[163] In Washington, D.C., and elsewhere, looters showed little remorse or tendency to conceal their looting activities from their peers.[164] These attitudes are very different from those of looters in natural disasters, who tend to be few in number and quite stealthy in their acts, which heavily offend the public conscience.[165]

Another evidence of norm emergence in protest is the fact of discrimination of protesters among potential victims of their protest actions. Rioters in Detroit and Los Angeles, among other cities, were shown to have spared most black businesses from looting and arson, as well as the businesses of those whites who had favorable reputations with clients in the local community.[166] This finding does not hold with all riots, however. Berson found that in Philadelphia in 1966 white stores were attacked without regard to quality of neighborhood relations, and even black business owners fared poorly if they lived so far from their businesses that they were unable to arrive in time to place black-identifying insignia on their stores.[167]

SOURCES OF INFLUENCE

It remains to discuss the contributions of different persons or agencies to the dynamics of protest development.

SOCIAL CONTROL AGENTS

Of special interest is the relation between protest episodes and the behavior of police and other authoritative agencies. As suggested above, the interaction of authorities may be an important consideration at every stage of protest process. We have already seen how official anticipation of a protest outbreak may contribute to the precipitation of a protest episode. Police presence at the scene of a "disturbance" may help to escalate the protest in at least two other ways: (1) The visible presence of police agents at the scene of an incident tends to generate a convergence of public interest on the incident, as people move toward a flashing police light or in the direction of a siren. If police are present at the scene of a confrontation and are visibly taking no action to restrain the protesters, this inaction may be taken as an indication of immunity of protesters to carry on their confrontational acts.[168] (2) On the other hand, police overreaction to confrontational acts may precipitate resentment of "police brutality" and mobilize new support for the protest by witnesses who were relatively indifferent to the original protest but indignant at excessive police action. Many students at Kent State were "radicalized" by their experience with police and military force on their campus,[169] and police action against Columbia University demonstrators tended to increase the degee of student support for the protest.[170] Stark thus describes the conversion of a sorority girl at Berkeley to sympathy with demonstrators upon observing police treatment of demonstrators and exclaiming, "Oh, my God, they are pigs!"[171]

Police may also use "inappropriate control strategies"[172] that escalate rather than reduce protest intensity. A common technique is that of demanding that crowds disperse and using coercive measures (tear gas, marches with fixed bayonets, etc.) if persuasions fail. Since people may simply disperse in all directions and gain new adherents in these directions, the dispersion may simply increase the amount of protest participation. It was said that "hell broke loose in Harlem" in 1964 from the moment that police charged into an intersection with the intention of clearing the street.[173] Marx suggests that the police dispersion tactic "may be somewhat equivalent to jumping on a burning log in order to put out a fire, only to have sparks and embers scatter widely."[174]

MASS MEDIA

Protest episodes are "news," and the news coverage of these episodes is often cited as having "inflammatory" consequences in the direction of spread of the protest. This effect is unlikely to occur at the very early stages of protest development, since these typically occur prior to the dissemination of news coverage.[175] A more realistic possibility is that news coverage at the early phases of protest contributes to the escalated phases. The coverage may make the intensity of protest appear greater than it is and lead, perhaps, to official overreaction and the cycle of interaction of protest defiance and official repression. Some violent protest may in fact be "staged" in the presence of reporters and cameras by protesters who wish to promote such escalations.[176]

Fear of such escalating effects of news coverage has led some officials to request or impose what amounts to a news blackout on information on protests. This news suppression may have the desired effect in preventing the spread of protest, but it may in the process deprive protesters of a desperately needed channel of communication of their grievances to a wider public. This effect was shown, for example, in a decision by news media in Winston-Salem, North Carolina, not to "play up" the riots occurring in that community.[177]

News coverage may, however, have something of the opposite effect to that of escalation: people *avoiding* provocative acts if it is known that their acts will be reported as news. This may especially be the case where *police* violence is concerned, since police typically do not want any extreme acts toward protesters publicized. A realization of this may have been behind the insistence of Attica prison inmates that a *New York Times* reporter (Tom Wicker) join the panel of people negotiating between prisoners and officials, and that there be television coverage of the negotiations.[178]

DIRECT INTERPERSONAL CONTACTS

Many escalated protests break out in areas of high population concentration, and complex communications systems are not necessary to spread information and motivation to participate in the protest. The Washington, D.C., riot of 1968, for example, began as "the intersection of 14th and U. streets, N.W., was filling up with its customary nighttime crowd [on] . . . a balmy Washington spring evening."[179] The daily movement of people may result in the movement with them of communication about a protest. An anti-Nazi work strike in Dutch towns in 1943 spread easily into the countryside because of the many rural commuters to urban jobs and because the closing of dairy plants forced many town dwellers to travel to farms to get milk, carrying news of the strike with them.[180]

A rather different communication channel was apparently of critical importance in the Newark riot. The arrest of a black taxicab driver precipitated the riot. The radio network of local cabs was used as a source of communication about the protest that increased convergence of protesters on the scene of the disturbances, including a "caravan" of black-operated taxicabs.[181]

COUNTERPROTESTERS

The Kerner report credited "counterrioters" with a large role in controlling the street riots of the 1960s, as ghetto blacks walked the streets urging their fellows to refrain from violent protest.[182] Warren found that counterrioters in his Detroit sample tended to be native-born blacks who were long-term residents of their neighborhoods (as opposed to the rioters, who were mostly native-born short-term neighborhood residents), reflecting, perhaps, their greater attachment to their neighborhoods and their desire that these neighborhoods not be destroyed.[183] As we have seen, counterprotesters at Berkeley tended to be fraternity men; those who, perhaps, were more attached to loyalty to the university. Anderson, Dynes, and Quarantelli found a variety of orientations of couterrioters, including those who used their influence against rioting for personally opportunistic purposes, and those who believed in the riot "cause" but not in its tactics.[184]

Whatever their social origins and motives, counterprotesters tend to have much difficulty in legitimating their protest-dampening activities in the eyes of officials. Marx and Archer report on a number of citizen's-patrol-type groups in America.[185] Many of these groups maintain a competitive or "adversarial" relation with local police forces. During one antiwar demonstration in Seattle the police chief declined the policing "assistance" of one such citizen's patrol, saying he feared he would have to face two mobs rather than one. Many volunteers as counterprotesters were similarly turned down by police during the 1960s riots. In Milwaukee in 1967 youth workers and civil rights leaders offered to talk with a crowd of protesters but were told by police not to do so.[186] A Human Relations Council in Los Angeles tried to mediate between protesters and officals but found officials ultimately unwilling to honor commitments to meet with protesters.[187] A deputy police chief allegedly told the director of this council, "we know how to run a riot and we are going to handle it our own way."[188]

CONSEQUENCES

We turn now to the question of the effects of protest episodes on the social systems in which they occur. If protests are essentially *political* in nature, as we have emphasized throughout, it is a natural question to inquire of the effectiveness of protest in securing the demands of pro-testers. We shall consider, therefore, those conditions that seem to facilitate or hinder the success of protests in securing demanded responses. In addition we shall consider some "byproduct" conse-quences of protest that do not bear directly on the success or failure of their political demands.

FACTORS AFFECTING PROTEST
SUCCESS OR FAILURE

Protest represents the "politics of the powerless,"[189] and an analysis of protest success or failure must start from a recognition of the political problem of the powerless confronting powerful authorities. Welfare clients are supposedly at the "mercy" of welfare bureaucra-cies that decide on their benefit eligibilities; students must ultimately yield to the power of administration officials who can suspend them at a last resort; street civilians without weapons to match those of police must ultimately yield to those police. How do the powerless generate enough power to force authorities to yield to their demands? We shall examine now several possible answers to this question. The ability or inability of a given group of protesters to take advantage of these possibilities may be seen as a factor in the success or failure of that pro-test.

MORAL PERSUASION

Protesters may appeal to the consciences of authorities, a feeling by the latter of the justice of the claims that protesters are making. This feeling may be enhanced by dramatic demonstrations of the commitment of protesters to the cause for which they are acting. This was the tactic of Gandhi in protesting British colonial rule in India.[190] The suffering experienced by him (e.g., his food fasts) and his followers would presumably engender guilt feelings among officials "responsible" for this suffering through their intransigence in the face of protests. Bobby Sands and other militants of the Irish Republican Army used hunger-strike tactics in 1981 to protest alleged maltreatment of I.R.A. prisoners in Northern Ireland's prisons.

The tactics of Gandhi were employed with some success in the American civil rights movement by the Congress of Racial Equality (CORE) and by Martin Luther King and his followers.[191] Nonviolent civil rights demonstrations showed different degrees of success in promoting civil rights legislation. The protest at Selma, Alabama, in 1965 was perhaps the most successful such demonstration, leading directly to the very important Voting Rights Act of that year.[192] The sight of police officials using fire hoses and police dogs against unresisting demonstrators helped galvanize great public sympathy for the demonstrators and their cause. Earlier nonviolent demonstrations had been somewhat less successful. A demonstration in Albany, Georgia, had little public impact because police officials there were very careful not to engage in confrontational "point of no return" acts of violence against the demonstrators. Nonviolent civil rights leaders learned a lesson from this failure, the lesson that nonviolence elicits public sympathy only if it is displayed in the presence of "police brutality." The city of Birmingham, Alabama, was chosen as a demonstration site in 1963, apparently largely because the demonstrators knew they could "count on" the violence of the police establishment in that city. Although the Birmingham demonstrations generated the desired "suffering in the face of police violence" pattern, movement leaders had trouble translating this success into broad public support. One reason for this was that in Birmingham there were instances of violence by black civilians that were played up by the news coverage. Public sympathy for protesters can easily be lost if there is a perception that protesters "deserve" violent treatment by virtue of their own violence. The reader may learn with some shock that townspeople in Kent,

Ohio, far from sympathizing with students, four of whom were killed by National Guard fire, felt that the students deserved harsh treatment and some expressed regret that *more* students had not been killed.[193] The student "violence" that justified Guard violence entailed such horrendous behavior as spitting at Guardsmen and chanting their "obscene" slogan, "one, two, three, four—we don't want your fucking war." Black protester behavior at Selma, in contrast, was a model in nonviolent decorum, and blacks were able to use the methods of moral persuasion with very good effect.

Student protests in the United States were considerably successful in having certain reforms made in University practices: for instance, liberalized dormitory rules, more interesting and "relevant" courses and majors available, and greater participation by students in university decision-making.[194] These changes occurred, it might be argued, because university administrators were sympathetic (or at least indifferent) in their own attitudes toward these reforms, and they capitulated easily before the "suffering" of student demonstrators. Likewise, Soviet Baptist demonstrators against the governmental regime were more openly tolerated in outlying provinces in which officials were not so strongly committed ideologically to the Soviet system that was being protested against.[195] When officials *are* ideologically committed very strongly to values that protesters are questioning, the methods of moral persuasion are not so likely to succeed. The attempt by non-Europeans in South Africa to use Gandhi's passive resistance technique to protest the apartheid system illustrates this possibility.[196] The white regime in the country was totally opposed to any breach in that system and, far from touching the consciences of officials by their suffering, the demonstrators simply brought down ever more repressive action on themselves.

COERCION

Protesters may also be able to threaten officials in certain ways and thereby induce favorable outcomes to the protest. Indeed one political scientist virtually *identifies* protest with the use of such tactics. According to Eisinger, protest "is a device by which people manipulate fear of disorder and violence while at the same time they protect themselves from paying the extreme costs of acknowledging such a strategy.[197]

In a study of many "challenging" groups over the course of American history, Gamson observes that, in general, those groups have been most successful in promoting their demands if they have on occasion resorted to violent tactics.[198] Groups may, of course, avoid violence out of ethical considerations; Gamson observes that "virtue, of course, has its own intrinsic rewards. And a lucky things it does, too, since its instrumental value seems to be dubious.[199] Piven and Cloward have similarly argued that the use of "disruption" tactics has been a powerful tool of a number of groups in the struggle to secure recognition of their political demands.[200]

We commented above on the "invisibility" of many ethnic ghettos. Ghetto residents may recognize the necessity of disruptive acts to focus any kind of official attention on ghetto conditions. Thus a black resident of Richmond, California, says: "We're completely forgotten until something happens, and then everyone comes running wondering why it's happening.[201] Campus protests may likewise be more effective if they use disruptive tactics that threaten the continuation of university functions. One study of 129 campuses shows that some of the changes demanded by students in 1968–70 were made at 19 percent of the "no protest" campuses, at 33 percent of the "orderly protest" ones, and at 61 percent of the "civil disobedience" campuses.[202]

The element of threat is also involved, in a complex and controversial way, in studies of the aftermath effects of the American street riots of the 1960s. The political "message" of the riots as black protests seems to have gotten across sufficiently to political powerholders that significant responses were made to demands articulated during these protests. The "riot commissions" appointed by local, state, and national levels almost invariably recommended greater attention to the outstanding grievances of black Americans. Large amounts of "welfare" money poured into black ghetto areas, especially those that had been the scenes of destructive riots.[203] It was also true, in the Watts area of Los Angeles, that the local police maintained a remarkably subdued attitude toward ghetto blacks in the immediate aftermath of the 1965 riot.[204] It could certainly be argued that these authoritative responses represented concessions under the threat of renewed violence of the sort just experienced.

These "favorable" outcomes to the use of threat-inducing protest tactics must be balanced by some other considerations. It was observed in Watts, for example, that the tremendous input of programs designed to improve the lot of residents tended to taper off in a few months, and much of the community euphoria of having accomplished something by the riots tended to disappear.[205] Some time after the campus disturbances of the late 1960s, Nathan Glazer wrote that student demonstrators found it so much easier to change "the world" (e.g., to have an impact on the foreign policy of the United States) than to change "the campus," which Glazer found to remain about as it was before the demonstrations.[206]

One reason for the lack of longer-range success of black or campus protest is that officials not only made "liberal" concessions to protesters but also mobilized their social control forces to prevent further protests of the same sort. On the author's own college campus, the faculty in the spring of 1970 acceded to student demands to close the college early in protest of the Cambodian invasion. In the fall of 1970, the same faculty voted a "never again" resolution, indicating that it would not again yield in this way. Also, on this and most other campuses across the country, there were promulgated quite explicit rules of civic order on campus, forbidding disruptive tactics and spelling out definite sanctions for violation of these rules. In the aftermath of the street riots, city governments, according to one study, tended to increase their expenditures for police and fire protection rather than to increase their welfare expenditures.[207] Such increases in welfare expenditures in riot cities as *did* occur came primarily from federal funds rather than local ones.[208] The withdrawal of this outside assistance after the immediate national crisis had passed was the predictable result of this pattern of response to the riots.

ALLIANCES

A given group of protesters may find it lacks the resources either to threaten or shame officials into yielding to their demands. They may, however, attempt to enhance these resources by forging alliances with other groups of similarly aggrieved persons. Thus a reanalysis of Gamson's analysis of the success or failure of "challenging groups" indicated a greater success rate among those groups able to make such alliances.[209]

Two instances of effort at such alliances among the "powerless" were similar both in the nature of the effort and the outcome. These are: (1) the effort of various non-European groups in South Africa—natives, Indians, Coloureds (racially mixed)—to make common cause in a campaign to defy the country's apartheid laws,[210] and (2) the attempt by different groups of "coloured" Britons—mostly black West Indians, Pakistanis, and Indians—to resist racial discrimination in Britain, especially the move to restrict immigration from nonwhite nations of the British Commonwealth.[211] Both these movements failed, and partly for the same reason: that parochial differences and rivalries among members of the protesting federation made it very difficult for them to maintain unified action.[212]

In the United States, several alliances of protesting groups have been attempted, with limited success. Martin Luther King's personal commitment to antiwar protest helped to generate some degree of alliance between the black and antiwar movements. However, internal criticism by other black leaders of this activity as a diversion from truly "black" issues limited the influence of King's personal example. Leaders of the women's movement, cognizant of the historical affinity between feminist and abolitionist protest,[213] have hoped for vigorous support of their movement by blacks. Many blacks have, however, suggested some actual conflict of interest between the two movements. Specifically, a feminist movement that threatens the status of males may contrast with the felt need of many blacks, both male and female, to *enhance* the status of the black male, who has borne the brunt of racial discrimination in American society.[214] Alliances of poor people's protests with the black civil rights movement have apparently been more successful, as the needs of the poor and blacks (jobs and better housing, for example) seem to coincide well. This alliance was reflected, for example, in the rent strike protest in New York in the 1960s,[215] and, of course, in the poor people's campaign conceived by Martin Luther King and executed by his successors in leadership of the Southern Christian Leadership Conference. A source of tension in this alliance is indicated however, in Barbaro's analysis of "ethnic resentment:" the feeling of Jews, Puerto Ricans, and others that the black poor have gotten the lion's share of benefit from Great Society welfare programs, to the virtual exclusion of the poor of these other ethnic groups.[216] Finally, protest alliances may be weakened if there is resistance to the inclusion of people in the alliance who for one reason or another suffer a stigmatized social status. The difficulty of movement alliance between gay activists and the broader civil rights movement has thus been explained largely as a matter of reluctance of other protesters to make common cause with militant homosexuals.[217]

OUTSIDE ASSISTANCE

A final tactic of weak groups in enhancing their power to gain demands through protest is that of appealing for assistance to powerful outside groups. The black civil rights movement, in its preriot phases, depended heavily for its success on the support of "white liberals," especially of leaders and rank-and-file members of the Jewish community. In recent years, the black-Jewish connection has been seriously eroded if not annihilated by such developments as: (1) the attack by black street rioters on white-owned property in the ghetto, which happened frequently to be Jewish-owned property;[218] (2) black demands in New York and elsewhere for local community controls of schools in black ghettos, a development that would perhaps threaten the jobs of Jewish schoolteachers;[219] and (3) the demand by blacks for "affirmative action" programs that threatened Jews with exclusion from jobs and school admissions as black "quotas" were being filled.[220] With all these developments, the diminished support of Jews for the black civil rights movement is more understandable.

In some instances, protesters in one country may hope for support of their cause by powerful friends in other countries. Black South Africans, for example, have certainly entertained hopes that foreign powers would threaten and/or shame the South African government into abandoning the apartheid system. The United States and the Soviet Union as cold war competitors for Third World support may have been expected to give such support, as were certainly the new "black" nations of Africa. Yet for various reasons of "national interest" (especially the avoidance of cold war confrontations in Africa), these sources of external support have largely failed to develop.[221] The reluctance of the United States to intervene diplomatically on behalf of the Jewish minority in the Soviet Union (despite the demand for such intervention by Senator Jackson and others and despite President Carter's aggressive "human rights" stand in international relations) is another example of failure to elicit outside support when this conflicts with perceived "national interest."

The outside "power" to which many protests address themselves is the alleged power of "public opinion" to pressure officials to yield to protest demands. As we have noted, prison rioters at Attica were much concerned to gain wide publicity to their protest activity. The fact that only Governor Rockefeller, an elected official presumably responsive to the opinions of his constituents, could grant their demands accounts to some extent for the prisoners' interest in publicity.

The influence of public opinion on the outcome of protests is a very complicated matter. Its influence in the direction desired by protesters depends, in the first place, on the perceived "legitimacy" of protest in the public view.[222] Protest may be viewed as illegitimate if it is perceived that a protesting group's grievances are nonexistent or trivial.

Much student and youthful protest encounters a public perception that today's "kids" are really the overpampered children of affluence who have little right to bitch about marginally unsatisfactory conditions.[223] Even if the complaints of a group are seen as fully legitimate, their *tactics* in promoting their demands may be rejected by public opinion. This was in fact the reaction in American public opinion to the violent and disruptive tactics of both student and black demonstrators.[224] These public attitudes place would-be protesters in a severe tactical dilemma. They may, on the one hand, avoid tactics that will elicit public disapproval and risk having their claims ignored as public attention is lavished on groups using more striking and newsworthy tactics. On the other hand, they may use disruption tactics to bring their demands to public attention and risk having an indignant public pressure officials to engage in repressive acts against themselves.[225] The ever-presence of this dilemma is one factor in making the politics of the powerless the delicate art that it is.

BYPRODUCT EFFECTS

Like all "purposive action," episodes of protest action may have "unanticipated consequences."[226] Given the complexity of possible byproduct consequences of social events, we shall narrow our attention here to a single dimension of such consequences. A question of sociological interest about any group action is the effect of that action on the unity or solidarity of the group involved. It is only because of the ties that bind people to one another that social life exists at all, that people are not simply isolated atoms of existence. Sometimes actions are undertaken with their unity-enhancing functions in mind, as when recent Polish industrial worker protests were organized by a group called Solidarity. More typically, perhaps, we act with quite concrete ends in view—materialistic, religious, recreational, sexual—and the unifying or disunifying effects of such actions are simply byproducts.

In considering the solidarity effects of protest, we may examine a prominent proposition from general sociological theory. Protest action is typically a form of *conflict* action, since protests engender the several kinds of resistance that we have been considering. According to a perspective developed by Simmel and more recently by Coser, conflict action tends to have a unifying effect on groups engaged in conflict.[227] In this perspective, whether a group has succeeded or failed in its protest demands, it tends to generate a level of group solidarity that outlasts the relatively brief period of intense protest activity. We now subject this idea to some critical examination.

A tempting verification of the proposition being discussed is provided by an examination of the black protest movement in the United States. The decade of the 1970s in no way fulfilled the expectation of continued black militancy growing out of the tumultuous decade of the 1960s; nor has such militancy been prominent in the early 1980s, in spite of some severe provocations in the form of violence against blacks in American cities. As early as 1973, Julius Lester, for example, was raising the question of what had happened to black militancy.[228] Whatever happened to black protest, an arguable effect of the protest decade was that it spawned the black pride and unity that did seem to develop throughout the 1970s. Although sit-ins, riots, and marches are hardly part of the personal experience of young blacks today, they have parents who *did* live through those "glorious" days and who have established for themselves and their offspring a black identity that does not need reinforcement by further protest. This is a highly speculative interpretation of an outcome of the black protests, but it does seem more consistent with the *extended* cessation of black protest than is the more common "disillusionment with protest" interpretation of that cessation.

Less sanguine outcomes of protest episodes in terms of group unity must also be considered. If a protest results in a *severely* repressive reaction by authorities, the repression may deprive a group of a major resource for its future solidarity. Prison riots typically result in the participants in the revolt being transferred to other prisons. Protesters against American military policy in Japanese relocation camps during World War II were "segregated" into special camps designed to deal with dissidents.[229] The "passive resistance" campaign of non-European against South African apartheid around 1950 led to a mass arrest and imprisonment of leaders that deprived these communities of some of their natural leaders for many years.[230] In all these instances it would by very difficult to say that the protest episodes had a unifying effect.

A final instance of a doubtful unifying effect of a protest episode may be cited. Unsystematic personal observations suggest that today's college students are almost totally uninfluenced in their morale or outlook by the protest activity on campuses a decade and more ago. Professors accustomed to glazed student looks when they refer to the ancient history of 1968–70 may see a deeper-than-expected glaze when the topic of reference is the student demonstrations of those days.[231] No informal lore of *those* glorious days seems to prevail in the college culture. This may be partly because students are a come-and-go group whose attachment to a school lasts the four or so years they are there; hardly a student may be found in a classroom today who was on the same campus in 1970. There are, of course, lores and traditions that survive over some years: those associated with the football team, the frat house, perhaps the academic department. But note that these are all traditions whose continuation is more or less programmed into the routine operation of the university. There will always (well, nearly always) be a Woody Hayes or a legendary professor of English literature. Protest episodes are generated by unique conditions that will not dependably recur. With a shifting population and a protest tradition not tied to institutional routines, the lack of long-term unifying effects of campus protest is not so difficult to understand.[232]

Notes

1. George Rudé, *The Crowd in History* (New York: Wiley, 1949); Theodore Lowi, *The Politics of Disorder* (New York: Basic Books, 1971).
2. Jerome Skolnick, *The Politics of Protest* (New York: Simon & Schuster, 1969).
3. For a collection of such reports, see Anthony Platt, *The Politics of Riot Commissions, 1917–1970* (New York: Macmillan, 1971).
4. Michael Lipsky, "Protest as a Political Resource," *American Political Science Review* 62 (1968): 1144–58.
5. Joe R. Feagin and Harlan Hahn, *Ghetto Revolts: The Politics of Violence in American Cities* (New York: Macmillan, 1973), p. 19.
6. Lewis S. Feuer, *The Conflict of Generations: The Character and Significance of Student Movements* (New York: Basic Books, 1969).
7. This view of the youth revolt as oriented to moral issues rather than the status enhancement of students must be qualified in two ways. First, student protests in America underwent considerable shift from student power and student rights (status issues) to the moralistic issue of the Vietnam war after 1969. Richard L. Gambrell, "Issue Dynamics in the Student Movement," *Sociological Focus* 13 (1980): 187–202. Second, student protest in other countries (perhaps those in which students are not

so privileged a group as in America) has taken more the form of demands for better living conditions for students. On the greater involvement of youth in "status" concerns in Sri Lanka (Ceylon), see Robert N. Kearney, "Youth Protest in the Politics of Sri Lanka," *Sociological Focus* 13 (1980): 265–72.

8. John M. Orbell, "Protest Participation Among Southern Negro College Students," *American Political Science Review* 61 (1967): 446–56; Barbara N. Geschwender and James A. Geschwender, "Relative Deprivation and Participation in the Civil Rights Movement," *Social Science Quarterly* 54 (1973): 403–11.

9. Catherine Arnott, "Feminists and Anti-Feminists as 'True Believers,'" *Sociology and Social Research* 57 (1973): 300–306; Jo Freeman, "The Origins of the Women's Liberation Movement," *American Journal of Sociology* 78 (1973): 792–811.

10. Ronald P. Abeles, "Relative Deprivation, Rising Expectations and Black Militancy," *Journal of Social Issues* 32 (1976): 119–37.

11. Stationery printed by an activist group, the National Organization for Women, carries the adapted slogan: Liberté, Equalité, Sororité; and the sororité may be especially important to the movement. Note, for example, the reluctant embracing by the movement of the rights of lesbians, surely a small minority of militant women.

12. Harold H. Kelley, "Two Functions of Reference Groups," in Guy E. Swanson, ed., *Readings on Social Psychology,* rev. ed. (New York: Holt, 1952), p. 412.

13. Emile Durkheim, *Suicide,* trans. by John A. Spaulding and George Simpson (Glencoe, Ill.: Free Press, 1951).

14. Robert Martinson, "Collective Behavior at Attica," *Federal Probation* 36 (1972): 3–7.

15. James C. Davies, "Toward A Theory of Revolution," *American Sociological Review* 27 (1962): 5–19.

16. Sports fans' protests that sometimes are reflected in the firing of managers or coaches seem to follow this pattern. When a person becomes manager of a very successful team, he or she is likely to be criticized very severely and even lose the job if the team does not maintain the level of performance its fans have come to expect. Jerry D. Rose, "The Attribution of Responsibility for Organizational Failure," *Sociology and Social Research* 53 (1969): 323–32.

17. William D. Pederson, "Inmate Movements and Prison Uprisings: A Comparative Study," *Social Science Quarterly* 59 (1978): 509–24.

18. The most destructive of such riots occurred in Harlem and Bedford-Stuyvesant in New York in 1964; in the Watts section of Los Angeles in 1965; in Detroit and Newark in 1967 and in Washington, D.C., and

many other cities following the assassination of Martin Luther King, in April, 1968. The year 1969 saw a larger *number* of disturbances, but they tended to be smaller in scale of destructiveness, more spread out over the year, and more off the streets and into the schoolhouses, which became the major locale of racial disturbances. For a careful inventory of racial disturbances, see Jane A. Baskin, Joyce K. Hartweg, Ralph G. Lewis, and Lester W. McCullough, Jr., *Race-Related Civil Disorders, 1967-1969* (Waltham, Mass.: Lemberg Center for the Study of Violence, 1971).

19. As noted above, the years 1968 and 1969 actually involved many racial disturbances in months other than those of summer.

20. Stanley Lieberson and Arnold R. Silverman, "The Precipitants and Underlying Conditions of Race Riots," *American Sociological Review* 30 (1965): 887-98.

21. Bryan T. Downes, "A Critical Re-examination of the Social and Political Characteristics of Riot Cities," *Social Science Quarterly* 51 (1970): 349-60.

22. Seymour Spilerman, "Causes of Racial Disturbances," *American Sociological Review* 35 (1970): 627-49.

23. Seymour Spilerman, "Structural Characteristics and Severity of Racial Disorders," *American Sociological Review* 41 (1976): 771-92.

24. David O. Sears and T. M. Tomlinson, "Riot Ideology in Los Angeles: A Study of Negro Attitudes," *Social Science Quarterly* 49 (1968): 485-503.

25. Feagin and Hahn, *Ghetto Revolts,* p. 122. "We have produced a situation in which the social and economic conditions 'necessary' for the outburst of disorders are so widespread that a potential for disorders exists in all regions of the country and in all types of cities" (Baskin et al., *Race Related Civil Disorders,* p. 65.)

26. John S. Adams, "The Geography of Riots and Civil Disorders in the 1960s," *Economic Geography* 48 (1972): 24-42.

27. Walter Williams, "Cleveland's Crisis Ghetto." *Trans-action* 4 (September 1967): 33-42. For a demonstration that economic indicators for black ghetto areas rose more slowly than for "whole city" black populations in Detroit, Washington, Los Angeles, and Newark between 1960 and 1970, see William R. Berkowitz, "Socio-economic Indicator Changes in Ghetto Riot Tracts," *Urban Affairs Quarterly* 10 (September 1974): 69-94.

28. Skolnick, *Politics of Protest.*

29. James C. Davies, "The J-curve of Rising and Declining Satisfaction as A Cause of Some Great Revolutions and a Contained Rebellion," in Hugh D. Davis and Ted R. Gurr, eds., *The History of Violence in America* (New York: Bantam Books, 1970), pp. 690-731.

30. Abraham Miller, Louis Bolce, and Mark Halligan, "The J-curve Theory and the Black Urban Riots: An Empirical Test of Progressive Relative Deprivation Theory," *American Political Science Review* 71 (1977): 964–82.

31. Miller, Bolce, and Halligan, "The J-curve Theory," p. 980.

32. Daniel P. Moynihan, *Maximum Feasible Misunderstanding* (New York: Free Press, 1969), p. 11.

33. Thomas A. Critchley, *The Conquest of Violence: Order and Liberty in Britain* (New York: Schocken, 1970). An interesting exception to British "orderliness" is the frequently rowdy behavior at soccer matches, a situation certainly not duplicated in North America. It has been suggested that soccer fan behavior in Britain is more disorderly, among other reasons, because many people stand in soccer stadiums, many fans make a "day" of a soccer match by liquid reinforcements at pubs before and after the games, and that Britons have only soccer as a major sport to be excited about, whereas North Americans have baseball, basketball, football, hockey, and so on. Alan Roadburg, "Factors Precipitating Fan Violence: A Comparison of Professional Soccer in Britain and North America," *British Journal of Sociology* 31 (1980): 265–76.

34. In discussing poor people's participation in rent strikes, Piven observes: "When people sit in, or refuse to pay the rent, they are breaking the rules. This means that effective disruption depends on the ability of leaders to induce people to violate rules of conduct that are ordinarily deeply ingrained. Somehow the normal pieties, and the normal mechanisms of social control that enforce these pieties, must be overcome. Moreover to break the rules ordinarily involves some danger; people must be induced to run the risk of provoking coercive and repressive forces" (Frances F. Piven, "Low Income People and the Political Process," in Richard A. Cloward and Frances F. Piven, eds., *The Politics of Turmoil* [New York: Random House, 1974], p. 86).

35. William A. Kornhauser, *The Politics of Mass Society* (Glencoe, Ill.: Free Press, 1959).

36. C. Wright Mills, *The Power Elite* (New York: Oxford, 1956).

37. Clark Kerr and Abraham Siegel, "The Interindustry Propensity to Strike: An International Comparison," in Arthur Kornhauser, Robert Dubin, and Arthur M. Ross, eds., *Industrial Conflict* (New York: McGraw Hill, 1954), pp. 189–212.

38. H. E. Ransford, "Isolation, Powerlessness and Violence," *American Journal of Sociology* 73 (1968): 581–91; James A. Geschwender and Benjamin D. Singer, "The Detroit Insurrection: Grievance and Facili-

tating Conditions," in James A. Geschwender ed., *The Black Revolt* (Englewood Cliffs, N. J.: Prentice-Hall, 1971), pp. 353–60.

39. National Advisory Commission on Civil Disorders, *Report* (Washington, D.C.: U.S. Government Printing Office, 1968). David O. Sears and John B. McConahay, *The Politics of Violence: The New Urban Blacks and the Watts Riot* (Boston: Houghton Mifflin, 1973).

40. Donald I. Warren, "Neighborhood Structure and Riot Behavior in Detroit: Some Exploratory Findings," *Social Problems* 16 (1969): 464–84.

41. Feagin and Hahn, *Ghetto Revolts,* p. 9.

42. Sears and McConahay, *The Politics of Violence.*

43. Charles S. Johnson, *Patterns of Negro Segregation* (New York: Harper, 1943).

44. Sears and McConahay, *The Politics of Violence.*

45. Gresham M. Sykes, *The Society of Captives* (New York: Random House, 1956).

46. New York State Special Commission on Attica, *Official Report* (New York: Praeger, 1972), pp. 116–18.

47. Robert M. Fogelson, *Violence as Protest* (Garden City, N.Y.: Doubleday, 1971), chap. 3.

48. Ibid., p. 110.

49. Ibid., p. 114.

50. Alan E. Bayer and Alexander W. Astin, "Violence and Disruption on the U.S. Campus, 1968–1969," *Educational Record* 44 (Fall 1969): 337–70.

51. A similar interpretation of "streaking" episodes on American college campuses in 1974 is offered in Robert R. Evans and Jerry L. L. Miller, "Barely an End in Sight," in Robert R. Evans, ed., *Collective Behavior,* 2d ed. (Chicago: Rand McNally, 1975), pp. 401–17.

52. National Advisory Commission on Civil Disorders, *Report.*

53. Leonard Berkowitz, "Frustrations, Comparisons and Other Sources of Emotional Arousal as Related to Social Unrest," *Journal of Social Issues* 28 (1972): 80, 81.

54. Jerry M. Lewis, "A Study of the Kent State Incident Using Smelser's Theory of Collective Behavior," *Sociological Inquiry* 42 (1972): 87–96.

55. Maurice Pinard, "Mass Society and Political Movements: A New Formulation," *American Journal of Sociology* 73 (1968): 682–90.

56. Roy S. Bryce-Laporte, "The American Slave Plantation and Our Heritage of Communal Deprivation," *American Behavioral Scientist* 12 (March–April 1969): 2–8.

57. E. Franklin Frazier, *The Negro in the United States* (New York: Macmillan, 1949); Daniel C. Thompson, *The Negro Leadership Class* (Englewood Cliffs, N.J.: Prentice-Hall, 1963).

58. Gary T. Marx, "Religion: Opiate or Inspiration of Civil Rights Among Negroes?" *American Sociological Review* 32 (1967): 64–72: Ronny E. Turner, "The Black Minister—Uncle Tom or Abolitionist?" *Phylon* 34 (1973): 86–95; Larry L. Hunt and Janet G. Hunt, "Black Religion as Both Opiate and Inspiration of Civil Rights Militance: Putting Marx' Data to the Test," *Social Forces* 56 (1977): 1–14.

59. T. B. Bottomore, ed., *Karl Marx: Selected Writings in Sociology and Philosophy* (New York: McGraw-Hill, 1964).

60. Karl Mannheim, *Ideology and Utopia,* trans. Louis Wirth and Edward Shils (New York: Harcourt, Brace, 1946).

61. Crane Brinton, *The Anatomy of Revolution* (New York: Vintage, 1952).

62. David Felix, *Protest: Sacco-Vanzetti and the Intellectuals* (Bloomington: Indiana University Press, 1965).

63. Serge Denisoff, "Protest Movements: Class Consciousness and the Propaganda Song," *Sociological Quarterly* 9 (1968): 228–47.

64. David Kowalewski, "The Protest Uses of Symbolic Politics: the Mobilization Functions of Protestor Symbolic Resources," *Social Science Quarterly* 61 (1980): 95–113.

65. Sears and Tomlinson, "Riot Ideology in Los Angeles."

66. Amitai Etzioni, *Demonstration Democracy* (New York: Gordon and Breach, 1970), p. 27. Etzioni's question may not be quite as rhetorical as he seems to think. Some protesters may *prefer* "the street" as a mode of political expression because of the intrinsic gratifications of this kind of activity.

67. Robert A. Dahl, *Pluralist Democracy in the United States* (Chicago: Rand McNally, 1967). For a general critique of pluralism as a description of American politics, see Richard E. Rubenstein, *Rebels in Eden: Mass Political Violence in the United States* (Boston: Little, Brown, 1970), chap. 1.

68. Tony Castro, "Nixon's Minority Responsiveness Program," *Race Relations Reporter* 5 (July 1974): 25–29.

69. Jewel Bellush and Stephen David, eds., *New York City: Five Studies in Policy-Making* (New York: Praeger, 1971).

70. Edward Greer, "The 'Liberation' of Gary, Indiana," *Trans-action* 8 (January 1971): 30–39.

71. Richard A. Cloward and Richard M. Elman, "Poverty, Injustice and the Welfare State," in Cloward and Piven, *Politics of Turmoil,* p. 28.

72. Steven Box and Ken Russell, "The Politics of Discreditability: Disarm-

ing Complaints Against the Police,'' *Sociological Review* 23 (1975): 315–46.

73. Judith Lorber, ''Good Patients and Problem Patients: Conformity and Deviance in a General Hospital,'' *Journal of Health and Social Behavior* 16 (1975): 213–25.

74. James M. Buchanan, ''Student Revolts, Academic Liberalism and Constitutional Attitudes,'' *Social Research* 35 (1968): 666–80.

75. New York State Special Commission on Attica, *Official Report,* pp. 19–21.

76. Sears and McConahay, *Politics of Violence,* pp. 134–38.

77. William L. Partridge, *The Hippie Ghetto: The Natural History of a Subculture* (New York: Holt, 1973).

78. Arthur J. Vidich and Joseph Bensman, *Small Town in Mass Society* (Princeton, N.J.: Princeton University Press, 1958).

79. On Berkeley, see Seymour M. Lipset and Sheldon S. Wolin, eds., *The Berkeley Student Revolt* (Garden City, N.Y.: Doubleday, 1965), and Max Heirich, *The Spiral of Conflict* (New York: Columbia University Press, 1971). On San Francisco State, see William H. Orrick, *Shut It Down! A College in Crisis,* Report to the National Commission on the Causes and Prevention of Violence (Washington, D.C.: U.S. Government Printing Office, 1969).

80. New York State Special Commission on Attica, *Official Report,* pp. 132, 133.

81. Michael Lipsky, *Protest in City Politics: Rent Strikes, Housing and the Power of the Poor* (Chicago: Rand McNally, 1969).

82. Frances R. Cousens, *Public Civil Rights Agencies and Fair Employment* (New York: Praeger, 1969); Morroe Berger, *Equality by Statute,* rev. ed. (Garden City, N.Y.: Doubleday, 1967).

83. Galen Martin, ''New Civil Rights Coverages—Progress or Racism?'' *Journal of Intergroup Relations* 4 (April 1975): 14–37.

84. Daniel Bell and Virginia Heald, ''The Community Revolution,'' in Ralph Turner and Lewis Killian, eds., *Collective Behavior,* 2d ed. (Englewood Cliffs, N.J.: Prentice-Hall, 1972), p. 208.

85. Lester W. Milbrath *Political Participation,* (Chicago: Rand McNally, 1965) p. 18

86. Lewis, ''A Study of the Kent State Incident.''

87. The highly dispersed character of the various riotous acts that made up the Los Angeles riot in 1965 is demonstrated in Margaret J. A. Starkey et al., ''Some Empirical Patterns in a Riot Process,'' *American Sociological Review* 39 (1974): 865–75.

88. Gerald D. Sturges, ''1000 + 1000 = 5000: Estimating Crowd Size,'' in

Irving L. Horowitz and Charles Nanry, eds., *Sociological Realities II* (New York: Harper & Row, 1975), pp. 166-168.

89. Lipsky, *Protest in City Politics,* chap. 3.

90. Rude, *The Crowd in History;* George Rude, *Protest and Punishment: The Story of the Social and Political Protesters Transported to Australia, 1788-1868* (Oxford: Oxford University Press, 1978).

91. Fogelson, *Violence as Protest,* pp. 27, 28.

92. National Advisory Commission on Civil Disorders, *Report,* pp. 127-33.

93. Sears and McConahay, *Politics of Violence*; Nathan S. Caplan and Jeffrey M. Paige, "A Study of Ghetto Rioters," *Scientific American* 219 (August 1968): 15-21.

94. Caplan and Paige, "Study of Ghetto Rioters."

95. Bayard Rustin, "The Watts Manifesto and the McCone Report," in Robert M. Fogelson, ed., *The Los Angeles Riots* (New York: Arno Press, 1969), p. 154.

96. National Advisory Commission on Civil Disorders, *Report,* p. 202.

97. Governor's Select Commission on Civil Disorder, State of New Jersey, *Report for Action* (New York: Lemma Publishing, 1968), p. 142.

98. U.S. President's Commission on Campus Unrest, *The Scranton Report* (Washington, D.C.: U.S. Government Printing Office, 1968), p. 7.

99. Heirich, *Spiral of Conflict;* Daniel Bell, "Columbia and the New Left," in Daniel Bell and Irving Kristol, eds., *Confrontation: The Student Rebellion And the Universities* (New York: Basic Books, 1968), pp. 67-107.

100. Fogelson, *Violence as Protest,* p. 51.

101. Angus Campbell and Howard Schumann, "Racial Attitudes in Fifteen American Cities," *Supplemental Studies for the National Advisory Commission on Civil Disorders* (Washington, D.C.: U.S. Government Printing Office, 1968).

102. *The Scranton Report,* p. 49.

103. Allen H. Barton, "The Columbia Crisis: Campus, Vietnam and the Ghetto," *Public Opinion Quarterly* 32 (1968): 333-51.

104. Robert M. Fogelson and Robert B. Hill, "Who Riots? A Study of Participation in the 1967 Riots," *Supplemental Studies for the National Advisory Commission on Civil Disorders* (Washington, D.C.: U.S. Government Printing Office, 1968).

105. National Advisory Commission on Civil Disorders, *Report,* p. 132; Nathan Caplan, "The New Ghetto Man: A Review of Recent Empirical Studies," *Journal of Social Issues* 26 (1970): 59-73.

106. Fogelson, *Violence as Protest,* p. 41, reviews some of this evidence and suggests, in criticism, that the high unemployment rates of blacks may reflect simply the concentration of rioting activity among young adults,

who have high unemployment rates. The Kerner report (p. 132) found no employment difference between rioters and nonrioters but did find that rioters tended to have more "intermittent" employment.

107. Gerhard Lenski, "Status Crystallization: a Non-Vertical Dimension of Social Status," *American Sociological Review* 19 (1954): 405–13.

108. Shirley M. Moinat, Walter J. Rains, Stephen L. Burbeck, and Keith K. Davison, "Black Ghetto Residents and Rioters," *Journal of Social Issues* 28 (1972): 45–62.

109. David O. Sears and John B. McConahay, "Racial Socialization, Comparison Levels and the Watts Riot," *Journal of Social Issues* 26 (1970): 121–40.

110. Moinat et al., "Black Ghetto Residents and Rioters," p. 58.

111. Feagin and Hahn, *Ghetto Revolts,* pp. 165, 166.

112. Richard Flacks, "The Liberated Generation: Exploration of the Roots of Student Protest," *Journal of Social Issues* 28 (July 1967): 52–75.

113. Milton Mankoff and Richard Flacks, "The Changing Social Base of the American Student Movement," *Annals of the American Academy of Political and Social Science* 395 (1971): 54–67.

114. Howard Schumann, "Two Sources of Antiwar Sentiment in America," *American Journal of Sociology* 78 (1972): 513–36.

115. Very much as it is the common view that "deviants" commit their deviant acts and only *then* do control agents get into the "act" by trying to suppress or control deviant behavior.

116. Very much as it is the case that the "societal response" to deviance is a vital factor in the process by which deviance develops as a "career" for some persons.

117. Feagin and Hahn, *Ghetto Revolts,* pp. 144–47.

118. Anthony Oberschall, "The Los Angeles Riot of 1965," *Social Problems* 15 (1968): 322–41.

119. National Advisory Commission on Civil Disorders, *Report,* pp. 84, 85.

120. Fred C. Shapiro and James W. Sullivan, *Race Riots: New York 1964* (New York: Crowell, 1964), chap. 1.

121. The Kerner report shows, for example, that the precipitating incidents in riots tended to be very similar to a *series* of such incidents that had occurred in a given city. National Advisory Commission on Civil Disorders, *Report,* pp. 117, 118.

122. For an extended discussion of ghetto resident "resentment" against police activity in the ghetto, see Fogelson, *Violence as Protest,* chap. 3.

123. Heirich, *Spiral of Conflict.*

124. Henry L. Mason, *Mass Demonstrations Against Foreign Regimes* (New Orleans: Tulane University Press, 1966), pp. 22, 23.

125. *New York Times,* 18 May 1980, p. 24.

126. Oberschall, "The Los Angeles Riot of 1965," Lenora E. Berson, *Case Study of a Riot: the Philadelphia Story* (New York: Institute of Human Relations Press, 1966).

127. Mason, *Mass Demonstrations Against Foreign Regimes,* p. 48.

128. Robert Kapsis et al., *The Reconstruction of a Riot: A Case Study of Community Tensions and Civil Disorder* (Waltham, Mass.: Lemberg Center for the Study of Violence, 1970), p. 21.

129. Louis C. Goldberg, "Ghetto Riots and Others: The Faces of Civil Disorder in 1967," in David Boesel and Peter H. Rossi, eds., *Cities Under Siege: An Anatomy of the Ghetto Riots, 1964–1968* (New York: Basic Books, 1971), p. 144.

130. Ralph W. Conant, *The Prospects for Revolution* (New York: Harper & Row, 1971), pp. 33–40.

131. Paul E. Zinner, *Revolution in Hungary* (New York: Columbia University Press, 1962), p. 239.

132. New York State Special Commission on Attica, *Official Report,* pp. 204–6.

133. Mason, *Mass Demonstrations Against Foreign Regimes,* p. 51.

134. Donald W. Light Jr., "University of Chicago; Strategies of Protest: Developments in Conflict Theory," in James McEvoy and Abraham Miller, eds., *Black Power and Student Rebellion* (Belmont, Cal.: Wadsworth, 1969), pp. 83–92. Chicago officials apparently remembered the lesson again in 1969 when they avoided confrontational mobilizaton of police action against protesting students. Rodney Stark, "Protest + Police = Riot," in McEvoy and Miller, *Black Power and Student Rebellion,* p. 171.

135. Frances F. Piven and Richard A. Cloward, *Poor People's Movements: Why They Succeed, How They Fail* (New York: Pantheon, 1977), p. 29.

136. Mason, *Mass Demonstrations Against Foreign Regimes.* pp. 77–83.

137. Ibid., p. 51.

138. Joseph Boskin, "Aftermath of an Urban Revolt: the View From Watts," in Donald E. Gelfan and Russell D. Lee, eds., *Ethnic Conflict and Power: A Cross-National Perspective* (New York: Wiley, 1973), pp. 310–18.

139. Conant, *Prospects for Revolution,* p. 34.

140. Goldberg, "Ghetto Riots and Others," p. 155.

141. Lewis, "A Study of the Kent State Incident," p. 90.

142. Mason, *Mass Demonstrations Against Foreign Regimes,* p. 60.

143. Heirich, *Spiral of Conflict.*

144. New York State Special Commission on Attica, *Official Report,* chaps. 3–8.

145. Etzioni, *Demonstration Democracy,* p. 27.

146. Robert Coles, "Social Struggle and Weariness," *Psychiatry* 27 (1964): 305–15.

147. Ralph H. Turner, "Campus Peace: Harmony or Uneasy Truce?" *Sociology and Social Research* 57 (1972): 5–21.

148. Albert K. Cohen, "The Social Problems of the University: Two Crises of Legitimacy," *Social Problems* 20 (1973): 276–81.

149. James D. Orcutt and James M. Fendrich, "Student's Perceptions of the Decline of Protest: Evidence from the Early Seventies," *Sociological Focus* 13 (1980): 203–14.

150. Ralph H. Turner, "Collective Behavior," in Robert E. L. Faris, ed., *Handbook of Modern Sociology* (Chicago: Rand McNally, 1964), p. 407.

151. Heirich, *Spiral of Conflict.*

152. James R. Hundley Jr., "The Dynamics of Recent Ghetto Riots," in Richard A. Chikota and Michael C. Moran, eds., *Riot in the Cities* (Rutherford, N.J.: Fairleigh Dickinson University Press, 1968), pp. 137–49.

153. Shapiro and Sullivan, *Race Riots,* pp. 13, 14.

154. Ben W. Gilbert, *Ten Blocks from the White House: Anatomy of the Washington Riot of 1968* (New York: Praeger, 1968), pp. 16–24.

155. Heirich, *Spiral of Conflict.*

156. Joseph M. Firestone, "Theory of the Riot Process," *American Behavioral Scientist* 15 (July–August 1972): 859–82.

157. Anthony J. Balzer, "Reflections on Muddling Through," *Public Administration Review* 39 (1979): 537–45.

158. See the account of the extended discussions of Detroit officials in 1967 in Hubert G. Locke, *The Detroit Riot of 1967* (Detroit: Wayne University Press, 1969).

159. New York State Special Commission on Attica, *Official Report,* pp. 313–30.

160. The controversial "Walker report" on the disturbances in Chicago during the Democratic National Convention in 1968 characterized the behavior of Chicago police as exemplifying a "police riot." Chicago Study Team, *Rights in Conflict,* Report submitted to National Commission on the Causes and Prevention of Violence (New York: Dutton, 1968).

161. Ralph Turner, "Collective Behavior."

162. Russell Dynes and E. L. Quarantelli, "What Looting in Civil Disturbances Really Means," *Trans-action* 5 (May 1968): 9–14.
163. James A. Geschwender, "Civil Rights Protest and Riots: A Disappearing Distinction," *Social Science Quarterly* 49 (1968): 474–84.
164. Gilbert, *Ten Blocks from the White House,* chap. 9.
165. E. L. Quarantelli and Russell R. Dynes, "Property Norms and Looting: Their Pattern in Community Crises," *Phylon* 31 (1970): 169–82. As we noted in the last chapter, the extensive looting during the 1977 blackout in New York City was a major exception to usual behavior during disasters.
166. Geschwender, "Civil Rights Protest and Riots," p. 303.
167. Berson, *Case Study of a Riot,* pp. 40, 41.
168. Hundley, "Dynamics of Recent Ghetto Riots."
169. Raymond J. Adamek and Jerry M. Lewis, "Social Control Violence and Radicalization: the Kent State Case," *Social Forces* 51 (1973): 342–47.
170. Barton, "The Columbia Crisis."
171. Stark, "Protest + Police = Riot," p. 178.
172. Gary T. Marx, "Civil Disorder and the Agents of Social Control," *Journal of Social Issues* 26 (1970): 19–57.
173. Shapiro and Sullivan, *Race Riots,* p. 50.
174. Marx, "Civil Disorder and the Agents of Social Control," p. 38.
175. Gladys E. Lang and Kurt Lang, "Some Pertinent Questions on Collective Violence and the News Media," *Journal of Social Issues* 28 (1972): 93–110.
176. Ibid.
177. David L. Paletz and Robert Dunn, "Press Coverage of Civil Disorders: A Case Study of Winston-Salem 1967," *Public Opinion Quarterly* 33 (1969): 328–45.
178. New York State Special Commission on Attica, *Official Report,* pp. 205, 221.
179. Gilbert, *Ten Blocks from the White House,* p. 13.
180. Mason, *Mass Demonstrations Against Foreign Regimes,* pp. 62, 63.
181. National Advisory Commission on Civil Disorders, *Report,* pp. 60–62.
182. Ibid., p. 129.
183. Warren, "Neighborhood Structure and Riot Behavior in Detroit."
184. William A. Anderson, Russell R. Dynes, and E. L. Quarantelli, "Urban Counterrioters," *Society* 11 (March–April 1974): 50–55.
185. Gary T. Marx and Duane Archer, "Citizen Involvement in the Law

Enforcement Process," *American Behavioral Scientist* 15 (September–October 1971): 52–72.

186. Frank A. Aukofer, *City With a Chance* (Milwaukee: Bruce Publishing, 1968), pp. 16–20.

187. John A. Buggs, "Report form Los Angeles," *Journal of Intergroup Relations* 5 (1966): 27–40.

188. Marx, "Civil Disorder and the Agents of Social Control," p. 39.

189. Lipsky, "Protest as a Political Resource." All the analysis in this section is heavily influenced by Lipsky's article.

190. Joan V. Bondurant, *Conquest of Violence: The Gandhian Philosophy of Conflict* (Berkeley: University of California Press, 1965).

191. Inge Powell Bell, *CORE and the Strategy of Nonviolence* (New York: Random House, 1968).

192. David J. Garrow, *Protest at Selma: Martin Luther King Jr. and the Voting Rights Act of 1965* (New Haven: Yale University Press, 1978.)

193. Elliott Rudwick and August Meier, "The Kent State Affair: Social Control of a Putative Value-Oriented Movement," *Sociological Inquiry* 42 (1972): 81–86. This public hostility toward the demonstrators was depicted later when there was a memorial service for the slain students and the ceremony was picketed with such signs as "The Kent State Four Should Have Studied More." James A. Michener, *Kent State: What Happened and Why* (New York: Random House, 1971), pp. 263–76.

194. Alexander W. Astin, Helen S. Astin, Alan E. Bayer, and Ann S. Bisconti, *The Power of Protest* (San Francisco: Jossey-Bass, 1975).

195. David Kowalewski, "Religious Protest Outcomes: The Soviet Baptist Case," *Review of Religious Research* 22 (1980): 198–206.

196. Leo Kuper, *Passive Resistance in South Africa* (New Haven: Yale University Press, 1957).

197. Peter Eisinger, "The Conditions of Protest Behavior in American Cities," *American Political Science Review* 67 (1973), p. 14.

198. William A. Gamson, *The Strategy of Protest* (Homewood, Ill.: Dorsey Press, 1975). For a recent review of the controversy on the validity of Gamson's thesis, including a response to critiques by Gamson, see Jack A. Goldstone, "The Weakness of Organization: A New Look at Gamson's *The Strategy of Social Protest,*" *American Journal of Sociology* 85 (1980): 1017–42; and Gamson's reply, pp. 1043–60.

199. Gamson, *Strategy of Protest*, p. 87.

200. Piven and Cloward, *Poor People's Movements*.

201. Kapsis, *Reconstruction of a Riot*, p. 5.

202. William R. Morgan, "Campus Conflict as Formative Influence," in James E. Short, Jr., and Marvin E. Wolfgang, eds., *Collective Violence* (Chicago: Aldine, 1972), pp. 278–91.

203. Michael Betz, "Riots and Welfare: Are They Related?" *Social Problems* 21 (1974): 345–55. For an exchange between Betz and M. Richard Cramer on the validity of his findings, see *Social Problems* 22 (1974): 304–10.

204. Boskin, "Aftermath of an Urban Revolt."

205. Ibid.

206. Nathan Glazer, "'Student Power' in Berkeley," in Bell and Kristol, *Confrontation*, pp. 3–21.

207. Susan Welch, "The Impact of Urban Riots on Urban Expenditures," *American Journal of Political Science* 19 (1975): 741–60.

208. Edward T. Jennings, "Urban Riots and the Growth of State Welfare Expenditures," *Policy Studies Journal* 9 (1980): 34–40.

209. Homer R. Steedly and John W. Foley, "The Success of Protest Groups: Multivariate Analysis," *Social Science Research* 8 (1979): 1–15.

210. Kuper, *Passive Resistance in South Africa.*

211. Benjamin W. Heineman, Jr., *The Politics of the Powerless: A Study of the Campaign Against Racial Discrimination* (London: Oxford University Press, 1972).

212. In the British case, the factionalism within the protesting federation is a partial explanation of the fact that, according to Patterson, civil rights agitation in Britain by ethnic minories played a relatively minor role in the politics of the process by which civil rights legislation was enacted. Sheila Patterson, *Immigration and Race Relations in Britain, 1960–1967* (London: Oxford University Press, 1969), p.412.

213. An affinity noted, for example, in the appendix to the classic work on race relations in America: Gunnar Myrdal, *An American Dilemma* (New York: Harper, 1944).

214. See the discussion of this issue in Linda J. M. LaRue, "Black Liberation and Women's Lib," in Horowitz and Nanry, *Sociological Realities II*, pp. 282–87.

215. Lipsky, *Protest in City Politics.*

216. Fred Barbaro, "Ethnic Resentment," in Norman R. Yetman and C. Hoy Steele, eds., *Majority and Minority*, 2d ed. (Boston: Allyn Bacon, 1975), pp. 606–17.

217. Carol A. B. Warren and Jann S. DeLora, "Student Protest in the 1970s: The Gay Student Union and the Military," *Urban Life* 7 (1978): 67–90.

218. Resentments of blacks against Jews as merchants are indicated in Ger-

trude Selznick and Stephen Steinberg, *Tenacity of Prejudice* (New York: Harper & Row, 1969), pp. 117–31.

219. Herbert J. Gans, "Negro-Jewish Conflict in New York City: a Sociological Evaluation," in Gelfan and Lee, *Ethnic Conflicts and Power,* pp. 218–30; Peter G. Sinden, "Anti-Semitism and the Black Power Movement," *Ethnicity* 7 (1980): 34–46.

220. A number of articles in *Commentary,* published by the American Jewish Committee, were highly critical of "quota" versions of affirmative action programs (which have now, of course, been declared unconstitutional in the Bakke case). See, for example, Elliott Abrams, "The Quota Commission," *Commentary* 54 (October 1972): 54–58; and Paul Seabury, "HEW and the Universities," *Commentary* 53 (February 1972): 38–44.

221. Colin Legum, "Color and Power in the South African Situation," *Daedulus* 96 (spring 1967): 483–95.

222. Marvin E. Olsen, "Perceived Legitimacy of Social Protest Actions," *Social Problems* 15 (1968): 287–310.

223. Ralph H. Turner, "The Public Perception of Protest," *American Sociological Review* 34 (1969): 815–31.

224. On white attitudes toward black protest actions, see Skolnick, *Politics of Protest,* pp. 184–88. On the negative reaction in general public opinion to "radical" tactics in the student and antiwar demonstrations, see Lipset and Wolin, *Berkeley Student Revolt* and Etzioni, *Demonstration Democracy.*

225. One study of the success of protest groups in achieving "responsiveness" to their demands thus indicates that, contrary to Gamson, Piven and Cloward, and others, there is a slight disadvantage accruing to those protesters who use "militant" tactics. Paul D. Schumaker, "Policy Responsiveness to Protest Group Demnands," *Journal of Politics* 37 (1975): 488–521. Even Gamson's data shows, upon reanalysis, that those groups are *least* successful that seek "the destruction or replacement of antagonists." Goldstone, "A New Look at Gamson's *The Strategy of Social Protest.*"

226. Robert K. Merton, "The Unanticipated Consequences of Purposive Social Action," *American Sociological Review* 1 (1936): 894–904.

227. Georg Simmel, *Conflict,* trans. Reinhard Bendix (Glencoe, Ill.: Free Press, 1955); Lewis A. Coser, *The Functions of Social Conflict* (Glencoe, Ill.: Free Press, 1956).

228. Julius Lester, "The Current State of Black America," in Norman R. Yetman and C. Hoy Steele, eds., *Majority and Minority: the Dynamics of Racial and Ethnic Relations* (Boston: Allyn & Bacon, 1975) pp. 578–84.

229. Roger Daniels, *Concentration Camps USA: Japanese Americans and World War II* (New York: Holt, 1971).

230. Leo Kuper, "Nonviolence Revisited," in Robert I. Rotberg and Ali A. Mazrui, eds., *Protest and Power in Black Africa* (New York: Oxford University Press, 1970).

231. Pinkser thus comments on the recent appearances of Mark Rudd and Jerry Rubin at the University of New Mexico and the sense of a lack of rapport of contemporary students with the causes for which these militants stood. Sanford Pinkser, "Erasing the Sixties; or Whatever Happened to Mark Rudd?" *Dissent* 27 (winter 1980): 100–3.

232. There are, to be sure, other explanations of the recent moribund state of student protest, especially that, by virtue of a change in "values," students today are simply less interested in the causes that motivated those in the late 1960s. Thus students themselves at Florida State University explained the student protest decline by suggesting, for example, that "drug use has mellowed students," that there was now "more emphasis in changing self" than changing society. Orcutt and Fendrich, "Student's Perceptions of the Decline of Protest." For a study that compares the values at Bowling Green State University in 1970 and 1980 with similar findings, see Eldon E. Snyder, Joseph B. Perry, Jr., Meredith D. Pugh, and Elmer A. Spreitzer, "A Note on Change in the Value Orientations of College Students Between 1970 and 1980," *Sociological Focus* 13 (1980): 203–14.

Chapter 4
Persecutions

WE CONSIDER NOW outbreaks of persecution of persons who come to be defined as dangerous public enemies requiring severe repressive action.

THE NATURE OF PERSECUTION

The first thing to observe is that social control of deviant or socially harmful behavior is one of the functional requirements of "normal" social situations. Police, judges, and jails are all maintained routinely on the justifiable assumption that some persons will behave in ways requiring arrest, conviction, and incarceration. There are, of course, waves of law enforcement—"crackdowns"—that bear some relation to our subject of extraordinary behavioral episodes.[1] Persecutions typically go a step beyond crackdowns, however, to the point of an almost obsessive public fear of the dangers emanating from some category of persons: witches, Jews, Masons, or Texas oil millionaires. These obsessions often eventuate in mass "hunts" or in "anti-" movements of various sorts, such as witch hunts, anti-Semitism, anticommunism, and campaigns against pornography or prostitution.

In the course of our discussion of persecutory episodes, we shall focus on several well-studied and popularly notorious episodes of this sort. While these by no means exhaust the empirical references for the concept of persecutions, they will give the reader some idea of the scope of persecutory outbreaks in human history.

WITCHES AND HERETICS

The term *witch hunt* has come to be used to cover a number of persecutory episodes in which witches are not actually the victims. Witches were imagined to be the human agents of the Devil, sworn by a pact with the Evil One to do his work on earth. The fear of witches and their persecution reached its height in Europe in the fifteenth, sixteenth, and seventeenth centuries.[2] During this period, perhaps as many as a half million people were executed as witches.[3] Many witch hunts were conducted by special tribunals with a mandate from the Church to extirpate witchcraft in particular communities or regions. Determined to find witches, these witch finders often found them in great numbers. Confessed witches were required, often under torture, to implicate their co-conspirators in evil and, by this judicial practice, the circle of accused witches in a given community often widened to include hundreds of people, including some very prominent ones. The notorious trials at Salem, Massachusetts, in 1692 came after witch trials had abated in Europe, and the doubts that had developed about witch-hunting methods in Europe spread to the colonies and help explain why "only" twenty people died in that episode.[4]

The witch trials were actually a contination of an equally violent effort of the Church several centuries earlier to root out heresy—the crime of the nonbeliever—by the actvities of the Inquisition.[5] Sometimes the Inquisition was dealing with genuine nonbelievers in Christianity. In other instances royal and/or papal animosity against such impeccably Christian organizations as the Knights Templar led to the victimization of these Christian soldiers as members of a subversive organization.[6]

ANTI-SEMITISM

The Jews are a religious "enemy" familiar throughout the history of Christianity.[7] Early Christians tended to identify Jews with the sufferings inflicted on Christ (conveniently ignoring the Jewish origin of Christ himself). Jews were later accused of sacrilegious acts very much like those of the Devil, and anti-Jewish "pogroms," mass murders by popular action, were often the result. Demagogues could blame Jews for all the dislocations of modern urban industrial life and appeal to a reactionary constituency on that basis. Jews were blamed for anti-tsarist revolutionary activity in Russia, and the need of Russian reactionaries to counter the revolution led to the fabrication of the notorious Protocols of the Elders of Zion, a fictitious account of a Jewish world revolutionary plot.[8] Above all, of course, Hitler and his German Nazi regime made political capital from blaming Jews for German sufferings, a maneuver that produced the Holocaust, the systematic extermination of European Jews.

POLITICAL PURGES

Some of the most dramatic contemporary instances of persecutions involve the efforts of revolutionary political regimes to "purge" themselves of alleged counterrevolutionary enemies. The advent of a new regime is often the signal for a reign of terror against such enemies: thus the anti-Chinese pogroms following the coup against the Sukarno government in Indonesia and the mass executions of pre-revolutionary leaders in Cuba, Iran, and many other places. One of the more dramatic episodes occurred in the Soviet Union in the 1930s, when Joseph Stalin determined to consolidate his hold on the Communist party by exiling or executing a great part of the membership of the party.[9] In a series of spectacular Moscow trials, leaders of the party confesssed openly and profusely to various "Trotsky-ite" and other misguided crimes against the Soviet people. These confessions did not save their lives, of course, but they were encouraged by their prosecutors to make these confessions as a last patriotic act on behalf of the revolution.

RACE RIOTS

In the last chapter we gave much attention to riots of racial minorities as a form of protest by these minorities. Riots have been at least as often the actions of *dominant* races, designed to punish minorities for some offense and/or to preserve the dominant groups from minorities that threaten to abandon their subordinate "place."[10] The so-called draft riots in New York in the 1860s became in fact occasions for Irish Americans to vent their hostilities against blacks.[11] The heavy urban migration of blacks to northern cities around the time of World Wars I and II produced explosively hostile race relations in American cities. Under slight provocation, blacks were attacked by white mobs in East St. Louis, Illinois, in 1917, in Chicago in 1919, and in Detroit in 1943, as well as in many other American cities.[12] Also in 1943, Mexican-Americans in Los Angeles were attacked by marauding bands of sailors and other whites.[13] These urban riots had their counterparts in the rural South in the terrorist activities of the Ku Klux Klan and other white supremacist groups.[14] In Britain in 1958 and 1959, growing animosity between whites and recent "coloured" immigrants led, in Nottingham, London, and elsewhere, to riots against West Indians that were mild by American standards but quite shocking to Britons, with their recent tradition of nonviolence.[15]

ANTI-COMMUNIST OUTBREAKS

The hostility against such political deviants as communists may have much the same emotional quality as that against such religious entities as the heretic, the Devil, the Jew. Twice in twentieth-century American history, the nation has been convulsed with fear of "reds" as supposed subversives. Shortly after World War I, with the Russian revolution still being fought and with the severe internal postwar dislocations, an anxious public was encouraged by its political leadership to believe that a small band of enemy aliens was subverting American society toward the end of a communist revolution.[16] The Attorney-General of the United States rounded up noncitizens with little concern for due process of law and deported hundreds of those thought to harbor subversive intentions. After World War II, the cold war relation of the United States and the Soviet Union prompted again much concern about communist subversives.[17] A congressional Committee on Un-American Activities made inquisitorial raids of such supposed hotbeds of communist influence as Hollywood, and in the early 1950s, Senator Joseph McCarthy made a brief but spectacular career of charging communist influence in the American government. In this era of "McCarthyism," loyalty oaths were instituted for teachers, scientific workers, and many others; and Julius and Ethel Rosenberg were executed as spies for having allegedly participated in an espionage ring that gave to the Soviet Union the "secret" of the atomic bomb.[18]

ANTI-CULT MOVEMENTS

Throughout human history, people have felt threatened by religious "radicals" whose beliefs and practices have seemed sacriligious in terms of their own conceptions of the "true" religion. The witch hunts in Europe were preceded by several centuries of effort to combat the supposed evil of such as the Waldensians and the Cathars.[19] Seventeenth-century England produced such religious groups as the Quakers, the Diggers, and the Ranters, and each of these was subjected to savage repression at the hands of outraged mobs.[20] Slightly later the Methodist religious societies founded by John Wesley experienced the same persecutory fate.[21] The roster of persecuted religious sects or cults is seemingly endless; it includes such groups as Mormons and Hutterites in North America, whose movement across the continent was impelled by the "encouragement" of their moving by their indignant neighbors.[22]

In recent years in America, members of established religious bodies have felt severely threatened by the rise of "new religions" of the sort we shall be discussing in the next chapter. Whether this threat is due primarily to the "heretical" beliefs of such groups or to the allegedly coercive methods of recruitment and harsh control exercised over followers is a matter of some uncertainty. The hostility aroused by Hare Krishna, the Unification Church (Moonies), and other groups is complicated by the tendency of these groups to involve themselves in the purchase of expensive real estate and/or business enterprises in the communities in which they operate. Thus, the Moonies' action in purchasing a villa and a seaside restaurant in Gloucester, Massachusetts, generated a characteristic community response: the formation of a "Coalition for a Free Gloucester" to try to reduce Moonie economic and religious influence.[23] Such cults have faced a congressional investigation (in the case of the Unification Church) and numerous lawsuits to prevent street solicitation and other "annoying" practices. In Denver a Christian "truth squad" has tailed the Hare Krishna group to try to reduce the recruiting effectiveness of the group.[24] They have also been subjected to the harassments of Ted Patrick and other "deprogrammers" who have, at the instigation of parents whose children have been "brainwashed" by cults, actually kidnapped young members in order to carry out their deprogramming work.[25]

MORAL CRUSADES

Finally, we may note a type of persecutory episode that focuses on the attempt of outraged people to eradicate some social "evil." Temperance and abolitionist movements of earlier times illustrate outbreaks of effort to eliminate such evils,—alcoholic consumption and slavery in these two cases.[26] The saloon-raiding activities of Carrie Nation in Kansas and attacks by "respectable" women on the red-light prostitution districts in Western towns illustrate the extra-legal or vigilante character of much of this crusading activity.[27] In recent years, the "upright" citizens of many communities have defined pornographic literature as a pervasive evil and have organized more or less vigilante campaigns to harass the participants in "indecent" activity of this sort.[28] "Crusaders" of this sort should be distinguished from the renewal-oriented activists (e.g., social reformers, hell-and-brimstone revivalist preachers) discussed in the next chapter. As Wallis and Bland note in characterizing participants in the 1976 "National Festival of Light" rally in Trafalgar Square, London, the protesters were oriented to "coercion" rather than "conversion" of the "sinners" involved in the likes of pornography, homosexuality or abortion.[29]

BACKGROUND

We begin, as we did in the analysis of protest background, with a general hypothesis which states three necessary factors or conditions for producing a persecutory episode. This hypothesis:

Persecution occurs when: (1) significantly large groups experience severely threatening social conditions; and (2) the source of this threat is defined as the result of the willful actions of an identifiable group of sub-human evil-doers; and

(3) it is possible to mobilize effective collective action against a group of such enemies.

The reminder of this section is a discussion of the elements of this hypothesis.

THREAT

All the types of persecution we have discussed occur in atmospheres marked by great social insecurity. Referring to witch hunting of both the religious and the anticommunist varieties, Carey McWilliams writes: "When old worlds are dying and new worlds are struggling to be born, there is always a prevalence of witches. . . The season for hunting witches is a season of terror and alarm, when 'fear hath a hundred eyes' and 'good and evil interchange their names'; when people, 'wearied out with contrarieties,' yield up moral questions in despair."[30]

Some persecutions reflect anxiety about sweeping social changes associated with the *modernization* of social life. When the old world of agrarian feudalism was dead or dying and the new world of industrial capitalism was struggling to be born in the fifteenth, sixteenth, and seventeenth centuries, Europe went through its most violent period of witch hunting. The modernization tensions in Salem, Massachusetts, at the end of this period are a dramatic illustration of this point. As Boyer and Nissenbaum show, accused witches, as well as those who testified on behalf of the accused, tended to be people who were geographically and socially close to the industrial-commerical *town* of Salem, while their accusers were more traditional farmers from the *village* of Salem.[31] The local minister, Samuel Parrish, who fanned the flames of the witchcraft conflagration, was himself an ex-capitalist who illustrated in his own life the sharp ambivalence of Salem villagers toward the modern capitalist world. Similarly, in a Hindu village undergoing transition from a subsistence to a cash economy, some women were able to use cash assets in exploitative ways and these women tended to be the accused witches of the village.[32] The frequent victimization of Jews in anti-Semitic persecutions reflects largely the association, in the public mind, of Jews as traders, industrialists, and urban people generally.[33] European anti-Semitism tended thus to appeal primarily to a rural constituency and, in America, antiblack, anti-

Catholic, and anti-Semitic feelings have found a common breeding ground in the social attitudes of rural southerners.[34]

Other social insecurities not so directly related to modernization may be cited. Revolution, war, and population migrations are examples of such persecution-generating conditions. The extended agitation against the tsarist regime, culminating in the Russian Revolution, was a major influence in promoting European anti-Semitism. The assassination of Tsar Alexander II of 1881 led to governmentally encouraged pogroms against Russian Jews. Tsarist regimes thus "pretended that all opposition to the regime, and particularly all terrorism, was the work of the Jewish world-conspiracy."[35] Likewise noting that the European witch trials coincided with an era of popular revolt against both church and state, Harris observes that "the principal result of the witch-hunt system (apart from charred bodies) was that the poor came to believe that they were being victimized by witches and devils instead of princes and popes."[36]

Wars have had a number of persecution-generating effects. Most obviously, groups within a country suspected of collaboration with an enemy may be targets of persecutory action. Japanese-Americans on the West coast of the United States automatically became "security risks" in the eyes of the American public and of government officials in 1941, and these people were "relocated" at detention areas far inland and allowed to leave only upon executing prescribed loyalty oaths.[37] It is interesting to observe that Italian-and German-Americans were not similarly treated during World War II. Their immunity from this kind of persecution may have resulted from their greater numbers, their lesser racial visibility, and the fact that they were less concentrated in one area, such as California with its long history of anti-Oriental agitation.[38]

Postwar effects tend to be important as well in the encouraging of persecution. Whether winners or losers, belligerents tend to experience insecurities in the postwar period. Defeats in war may produce traumatic crises in national self-confidence. Anti-Semitic persecutions thus occurred in three times and places in which countries had suffered disastrous military defeats: in France after the defeat by Germany in 1870, in Russia after a losing war with Japan in 1905, and in Germany after World War I.[39]

Even the victors in war are not immune from the persecution-generating effects of postwar conditions. The outbreaks of anticommunism in the United States following both World War I and World

War II illustrate this point. After World War I there was much tension associated with rapid demobilization and also a significant holdover effect from the state of public opinion generated by that war. To promote public support of the war effort, government agencies kept up a running stream of anti-German propaganda aimed at generating national unity focused on hatred of the enemy. As Levin suggests, "It must have been difficult to relinquish a pleasurable belligerent nationalism and the excitation of hatred and the gratification of *communitas*. It must have been difficult to give up simple conspiratorial explanations which left no doubt about good and evil."[40] With the specter of the recent Russian revolution at hand, it was apparently easy to transfer hostilities from Germans to communists. Commenting on the continuity between anti-German and antiradical agitations, Higham remarks that "no date marks the end of one or the beginning of the other."[41]

The anticommunist outbreak after World War II resulted from quite different postwar tensions. In the latter period, fear of an internal communist revolution was relatively slight, but the fear of aggressive military action by the Soviet Union was very great. The concern now was with military (especially atomic weapons) secrecy. Senator Joseph McCarthy's charges of communists in government turned on alleged "security risks," and the spy trial that resulted in the execution of the Rosenbergs followed the explosion of an atomic bomb by the Soviet Union and a reportedly severe pressure on the FBI to discover the ring of spies who had supposedly given away the secret of the bomb.[42] This public obsession with secrecy and security risks has been related to the postwar "strain" of the United States in assuming a newly prominent role in international diplomacy.[43] With the good-and-evil dichotomies of war again fresh in the public consciousness, Americans were not prepared to wage a war (even a "cold" one) that they could not *win*.[44] This intolerance for international ambiguity was well illustrated in the public reactions to communist takeover in China in 1949. Unable to see the event as involving any elements of communist virtue or of Nationalist failure, McCarthy and other redbaiters were especially insistent that traitors in the Far East section of the State Department were the villains who "gave" China to the reds.[45]

Another factor in some persecutions is the insecurity produced by massive population movements. The relatively rapid movement of Chinese and, later, Japanese workers into California produced a threat to the privileges of the native labor force and provided the motive for the notorious anti-Oriental agitation in that state.[46] The violent race riots around the time of World War I and again in Detroit in 1943 reflected the tension of rapid wartime migrations of blacks to northern cities.[47] The interracial frictions in Detroit, for example, were illustrated shortly before the 1943 riot when a housing project built for black residents became the focus of bitter white-black contest in a situation of severe housing shortages.[48] White insecurities in the face of black urban migration were further exaggerated by the practice of some employers of using blacks as strikebreakers to combat the influence of labor unions.[49] The riots against "coloured" residents in Britain in the 1950s occurred in a context of fear by many Britons that their tight little island was being "inundated" by nonwhite immigrants.[50]

Virtually all the threatening background conditions we have so far discussed involve some degree of fantasy or exaggeration of danger. The post–World War II fear of loss of the "secret" of the atomic bomb was, according to some physicists, a fantastic fear, since the only real secret the United States ever possessed was the knowledge that a bomb could be made, and that secret was let out at Hiroshima in 1945.[51] There was never any dangerous Jewish world conspiracy, Japanese-Americans on the West coast during World War II were not really inclined to support the enemy war effort, and so on. The persistence of persecution delusions has been called a "paranoid" tendency in social thought.[52] To the extent that delusionary threat is a strongly *American* phenomenon (Hofstadter, for one, denies this), it may be a result of some uniquely American social conditions. The fear of the "un-American," for example, could only develop in a country in which people do not, as in Britain, take for granted the national loyalty of their countrymen. The very ambiguity of what is American may produce the situation in which, as Shils says, "It is natural for human beings who are uncertain of the stability of their own conformity with a given standard to abuse others for inadequate conformity with it."[53]

Beyond such paranoid exaggerations that may be built into a national culture, we should observe as well the tendency of certain vested interests to exaggerate a threat for their own benefit. Californians led the fight for military exclusion of Japanese from the West coast in the 1940s,[54] and there is more than a little suspicion that this reflected a longstanding effort to reduce Oriental economic competition in the area. The amount of black migration to East St. Louis was grossly overstated by political parties and candidates hoping to gain white votes by alleging that blacks were being "colonized" (brought in by trainloads from outside) to vote for the opposition.[55] Senator Joseph McCarthy's zeal for fighting communists came only after a few years of such poor performance that he was voted the worst of senators, and after a strategy meeting with advisers in which the participants fished for an issue on which to build a more popular image.[56]

Before closing this discussion of persecution-generating threats, we should note some conditions in which very real dangers may provoke persecutory outbreaks, however fantastic may be people's understanding of these dangers. The bubonic plague—the Black Death of the middle ages—was a cause of scapegoating of Jews, who were thought to spread the plague by poisoning water wells.[57] Similarly, Midelfort notes the strong correlation in Germany between witchcraft persecutions and such calamities as crop failures, storms, and disease epidemics.[58] Very realistic, too, were certain fears of white Americans around the time of World War I that blacks were becoming very militant and forgetting their subordinate "place." Blacks were, in effect, promised greater racial justice at home in exchange for their active contribution to the war effort. A hero's welcome parade in Chicago for a returning all-black combat unit was hardly consistent in the minds of blacks with the racial discrimination experienced both in the army and back home in Chicago.[59] Such militant black activities as the founding of a black cooperative in Longview, Texas, and the organizing of a protest against sharecropper conditions in Elaine, Arkansas,[60] were instances contributing to a very realistic white fear of danger to white privileges emanating from black Americans. There may thus be a strong reality basis to the threats in the background of persecutions. Whether the persecutions are a realistic response to the threats is another question. Certainly the burning of witches did not cure disease epidemics or stop storms. The repressive riots of whites against blacks may, as we suggest below, have had the self-defeating effect of escalating the very black militance that whites so greatly feared.

In identifying these various threat elements in the background of persecution, it may be well to refer to the distinction in the last chapter between *status* and *moral* types of deprivation in the background of protest episodes. Similarly, people may engage in persecutions through some combination of threats to their personal status or the "fraternal" status of their nations, communities, or social groups. The actions of white rioters against blacks who forgot their "place" will illustrate persecutions based on such status threats. Moral crusades (against pornography, prostitution, etc.) almost by definition involve threats to the cultural values of a people.[61] In some persecutory episodes, as in some protest episodes, it is extremely difficult to determine the relative importance of status and moral threats. Jews in a Venezuelan town were resented by Christians for the fact that "they are already in control of business and money" and "they take the wealth of our own country to their own" (status threats) but also because "they ridicule our religion and the Church's saints" (a moral threat).[62] Agrarian fears of modernization incorporate elements of fear of status loss at the hands of up-and-coming commercial-industrial interests, but they reflect as well the sense of loss of a valued way of life. Witches were long condemned for the personal harm that they were alleged to perpetrate against their victims, but massive witch hunts occurred only when the image of the witch was assimilated to that of the heretic.[63] The witch became thereby a threat to the Christian way of life. When the devil and his legion of witches were seen as would-be destroyers of Christianity, the church and its highly efficient Inquisition took over the task of rooting out this evil.[64]

SOCIAL DEFINITION OF ENEMIES

A strong sense of insecurity, if a necessary factor in producing persecution, is clearly not sufficient in itself to generate such outbreaks. It is necessary as well that a category of people become defined as a likely causal agent in producing current social misfortunes. Middlefort illustrates this fact in his study of German witch hunting. The 1630s were among the worst years of insecurity in Germany, but they were also years of Swedish military occupation, and the Germans knew exactly whom they should blame for their misfortunes—the Swedish occupation army—so witches were not required as scapegoats.[65] In the following discussion we shall describe two apparently essential definitional processes as background to persecution: (a) the identification of a group as a social enemy: the scapegoating process; and (b) the definition of this group as composed of people who have forfeited any right to humane treatment: the dehumanizing process.

SCAPEGOATING

The need to *blame* someone for social misfortune is apparently a very strong human tendency. We have already seen that in the immediate aftermath of disaster there is a strong likelihood that efforts will be made to assess human responsibilities for allowing the disaster to occur. We also saw that "riot commissions" tend to become heavily involved in responsibility assessments. In the recent energy shortage crisis, officials and citizens alike have suspected that the shortage is manipulated by profit-hungry oil companies or have blamed government officials for lack of the foresight that would have averted the crisis. It seems very difficult for people to look within themselves and attribute misfortune to their own behavior, or even attribute it to impersonal forces.

Given the importance, then, of determination of an enemy as a prelude to persecution, it is necessary to consider how the fantasies from an enemy come to be constructed. In the case of witch persecutions, it was of extreme importance that witches came to be associated with heresy and the idea of a Devil-led conspiracy against the Christian faith. Early in its history, the church took a relatively relaxed attitude toward the dangers emanating from the devil and his earthly adherents, the witches. In particular, the church distinguished between white, or beneficial, magical practice and black magic with malevolent intent, severely punishing only the latter. In the latter days of the Inquisition against heretics, inquisitors began to formulate the crime of witchcraft as essentially one of apostasy, in which *any* traffic with supernatural forces other than God was defined as an antireligious threat.[66] Once the witch became an enemy of "the faith," people whose own faith might have been wavering in a period of religious change could project their own insecurities upon the hapless witch.

Especially intense fear of a social enemy can be generated if it can be shown that there is a secret and powerful conspiracy among evildoers. Robert Welch's Blue Book, which provides the John Birch Society with details of a communist conspiracy,[67] is by no means the first such conspiracy fantasy. The plot of a Jewish world conspiracy was put forth in a fictitious document called Protocols of the Elders of Zion.[68] An obvious plagiarism from a purely fictional writing of a French satirist, the Protocols were apparently fabricated by the Paris branch of the Russian secret police in response to tsarist Russia's need for an anti-Semitic document to facilitate making the Jews a scapegoat on which to blame the antitsarist revolution. However dubious their origin, the Proctocols were translated and printed in many languages as though they were an accurate representation of a Jewish conspiracy. Ideas lifted from the Proctocols were used to construct the conspiracy plot detailed in *The International Jew*, an "expose" by Henry Ford's newspaper, the *Dearborn Independent*. [69] These protocols were also used with especially lethal effect by the Nazi propaganda minister, Alfred Rosenberg, in the Nazi program of anti-Semitic persecution in Germany.

Such propaganda efforts at scapegoating may succeed by virtue of the elaborate documentation and "pseudo-scholarship"[70] that characterizes the "evidence" of such conspiracies. Noting, for example, that a 96-page anticommunist pamphlet by McCarthy contains 313 footnote references, Hofstadter observes that "the entire right-wing movement of our time is a parade of experts, study groups, monographs, footnotes and bibliographies."[71] Not only in "our time" is this the case. In the same style of pseudo scholarship, the Lusk Committee of the New York State legislature made a heavily documented 4456-page report on "revolutionary radicalism" in 1920.[72] Persecution propagandists can thus borrow the prestige attached in modern culture to science and scholarship to bolster their conspiracy fantasies.

DEHUMANIZATION

When human beings are subjected to torture, killing, and public humiliation as they are during persecutions, they are experiencing violations of generally recognized human rights (to life, dignity, etc.). It greatly facilitates persecution, therefore, if victims can be labeled as something less than human, people who have forfeited any rights to humane treatment. It would be difficult to exaggerate the intensity of inhuman atrocities that have been attributed to persecution victims. Jews in the middle ages and into the nineteenth century were believed to engage in the "ritual murder" of Christian children.[73] Witches' meetings with the devil were thought to be characterized by all kinds of obscenities and crimes: promiscuous and incestuous copulation, kissing the devil's anal orifice, the killing and eating of babies, and so on.[74] Anti-Catholic agitation was stimulated by the "awful disclosures" of a renegade nun of the immoralities of behavior in monasteries.[75] Anti-Mexican riots in Los Angeles in 1943 were facilitated by the tendency to equate Mexicans with "zoot suiters," a fashion of the times.[76] Symbolic of this exclusion of the persecution target from the realm of the human is Hitler's report in *Mein Kampf* of his first encounter with Jews in Vienna. Hitler asked himself first if this was a Jew then if he was a German then if he was a man. The Nazi treatment of the Jews indicates an ultimate negative answer to the last question.

The dehumanization of potential persecution victims is facilitated if they can be associated symbolically with distinctively subhuman phenomena. At the time of the Soviet purge trials, the Soviet press was accustomed to refer to alleged counterrevolutionaries as "mad dogs," dangerous beasts for whom killing is only appropriate.[77] The covers of some editions of the Protocols of the Elders of Zion depicted the Jewish world conspiracy as a venomous snake or spider.[78] Identification of "radicals" with vermin and even feces was characteristic of the anticommunist propaganda after World War I.[79] It may be some measure of human progress from 1920 to 1950 that, when Senator McCarthy, in testimony to a Senate committee, referred to some of his victims as "slimy creatures," he produced a "stunned silence" in the committee that led the master redbaiter to tone down his characterization.[80]

MOBILIZATION

The final background factor for an outbreak of persecution is the possibility of mobilizing collective action against defined enemies of the people. The *motivation* for a certain kind of human action is insufficient as an explanation of that action; it must also be *possible* in the given social situation. We are interested here in social conditions that make persecutory actions possible and even highly likely when other background factors are present.

GOVERNMENTAL AGENCIES AS FACILITIES

Outbreaks of persecution are characterized by different degrees of official sanction for the activities of persecutors. We may hypothesize that no sustained persecution can occur without a degree of approval by agencies of government. The disposition of these agencies to tolerate or encourage persecution is one vital "facility" in the background of an outbreak of persecution.

This assertion may be challenged when one considers those persecutions with a *vigilante* character, in which mobs take the law into their own hands and punish "enemies" without any official sanction to do so. Most of the race riots described above have this character. However, it has often been noted that sustained riots occur only when police and other officials give tacit support to the rioters by, for example, arresting *blacks* during antiblack riots (as in East St. Louis);[81] or when they fail to take effective action to restrain rioters (as happened in Chicago in 1919, Detroit in 1943 and in many other riots).[82] In one of the seven major American riots in 1919, that in Charleston, South Carolina, law enforcement officials *did* act decisively and quickly to restrain rioters; the other riots of that year were notable for a lack of police neutrality in dealing with law violators.[83] Waskow suggests that local police officials could take this stance in Charleston, since the white perpetrators of the riot were sailors from a nearby naval station, "outsiders" who could not enjoy the immunity of respectable local citizens.

In many persecutions, officials (sometimes church or other nongovernmental officials) are themselves the persecutors and there is no question of official support for the persecution. In this instance, the question is whether officials have at their disposal a set of devices that will be *effective* in carrying on the persecution: how successful may they hope to be in finding their witches, heretics, communists, or counter-revolutionaries? An obvious problem in many political systems is the constitutional protection of citizens against arbitrary governmental action. People may not be deprived of life, liberty, or property without due process of law, and this due process is a thorn in the side of many would-be persecutors who claim that public enemies can use the cloak of civil liberties to avoid their being brought to heel. Any device that is discovered to circumvent due process accordingly is a giant step forward for persecutors. Attorney-General Palmer, using a "clear and present danger" definition of the Supreme Court of conditions under which he might take unusual legal action, was able to deport many "enemy aliens" with minimal due process.[84] Congressional committees found in the 1940s and 1950s that, while they could not compel suspected communists to reveal their political beliefs, they could expect that reluctant witnesses would be labeled as "5th amendment communists."[85] Prosecutors of Soviet spies discovered that it was easier to convict people for a conspiracy to commit espionage than to convict them for any overt acts of espionage.[86] Court decisions tolerant of anticult "deprogramming" have been able to distinguish between the constitutional right of cults to their religious beliefs on the one hand and the illegitimacy, on the other hand, of their alleged "brainwashing" techniques of promoting those beliefs.[87]

In the long history of persecutions, perhaps the most persecution-enchancing such "discovery" was the development of an *inquisitorial* technique of prosecuting enemies. The prototype of this device, the papal Inquisition of the middle ages, had two vital features that were adapted to later inquisitions.

First, the inquisition made the detection and accusation of enemies the responsibility of a special tribunal or committee, not an individually aggrieved person. Inquisitors visited a territory with a mandate to seek out and punish heretics, it having been predetermined that heresy was a problem in the territory.[88] The major witch hunts of three to four centuries later were similarly often conducted by such special witch-hunting tribunals.[89] In England, there were a number of such "witch-finders general," of whom the most notorious, Matthew Hopkins, was responsible for the execution of perhaps 300 witches.[90] The investigations of the House Committee on Un-American Activities adopted the same inquisitorial stance. As Caute describes it, "Geographical inertia was not one of HCUA's vices. The Committee and its subcommittees customarily rode into town like a sheriff's posse. . . . Sometimes the rough riders focused on Communist infiltration of a geographical area, but usually the area dimension was linked to a professional one: defense industries, longshoremen, lawyers, the press, radio and television, the film industry, teachers, social workers,"[91] This feature of the inquisition contributed to persecutions in two ways: (1) it professionalized the finding of enemies, placing it in the hands of people with vested interests in finding the evil being investigated; and (2) it contributed an element of irresponsibility in the making of accusations. In the early history of witchcraft trials, if an individual accused another of witchcraft and the accused was found innocent, the accuser was typically punished for that false accusation.[92] Later, when church officials themselves were hunting witches to fulfill the inquisitorial mandate, witchcraft accusations became much less hazardous to the individual. In the more recent anticommunist persecutions, perjury for false accusations was not an unknown occurrence. However, most perjury trials were for those (like Alger Hiss) who had *denied* communist connections. When Harvey Matusow, one of the "professional" informers against communists, later testified that he had been paid by the government to give false accusations, he was prosecuted for perjury in denying the validity of his original charges. Prosecutors, in other words, chose to believe that he was lying when he said he gave false witness, not that he lied when he made his accusations.[93]

A second feature of the inquisition seems to follow from the first. If inquisitors begin their investigations already convinced that they are dealing with a widespread danger, they will be likely to demand that discovered enemies confess their crimes and name their co-conspirators. This demand may, as in the Inquisition itself and in the witch trials, result in the use of torture to induce such confessions.[94] In another famous case of mass confessions, the Moscow purge trials of the 1930s, defendants were not only "subjected to the standard pressure devices of the NKVD: very protracted interrogations, deprival of sleep, constant exposure to a powerful glare, much standing, and simulations of impending execution."[95] They were subjected as well to prolonged guidance by their interrogators toward the view that their confessions would render a last valuable service to the party. Confessions that implicate co-conspirators may, of course, be based on another discovery in the arsenal of the modern prosecutor: a plea-bargaining arrangement in which a defendant accuses others in exchange for immunity from prosecution or the privilege of pleading guilty to a lesser charge. In the Rosenberg espionage trial, such promises to David and Ruth Greenglass may have been a factor in their damaging testimony against their kinfolk, the Rosenbergs.[96]

PUBLIC OPINION AND THE MASS MEDIA

Whatever the "official" involvement in persecution, these episodes appear to require as well the support of a substantial part of the general public. Had Senator McCarthy not been reelected from Wisconsin in the midst of his anticommunist crusade, his career would have been cut short. Race riots and pogroms, however much they may be instigated by official policy, must depend on a body of citizenry to carry out destructive acts. The condemnation of witches, even when conducted by inquisitorial tribunals, requires a mass of people acting as accusers. The degree of popular support for a given persecution is clearly an important background factor.

The dispositions of the popular press are one significant factor in this regard. Book publishers may help incite popular indignation, as in the rash of "devil books" that were published at around the time of the witch hunts in Germany.[97] As we shall note below, newspapers, radio, TV, and so on are often important elements in the process of development of a persecutory episode. These agencies may serve as well as significant background for many persecutions. The anti-Mexican riots in 1943 followed a period of some months in which the Los Angeles press had increasingly been reporting Mexican-American news in terms that minimized the favorable connotations of "Mexican" in the minds of non-Mexicans.[98] The popular press in 1919 prepared the public opinion ground for the anticommunist deportation proceedings by playing up the theme of communist influence on the labor disputes of that period.[99] In the 1950s, the stealing of atomic "secrets" by British, Canadian and American spies became big news, and this news reporting set the stage for the blaming of spies for the Russian development of the bomb and even (in the case of the Rosenbergs) for the Korean War.[100]

A STRUCTURE OF SUPPORTING SOCIAL ORGANIZATIONS

Many persecutions are highly organized affairs and not simply a reflection of sudden outbursts of general public rage. To succeed, therefore, they often require access to support from various organized groups. We may refer again at this point, as in the last chapter, to the criticism of the "mass society" view of conditions that encourage collective behavior. This view, that collective behavior is the product of action by socially *isolated* individuals, is supported in the case of persecutions even less than in that of protests. The Nazi German persecution of Jews, perhaps the most intense persecutory outburst, occurred in a society *not* characterized by a low degree of social organization.[101] In fact, like Americans, Germans are notorious "joiners" of various organizations. However, these organizations, far from inhibiting radical action by their members, tend to promote such action in many cases. In Germany, as in many other European countries, the organizations to which an individual belongs (churches, political parties, unions, etc.) tend to segregate him or her into groups of like-minded individuals, setting the person apart from other individuals in other groups. Radical political action of all sorts—including radical persecutory action—is the likely result of this pattern of social organizations. The United States, in contrast, is often characterized as having an organizational pattern in which membership in any group cuts across the broad spectrum of social types.[102] The political parties and the churches of the country, for example, have members from all social classes, races, and regions of the country. In this situation, such organizations are unlikely candidates as points of mobilization against people in other organizations, since any given category will appear in all organizations.

While there is a element of truth to this characterization of American society as lacking a vital persecution-mobilizing factor, there is an obvious problem here. If American politics is, indeed, characterized by a recurring "paranoid style," then it appears that either: (1) this mobilization factor is *not* an essential element in the background of persecution; or (2) the characterization of American society as lacking political polarization on the basis of organizational memberships is not a wholly accurate one. Since we are arguing here that the given mobilization factor *is* a vital one, it is important to explore the second alternative.

Considering political parties and churches, the point is often made that the Republican and Democratic parties have memberships from all social classes, religions, races, regions of the country, and so on, and the various religious denominations have similar memberships across a broad spectrum of social types. A closer look, however, will show a southern and a northern "branch" of the Democratic party, and a distinction in Protestantism between "fundamentalist" groups, with a lower-class membership, and "progressive" groups, with a higher-class membership.[103] With a narrowed base of social support, one of these political or religious subgroups can easily appeal to a severe threat to the special interest of the particular type of membership. Let us consider two examples.

Antipornography campaigns in America are largely the product of middle-class crusaders, and these are often initiated by religious and other groups with a strongly middle-class membership. Such a crusade was launched by a group of the Knights of Columbus, a middle-class social action group of the Catholic church.[104] In another community, an antipornography campaign originated as a "project" of the local Methodist men's group.[105] Once such campaigns are under way, they may expect to mobilize support from a wide range of socially active "civic" organizations with middle-class members. In a meeting to plan an Uprising for Decency in a southern city, the following organizations are reported as sending representatives: "two American Legion posts; the Greenwood Baptist Church; the Catholic Daughters; the four Knights of Columbus councils of Southtown; Sertoma; the Michael Road Church of Christ; the Ben Hur Shrine Masons; the Civitan Club; three PTA chapters; the Holy Cross Parents' Club; the Boys' Club of Southtown; the Catholic Youth Organization; and the Independent Auto Repair Shop Association."[106]

A second example concerns the role of the Republican party in mobilizing support for Senator Joseph McCarthy's anticommunist crusade. By 1952 the party was deeply frustrated by its exclusion from the White House for the past twenty years.[107] Even highly respectable party leaders (including "Mr. Republican," Senator Robert Taft) saw in McCarthy's charges of communists in the government an issue on which they might finally win a national election. This mobilization for anticommunism through party channels was undoubtedly facilitated by the polarization of social-class support for the two parties that was introduced by the Depression and the New Deal era. Black and working-class support gravitated heavily to the Democratic party, leaving the Republican party as the stronghold of "free enterprise" and its middle-class adherents. The mobilization of party support against communism as an enemy of free enterprise was fairly easy among the constituents of this party.

In addition to the preexistence of organizations with members favorable to persecutory outbreaks, it should be noted that some organizations may be created ad hoc, for the specific purpose of fighting some menace. The American Legion came into existence in 1919 and immediately became deeply involved in combating the perceived red menace.[108] Anti-Semitic persecution in Russia was greatly facilitated by the formation in 1905 of a Union of the Russian People, popularly called the Black Hundreds, whose raison d'être was to carry on anti-Semitic agitations.[109] The John Birch Society was similarly founded in 1958 with an anticommunist program, and many organizations of the "Christian crusade" were similarly established with a specific communist-fighting purpose.[110] The riots against West Indians in Britain in 1958 were preceded by several years of agitation to "Keep Britain White" by such organizations as Sir Oswald Moseley's Union Movement.[111] The deprogramming efforts of anti-cultists have been promoted by such ad hoc groups as Free Children of God and Citizens Engaged in Freeing Minds.[112] Although a given organization may not have persecution aims in its avowed charter or program, such activity may be characteristic of its actual operation. Thus the various "athletic clubs" in Chicago were supposedly athletic rather than racist in orientation; they in fact had long engaged in anti-black street activity and, when a riot broke out in 1919, they quickly took advantage of the situation to escalate their customary activity.[113]

The *relative* importance to persecution mobilization of such groups, which make persecution a central part of their group life, and those for which persecution simply becomes a "project" at a particular time is an open empirical question. The relevant point here is that organiza-

tions of one or both types seem to be a vital factor in the array of
"facilities" without which an outbreak of persecution would be highly
unlikely.

PARTICIPATION

The question of participation in persecutory episodes is one about
which there is much controversy and inconclusiveness. Part of the
problem arises from lack of definition of precisely what is involved in
being a persecution participant. In discussing protest participation, we
suggested an active core-cheerleader-spectator continuum of degree of
involvement in an episode. Similarly for persecutions, there are the active *instigators*—congressional investigating committees, rioters, witch
finders, papal inquisitors, and so on. There are also, the *supporters* of
persecution, those who give money to antipornography campaigns,
applaud rioters in letters to newspapers, and vote for officials actively
engaged in persecutions. Finally there may be a tenuous but significant level of participation in which people simply *tolerate* or let pass the
persecutory acts of others. In discussing protest participation, we
observed that most sociological data on participation concerned active
core participants—for example, persons arrested as rioters. In the case
of persecutions, studies of core participants are a rarity, and most of
our data are based on studies of the "supporters." In most cases, we
are left to make inferences about likely patterns of instigator and
tolerance participation.

The question of "how many?" people participate in a persecutory
episode is especially lacking in answers based on empirical data.
Recorders of persecutions typically tell us with some accuracy of the
body count of *victims* of a persecution: the number of witches or
heretics executed during a trial, the number of people injured or killed
during riots and pogroms, the number of deported enemy aliens or
those dismissed from government jobs as security risks. Seldom is
there anything like comparable recording of the numbers of persecutors involved.[114] A reasonable formula (only an hypothesis,
without empirical verification) would be that any persecution involves
very wide popular support, at least at the level of "tolerance," but that
the overt acts of victimization are carried out by a much smaller
number of people. This formula seems to apply to every kind of

persecution we have discussed, though the actual counting has apparently not been done in any case.

The other kind of participation question—what kind of people? —has been given much more research attention, though the findings of different studies have been sharply contradictory. One version of persecution-participation is quite similar to a perspective on protest participation that suggests the socially *marginal* character of participants. In this view, persecution is the product of *status discontent* on the part of persons whose social positions are being threatened by current social changes. Crusades against evil are described as *symbolic* protests against broad social changes; temperance crusaders, for example, see their prohibitionist activity as a verification of the identification with a traditional way of life that is challenged by modernism.[115] Antipornography crusaders are similarly described as middle-class, small-town churchgoing Americans who strike at pornography as symbolic of newer life styles, as symbolized, for example, by the counterculture.[116] The witchcraft accusers in Salem, traditional farmers who accused people associated with modern commercial activity, were engaged in what could be called symbolic protest against modernization.[117] The persecutor, in this view, is the person whose days of status glory were in the past, who sees great threats to that status in the present and future.

One type of such status discontent featured in several analyses of persecution participation is the status situation of the "old middle class." This expression was popularized by C. Wright Mills in a study of the growing ascendency of a "new" middle class of white-collar employees as opposed to the "old" middle class of self-employed farmers and small businessmen.[118] As both their numbers and their economic situation have declined, this group is inclined to support persecutory actions against those who can be blamed for this decline. This old middle class has been asserted as an important base for support of National Socialism (Nazism) in Germany.[119] Similarly, the "agrarian radicalism" that once expressed itself in rural protest against urban dominance was allegedly translated into support of McCarthy, the John Birch Society, and other agents of more recent anticommunism.[120]

This "status discontent" interpretation of persecution participation has been challenged in the cases both of support for National Socialism in Germany and for anticommunism in the United States. While Hitler's *apparent* base of social support was largely from persons of marginal middle-class status, he was given a great deal of covert support by well-established and secure industrialists.[121] The identification of McCarthy's support with earlier agrarian radicalism is likewise challenged in a study that shows, for example, that there was little continuity in Wisconsin in voting patterns or newspaper support as between the agrarian radical LaFollette and the anitcommunist McCarthy.[122] What this study suggests, in contrast, is the strong association between support for McCarthy and support for the Republican party, tending to identify McCarthy with the desperation of the party to regain national political control.[123] Rogin suggests that liberal intellectuals of the 1950s—"pluralists" who insist that the American system normally works very well to protect minorities—could only attribute McCarthyism to an aberrant radicalism that ruptures and threatens this normal political functioning. As a matter of fact, quite established and respectable social groups support persecutory actions when they see it in their interest to do so. In this vein, a chapter on "white militancy" in *The Politics of Protest* suggests that right-wing radicalism has its respectable and its unrespectable branches.[124] In the South, status marginals support the physically violent Ku Klux Klan, and respectable businessmen and professionals support the White Citizens Councils, with their more "genteel" methods of economic coercion. Among northern anticommunists, the Minutemen were described as engaging the "lumpenbourgeoisie," while the John Birch Society, headed by a wealthy candy manufacturer, provided organizational support for paranoiacs of slightly higher social status.

A study of participants in a moral crusade rally in Trafalgar Square, London, in 1976 was also critical of the status discontent view of persecution participation.[125] For one thing, around 96 percent of these people claimed to be regular churchgoers, suggesting a very "respectable" group in a country in which churchgoing is not as common as in some other countries. For another, participants themselves (for whatever the observation is worth) indicated little consciousness of any "loss of valued status" as a motive for participation in the rally. Most gave highly moralistic explanations of their motives and believed the rally worthwhile even if it failed to contain the designated evils because a "moral stand had been made."

It must finally be said that the sociology of persecution participation remains a rather badly underdeveloped area of analysis. In our understandable concerns with *why* and *how* persecutions occur, we sometimes slight the question of *who* engages in them. Some elementary analysis of the modes of persecution participation, as suggested here, might be the starting point for more refined analysis. Beyond this, we shall need to remain sensitive to the interaction between participation and the persecution *process*, observing perhaps that, as a persecutory episode develops, the number and types of its participants may change rather radically. It is to the matter of persecution process that we now turn.

PROCESS

The development of a persecutory episode through its various stages may be considered in terms that parallel the analysis in the last chapter of protest stages. Persecutions have their points of origin, or *precipitation*, their process of expansion, or *escalation*, their points of *termination*.

PRECIPITATION

Persecutions tend to be precipitated by dramatic events that typify the threats being experienced by persecution-prone people. A drastic crop failure, storm, or disease epidemic often provoked an outbreak of witchcraft persecution in a given community. Thus, officials of a German town, Ellwangen, criticized in 1618 for the ferocity of their local witch hunt, replied in self-justification that "the large number of supernatural storms and mysterious diseases was ample proof. If officials had not acted quickly, they would have sinned against the innocent, whom they were obliged to protect."[126] In race riots, among the most intensely episodic of persecutions, aggressive acts by minority races are likely to activate dominant race fears. In East St. Louis in 1917, blacks fired upon and killed police officers in a car that they mistook for another car whose white occupants had fired upon black residences.[127] In the "jailhouse riots" of 1919 in Knoxville and Omaha, white lynching mobs invaded prisons where they believed blacks accused of crimes against whites were held in custody, and these lynchings escalated into repressive riots.[128] In Chicago in 1919 and in Detroit in 1943, black aggressiveness in claiming the right to use recreational facilities (beaches and parks) produced interracial altercations that became race riots.[129] When "coloured" people in Nottingham and London in 1958 acted aggressively in response to recurring assaults by whites, their acts became the pretexts for vigorous anti-"coloured" riots.[130]

As we noted in the case of precipitants of protest, there may be a *series* of provocative incidents rather than a single event that provokes persecution. The anticommunist outbreaks after both World War I and II illustrate this point. The red scare of 1919–1920 grew in intensity between about April and November 1919 as a series of aggressive acts attributed to radicals or communists occurred.[131] In April there was a shipyard strike in Seattle that its mayor and much of the press labeled as red-inspired. Bombs were set off or mailed to various public officials, again attributed to radicals; there were large May Day rallies of radicals, a general strike planned for July 4, and, in the fall, a frightening police strike in Boston and a nationwide steel strike. The anticommunist crusade of McCarthy followed a "year of shocks" (1949), marked by such events as the fall of China to the communists, the exploding of an atomic bomb by the Soviet Union, and the espionage-related trial of a former State Department official, Alger Hiss.[132]

An important feature of some persecutions is that they are apparently precipitated by the persecutors themselves, in dramatic events that are falsely blamed on persecution victims. The Russian anti-Semitic pogroms were often engineered by members of the Black Hundreds. In the typical scenario, "someone, supposedly of course a Jew, would fire upon a patriotic procession carrying a portrait of the tsar, and the mob, infuriated, would fall upon the Jewish population."[133] This tactic is one of the tricks of the trade of the *agent provocateur*: for example, the law enforcement agent who poses as a demonstrator and sets off a bomb, an act leading to repressive action against demonstrators.[134] In some cases, officials determined to undertake a persecution may use some relatively insignificant event as a pretext for persecution. Thus the Nazi official Goebbels planned in 1938 the destruction of Jewish synagogues in the Kristallnacht (Night of the Broken Glass), using as a pretext the murder in Paris of a German embassy official by a Polish Jew.[135]

ESCALATION

The buildup of persecutory action depends on a number of factors that facilitate the intensification of action.

NEWS AND ESCALATION

It may be noted, in the first place, that the character of "news" coverage of precipitating events may contribute to the development of full-scale persecutory retaliations by threatened persons. Whether the news coverage is print or electronic, it often conveys hysterically exaggerated versions of precipitating events. Newspaper headlines conveyed as facts the offhand speculations that strikes in 1919 were red-inspired.[136] Senator McCarthy's charges of communists in the government were duly reported in major news stories; the refutation of these charges seldom made the news.[137] The local press in Washington, D.C., in 1919 gave its readers such inflammatory headlines as "Negroes Attack Girl . . . White Men Vainly Pursue."[138] The same newspaper, the *Washington Post*, actually publicized a planned "mobilization of every available service man" in the Washington area at a given time and place for "a 'clean-up' that will cause the events of the last two evenings to pale into insignificance."[139]

Rumor or improvised news may also play an extremely important role in persecutory buildups. In both the Chicago riot of 1919 and that in Detroit in 1943, details of the initial racial altercations were wildly distorted by rumors among both blacks and whites.[140] As a result, members of both races overreacted to the aggressiveness of the *other* race in the precipitating incident, and many angry blacks and whites converged on the scene of confrontation with this misapprehension.

BEHAVIOR OF VICTIMS

In the process of escalation, there comes to be an exaggerated sense of the danger emanating from persecution victims. In many instances, the behavior of the victims reinforces these dangers as they cooperate fully in the process of their victimization. Many accused witches eagerly confessed their pacts with the devil, sometimes because they had delusions of being witches.[141] These confessions without torture were in fact very significant in convincing such intellectuals as Jean Bodin of the reality of witchcraft and of the necessity for condemning witches.[142] In the Moscow purge trials, the confessions of counterrevolutionaries were again an element in legitimating the mass purge.[143] When revolutionary radicals were blamed for the labor strike in Seattle in 1919, they obligingly claimed credit for this event, which was actually a strike over rather mundane issues of demands for better working conditions. The Industrial Workers of the World (Wobblies) engaged in much incendiary rhetoric about violent revolutionary intentions, though the Wobblies' deeds were far less violent than their words. The antiradical division of the Justice Department (headed by J. Edgar Hoover) frequently raided the headquarters of such organizations and was seldom disappointed in "proof" of a radical conspiracy. It was even said that the finest collection anywhere of radical literature was in Justice Department files.[144] During the anticommunist flurry after World War II, the truculent behavior of many witnessess before investigating committees must have reinforced in the minds of many the bad character of these witnesses and the heroic quality of the investigators who were confronting them. About the ten Hollywood figures singled out for special attention by the House Committee on Un-American Actitities, Caute says, "The Ten did themselves little credit, rolling in the mud with the Committee, kicking and biting."[145] Finally, residents of Gloucester, Massachusetts, had some of their fantasies of a Moonie religion "takeover" of their community confirmed by the deviousness of a real estate deal by which an important piece of property fell into the hands of the Unification Church.[146]

Neutralizing Opposition

Our discussion above of "mobilization" as a background factor to persecution suggested the importance of a preexisting social organization with people already disposed and organized to move into action against "enemies." Given sufficient provocation, it is not hard to understand how Chicago's athletic clubs, professional witch finders, or right-wing anticommunist groups become involved in a persecutory episode. The more difficult question is how other groups of people *not* disposed to such action become involved. With virtually every type of persecution we have considered, there were "liberal" forces which might have been expected to oppose the persecutory action. In the red scare after World War I, one might have imagined that organized labor unions would have had a vested interest in denying the connection between labor strikes and communist influence. One might have imagined that such a "respectable" newspaper as the *New York Times* would have used its stable of investigative reporters to check the validity of the actual danger of communist revolution in the United States. Such agencies, in fact, joined the crowd of redhunters and exercised an exacerbating rather than a restraining influence.[147] In some other instances, potentially influential forces in countering persecution seem to "stand by" and watch the persecution develop. Liberal Democratic senators whom one might have expected would nip in the bud the effort by Senator McCarthy and the Republicans to pin a treason label on Democratic administrations "just sat there" and let McCarthy use the Senate as a forum for presenting his charges.[148] At about the same time, "liberal" American universities like those of California and Washington were acquiescing to demands of anticommunists that communists not be allowed to speak on campus, that professors be required to take loyalty oaths, and that those whose loyalty was suspect be dismissed.[149]

In explaining this neutralization of liberal opposition, McWilliams suggests an interesting formula: at the height of a persecution, people are unsure of how far the persecution may go and are constrained to disidentify themselves from persecution victims.[150] The Democratic party after World War II realized that the Republicans had a powerful political weapon in their espousal of anticommunism. President Truman's executive order in 1947 setting up a "loyalty review board" followed the "disastrous" off-year election of 1946, in which the anticommunism issue was first successfully injected into an election.[151] As Cook summarizes the matter, "the Democratic-liberal establishment, which should have provided a rallying point, virtually disintegrated before the first onslaught and sought to camouflage itself by riding to hounds with the foe."[152]

Fear of association with persecution victims has other bases than concern for winning elections. Hollywood producers were fearful that investigations of communist influence on films would lead to government censorship of their product, and most succumbed easily to pressures from the redhunters.[153] Officials of the University of California were fearful that their budget would be mutilated by the state legislature unless they went along with a legislative committee demand for a loyalty oath for professors.[154]

Persecutors may, of course, play on this fear of association with victims to expand the circle of victims. Hollywood film writers, actors, and directors who were suspected of communist leanings were subject to being fired and blacklisted from further employment; only by naming other victims could they clear themselves and keep their jobs or find reemployment.[155] During the witch trials, medical practitioners were often called on to verify the "witch's mark" on the bodies of accused witches. Relatively few male doctors were able conscientiously to report such marks, but female paramedics, midwives, did freely give such diagnoses. An interesting interpretation is that midwives were *themselves* often suspected of witchcraft, and their identification of witches marks was a way of clearing themselves of accusation.[156]

TERMINATION

We consider now those various forces responsible for the termination of an episode of persecution. As in the case of protest, persecution seems to terminate as a result of some combination of internal and external forces.

INTERNAL FORCES

It is possible to take an essentially *dialectic* view that persecutions, like other human phenomena, generate the seeds of their own destruction. Begun in a small way, to promote the political or economic interest of its sponsors, a persecution may escalate to the point that it no longer serves these interests.

This possibility is illustrated in the Soviet counterrevolutionary purge of the 1930s. Initiated to consolidate the hold of Stalin over the Communist party and the party over the country, the purge created a massive police apparatus the power of which began to challenge the supremacy of the party itself. The purge also discouraged new people from joining the party, to the extent that its strength was severely weakened. The party then acted to condemn some of the excesses of the purge as the work of "enemies" who had infiltrated the party to promote mass expulsions. This party turnabout resulted, for example, in "numerous arrests among the NKVD [security police] personnel, who frequently joined their former victims in the cells."[157]

Sometimes the persecution expansion begins to challenge important vested interests that were immune from victimization at the start. The Republican sponsors of McCarthy withdrew their support and voted for his censure when his attacks were turned to a Republican administration and another powerful vested interest, the United States Army.[158] Both organized labor and major American newspapers, supporters of the red scare of 1919–20 in its early phases, turned against the persecution when, from their perspective, it turned nasty and began demanding a sedition law that would limit freedom of the press and place barriers in the way of labor's right to strike.[159] Midelfort gives a similar interpretation to the termination of witch trials in Germany.[160] The early witch victims were mostly poor old women, but as the hunts expanded, they included more socially prominent citizens, not excluding some trial magistrates. The trials terminated not because the judges no longer believed in witchcraft but because they came to doubt their own ability to extirpate witchcraft without destroying the foundations of their communities.

Rising opposition to persecution may also come from somewhat less self-interested motives. The liberal community, dormant in a persecution's early stages, may be revived as the persecutor's methods pass a threshold beyond the liberal's tolerance. In this regard we often find manifestos of "conscience" delivered in the midst of a persecutory episode. In 1692 Increase Mather, a minister and father of Cotton Mather, a proponent of the witch trials, issued his *Cases of Conscience Concerning Evil Spirits Personating Men*, and this essay was endorsed by fourteen Boston ministers.[161] His *Cases* is an indictment of the methods of proof being employed in the Salem trials of that year, and its publication was apparently influential in the later decision of the Massachusetts colony to suspend the prosecutions. In 1920 Charles Evans Hughes, former Justice of the Supreme Court and a liberal Republican, led a liberal attack on various manifestations of the red scare.[162] In a more dramatic event, a liberal Assistant Secretary of Labor, Louis Post, exercised his legal right to release people being held illegally in deportation cases. Congress angrily threatened to censure Post, who demanded the right to appear before a House committee, to which he gave so thorough an account of the illegalities of the deportation process that "the House, in a dramatic reversal, decided to investigate the Attorney General."[163] In a dramatic reversal of the same kind, the United States Senate voted a censure of Senator Joseph McCarthy in 1954. In the background of that censure was a "Declaration of Conscience" by Margaret Chase Smith and several other Republican senators which condemned the tactics of their colleague.[164]

EXTERNAL FORCES

Persecution may be contained by pressures external to the persecutors themselves. An obvious possibility is that victims themselves might find some way to strike back against their tormentors to force termination of the persecution. This possibility seems to be realized very seldom, perhaps because victims are frequently so powerless. One instance is the situation of an antipornography campaign in a midwestern community, featuring legal harassment against a bookstore. The bookstore entered a large suit against antipornography leaders for harassment and, while the suit did not stop the campaign, it did make the campaigners "more cautious," according to one leader.[165] Likewise, "new" religious groups like Hare Krishna and the Unification Church have countered harassments by, for example, filing a defamation suit against the publishers of a book by the notorious deprogrammer Ted Patrick.[166]

More often, external control emanates from forces outside the community or country in which the episode occurs. Police and military forces were called in, often reluctantly and slowly, in American race riots. While these agents of social control may be less than exemplary in their determination to stop riots,[167] in persecutory as in protest riots the effective deployment of police/military force is a key to riot containment. The decade of the 1830s in Germany was a period of much reduced witchcraft persecution, largely because of the suppression of such activity by the Swedish occupation army.[168]

To summarize the matter of termination of persecution: it may be that there are many self-limiting tendencies that indicate a persecution will burn itself out in the absence of external controls. However, this observation could hardly constitute a counsel of laissez faire to those concerned with ending persecutions, since millions of people may literally be burned before this burned-out point is reached.

CONSEQUENCES

We consider now the impact of persecutory episodes on the countries and communities in which they occur. As we did with protest, we shall first note effects as they bear on the success or failure of the aims of persecutors; then on some possible unintended or byproduct effects of persecution.

PERSECUTION SUCCESS AND FAILURE

If all persecution aims at the suppression of some social "enemy," it is an obvious question to inquire of the fate of whatever "dangerous" tendencies were being combated by the persecutors. As so much of this assumed danger is an exaggeration of reality, we must examine the related question of the *perception* of danger in the aftermath of a persecution. If witches never really threatened society except in the minds of witch hunters, it is important to survey changes in the public mind about witches in the aftermath of a major witch hunt.

Do persecutors succeed in their aims? The answer to this is highly variable with different persecutions. The red scare after World War I has been described as remarkably successful in accomplishing its aims.[169] The American Communist party went into severe decline in the 1920s. More important, if one credits the real aim of the scare as an effort by big business to stop the growing militancy of American labor, the red scare was a great success, as indicated by the heavy loss of trade union membership in the early 1920s. The enduring repression of "radicals" was reflected by the establishment of loyalty oaths for teachers and other public employees.[170] The fear of aliens promoted by the scare helped produce the Immigration Act of 1924, with its immigration quotas that discriminated sharply against immigrants from eastern and southern Europe, a supposed "hotbed" for the growth of radical politics.[171] Finally, as one scholar suggests, the red scare may have demonstrated, for the encouragement of such future persecutors as McCarthy, the "democratic capacity for repression," the ability to stifle dissent without resorting to obviously authoritarian political forms.[172]

The anticommunist outbreak following World War II had a more ambiguous relation to future persecutions. Since the American Communist party had already largely self-destructed after the Nazi-Soviet nonaggression pact in 1937, the continued weakness of the party is no indication of the success of redhunting. After about 1954, the "paranoid style" in American politics went into abeyance for about fifteen years. This may have been partly a backlash effect of the excesses of McCarthyism, a reverse guilt-by-association in which "respectable" redfighters may have feared identification with the now-unrespectable McCarthy. It is also worth noting that 1954 was the year of the Supreme Court decision invalidating school segregation. For the next several years, persecutory aggressiveness took largely the form of white resistance to the implementation of desegregation and civil rights for blacks.[173] Anticommunism was now relegated to the lunatic fringe of the paranoid delusions of ideologists of the Ku Klux Klan, Minutemen, John Birch Society, and various "Christian crusaders" such as Carl McIntire and Billy Joe Hargis.[174] No national spokesman appeared until near the end of the period when first Barry Goldwater and then George Wallace combined racist and anticommunist appeals into a degree of threat to the major political parties. The paranoid style was revived for a brief career of political prominence in 1968, when a serious Wallace campaign was countered with the "southern strategy" of the campaign of Richard Nixon, whose early career in the House and Senate and as vice-president was based on anticommunism and his willingness to act as "hatchet man" for respectable Republicans. Nixon's own hatchet man, Spiro Agnew, spearheaded objection to liberal—especially news media—opposition to the Nixon administration. Agnew's contributions to the English language included characterizations of intellectuals as "an effete corps of impudent snobs" and of opposition newspaper editorialists as "nattering nabobs of negativism."[175] The planned intensification of repression of dissent in the second Nixon administration failed only because of the incredible historical accident of the uncovering of the Watergate conspiracy. Continued East-West détente and a cooling of racial tensions led the 1970s to close on a remarkably nonpersecutory note.

The flurry of race riots around the time of World War I apparently had a very different outcome. Public reactions to the riots tended to divide sharply between those advocating legal measures to resubordinate blacks and those advocating greater racial equality and a more neutral police enforcement during racial conflicts.[176] Largely through the growing influence of W. E. B. Du Bois and the National Association for the Advancement of Colored People, the latter course predominated. Militant black intellectuals glorified the "fighting back" tendency of blacks in several of the riots.[177] The NAACP vigorously defended some of the victims of discriminatory law enforcement during the riots—for example, the twelve black men sentenced to die for alleged murders in the Elaine, Arkansas, riots.[178] In this case, federal agencies, including the Supreme Court, were forced virtually to admit the reality of racial repression in the country.

While racial repression was obviously not eliminated in the 1920s or in any time since, the extended anticommunist hysteria of the 1920s found no parallel in further antiblack repressions of that era. The difference may reflect the varying strengths of organizations representing the persecuted. The militant NAACP of the period found only a pale reflection in the efforts of the American Civil Liberties Union to defend the civil rights of "radicals."[179] In support of this suggestion, it might be noted that in the wake of riots against "coloured" immigrants in Nottingham, London, and other English cities in 1958, there was the familiar polarization of white responses: put them back in their place versus improve their social situation.[180] In England, long agitation on the matter resulted both in a 1962 law restricting further "coloured" immigration and 1965 civil rights laws outlawing certain forms of racial discrimination. The inability of the immigrants to organize effectively in their own behalf[181] was undoubtedly a reason for the "mixed" outcome of the English period of racial tension.

Finally, the aftermath of witch hunting will be considered in terms of whether the hunts resulted in an abatement of fear of witches. As already suggested, many witch hunts ended in frustration and fear that the persecution was engulfing the whole community. In this stage, it is easily imaginable that a renewal of witch hunting would require only a period of "recovery" from the ravages of the last persecution. Midelfort asserts that people continued to believe in witches long after they lost confidence in their ability to control them. Nevertheless, there was in both Europe and America an alternative religious inter- pretation of "misfortune" that, where it came to prevail, greatly dampened the fear of witches. Among German theologians, for exam- ple, there was a "providential" interpretation of misfortune that countered the interpetation of misfortune as the work of the devil and his witches.[182] In this view, misfortune is God's way of chastising man for sin and is a needed spur to self-examination and the mending of er- rant ways. The availability of this tradition may have helped prevent further lapses into witch hunting. In Salem there was an aftermath period of tension while the witch-baiting minister remained until fi- nally deposed in 1697. The minister who arrived in that year preached the providential message of the recent afflictions as God's signal for self-searching, not for accusations.[183] In 1734, in the Massachusetts town of Northampton, Jonathan Edwards used the cases of "afflicted" children as an exemplary manifestation of the Holy Spirit. He was a key figure in the Great Awakening of religious piety that was shortly to sweep through New England and sweep away most of the concerns with witchcraft. Even by 1711 witch hunting had become so disreputable in the colony that the General Assembly passed a "rever- sal of attainder" that condemned the Salem trials and exonerated all survivors against whom witch accusations had been made.[184]

BYPRODUCT EFFECTS

Like other "purposive actions" of human beings, persecutions may have their "unanticipated consequences."[185] One possibility is

that persecution increases the solidarity of its victims. The classic instance is the Jewish reaction to anti-Semitism, the binding effect of a
sense of common persecution. In the aftermath of the Holocaust, it is
said that "there is scarcely a Jewish family in the world which is not
personally linked to the tragedy by the loss of relatives in the prisons,
torture chambers and death camps of the Nazis."[186] This unity in
adversity is illustrated also in the case of some Indian tribes, about
whom it is said that their only real sense of Indian history is a historical
catalog of grievances against white persecutions.[187]

The effects of repressive riots on black racial solidarity is an important question. The militant racial organizations (like the NAACP) and
newspapers (like the *Chicago Defender*) of the time encouraged blacks to
believe that they had "fought back" during the riots and that similar
self-defensiveness would be the hallmark of the "new negro."[188] As
suggested in the last chapter, however, this black militancy was largely
confined to the North, at least until the time of Martin Luther King's
southern protest activity, beginning about 1957. In the last chapter we
reviewed evidence that the riots of the 1960s were predominantly nonsouthern, occurring outside the South and participated in by blacks
who had been socialized for some years in the northern black political
culture of militancy. The accommodating attitudes of such black
leaders as Booker T. Washington were by no means discredited in the
rural South by World War I–era disturbances, and a North-South
cleavage on the militancy issue clearly survived these persecutions.

Another possibility is that persecutory action may generate a
"tradition of violence," which may be used by victims when they later
engage in protest actions of their own. The violence of student, antiwar, and black demonstrators in the 1960s was justified in their own
minds by the history of "legal violence" as well as by vigilante
violence.[189]

Finally we may observe that, quite without anticipation of such an
effect, an acute persecutory outbreak may provide victims with a better social fate than they experienced before the persecution. The situation of Japanese-Americans in the United States illustrates this
possibility. Long concentrated on the West coast and in bitter competition with white Americans, these Americans were subjected to a brutal
removal to "relocation" camps inland at the start of World War II.
Upon their release from these camps, many Japanese-Americans
failed to return to areas in which their land, businesses, and homes
had been confiscated, and they tended to disperse in urban locations

throughout the United States.[190] This forcible removal of Japanese-Americans from areas in which they had been persecuted allowed some of the "natural" advantages of members of this group in striving for success to come to the fore—for example, a demonstrated affinity between traditional Japanese cultural values and those of the "Protestant ethic" in Western societies.[191] The net result of these developments was that, shortly after the war, Japanese-Americans began to emerge as a "model minority"[192] and have been strikingly successful in overcoming discrimination. The relocation persecution of World War II was an unwitting catalyst of this change.

Notes

1. H. Laurence Ross, Donald T. Campbell, and Gene V. Glass, "Determining the Social Effects of a Legal Reform: The Breathalyser Crackdown of 1967," *American Behavioral Scientist* 13 (1970): 493–509.

2. Studies of European witchcraft typically focus on a particular aspect of the trials, or they deal with trials in a particular country or region. In the first category are Norman Cohn, *Europe's Inner Demons* (New York: Basic Books, 1975); Richard Kieckhofer, *European Witch Trials* (Berkeley; University of California Press, 1976); and Marvin Harris, *Cows, Pigs, Wars and Witches: The Riddles of Culture* (New York: Random House, 1974), pp. 207–40. For major regional studies, see E. C. Erik Midelfort, *Witch Hunting in Southwestern Germany, 1562–1684* (Stanford: Stanford University Press, 1972); E. William Monter, "Patterns of Witchcraft in the Jura," *Journal of Social History* 5 (1971–72): 1–25; Alan D. F. MacFarlane, *Witchcraft in Tudor and Stuart England* (New York: Harper & Row, 1970); Christina Hole, *Witchcraft in England* (Totowa, N.J.: Rowman and Littlefield, 1977); George L. Kittredge, *Witchcraft in Old and New England*; and Wallace Notestein, *A History of Witchcraft in England from 1558 to 1718* (New York: Russell & Russell, 1965). For overall review, see Nachman Ben-Yehuda, "The European Witch Craze of the 14th to 17th Centuries: A Sociologist's Perspective," *American Journal of Sociology* 86 (1980): 1–31.

3. The half-million estimate is that of Harris, *Cows, Pigs, Wars and Witches*, p. 207. Calling such estimates "fantastic exaggerations," Cohn asserts that records are too defective to make any accurate estimate. Cohn, *Europe's Inner Demons*, pp. 253, 254.

4. Paul Boyer and Stephen Nissenbaum, *Salem Possessed: The Social Origins of Witchcraft* (Cambridge: Harvard University Press, 1974); Chadwick

Hansen, *Witchcraft at Salem* (New York: George Braziller, 1969); David Levin, ed., *What Happened at Salem?* 2d ed. (New York: Harcourt, Brace and World, 1960).

5. Henry C. Lea, *A History of the Inquisition in the Middle Ages* (New York: Russell & Russell, 1958).

6. Cohn, *Europe's Inner Demons*, pp. 75–98

7. James Parkes, *Antisemitism* (Chicago: Quadrangle, 1963); Vamberto Morais, *A Short History of Anti-Semitism* (New York: Norton, 1976); Paul E. Grosser and Edwin G. Halperin, *The Causes and Effects of Anti-Semitism: The Dimensions of a Prejudice* (New York: Philosophical Library, 1978); Helen Fein, *Accounting for Genocide: National Responses and Jewish Victimization During the Holocaust* (New York: Free Press, 1979).

8. Norman Cohn, *Warrant for Genocide: The Myth of the Jewish World Conspiracy and the Protocols of the Elders of Zion* (New York: Harper & Row, 1966).

9. Zbigniew K. Brzezinski, *The Permanent Purge* (Cambridge: Harvard University Press, 1956); Nathan Leites and Elsa Bernaut, *Ritual of Liquidation: The Case of the Moscow Trials* (Glencoe, Ill.: Free Press, 1954); Borys Levytsky, *The Stalinist Terror in the Thirties: Documentation from the Soviet Press* (Stanford: Hoover Institution Press, 1974).

10. For a general formulation of the nature of repressive riots, see H. Otto Dahlke, "Race and Minority Riots: A Study in the Typology of Violence," *Social Forces* 30 (1952): 419–25.

11. James McCague, *The Second Rebellion: The Story of the New York City Draft Riots of 1863* (New York: Dial, 1968).

12. Elliott M. Rudwick, *Race Riot at East St. Louis: July 2, 1917* (Carbondale: Southern Illinois University Press, 1964); William M. Tuttle, Jr., *Race Riot: Chicago in the Red Summer of 1919* (New York: Atheneum, 1970); on Detroit, Alfred M. Lee and Norman D. Humphreys, *Race Riot* (New York: Dryden Press, 1948); Arthur I. Waskow, *From Race Riot to Sit-In: 1919 and the 1960s* (Garden City, N.Y.: Doubleday, 1966).

13. Ralph H. Turner and Samuel J. Surace, "Zoot-Suiters and Mexicans: Symbols in Crowd Behavior," *American Journal of Sociology* 62 (1956): 14–20.

14. C. Vann Woodward, *The Strange Career of Jim Crow*, 2d ed. (New York: Oxford University Press, 1966).

15. Ruth Glass, *London's Newcomers: The West Indian Migrants* (Cambridge: Harvard University Press, 1961), pp. 127–46.

16. Robert K. Murray, *Red Scare: A Study in National Hysteria, 1919–1920* (Minneapolis: University of Minnesota Press, 1955); Murray B. Levin,

Political Hysteria in America: The Democratic Capacity for Repression (New York: Basic Books, 1971); William Preston, Jr., *Aliens and Dissenters: Federal Suppression of Radicals, 1903–1933* (Cambridge: Harvard University Press, 1963).

17. David Caute, *The Great Fear: The Anti-Communist Purge Under Truman and Eisenhower* (New York: Simon & Schuster, 1978); Fred J. Cook, *The Nightmare Decade: The Life and Times of Senator Joe McCarthy* (New York: Random House, 1971); Carey McWilliams, *Witch Hunt: The Revival of Heresy* (Boston: Little, Brown, 1950); Earl Latham *The Communist Controversy in Washington: From the New Deal to McCarthy* (Cambridge: Harvard University Press, 1966).

18. Walter Schneir and Miriam Schneir, *Invitation to an Inquest* (Garden City, N.Y.: Doubleday, 1965); Robert Meeropol and Michael Meeropol, *We Are Your Sons: The Legacy of Ethel and Julius Rosenberg* (Boston: Houghton Mifflin, 1975).

19. Cohn, *Europe's Inner Demons*.

20. A. L. Morton, *The World of the Ranters: Religious Radicalism and the English Revolution* (London: Lawrence and Wishart, 1970).

21. R. A. Knox, *Enthusiasm: A Chapter in the History of Religion* (London: Oxford University Press, 1931).

22. Leonard J. Arrington and Davis Bitton, *The Mormon Experience: A History of the Latter Day Saints* (New York: Knopf, 1979); Harry J. Sawatzky, *They Sought a Country:* (Berkeley: University of California Press, 1971).

23. *Washington Post,* 25 August 1980, p. 1.

24. *New York Times,* 23 December 1979, p. 7.

25. Anson D. Shupe, Jr., Roger Spielmann, and Sam Stigall, "Cults of Anti-Cultism," *Society* 17 (March–April 1980): 43–46.

26. Joseph R. Gusfield, *Symbolic Crusade: Status Politics and the American Temperance Movement* (Urbana: University of Illinois Press, 1963).

27. Marion Goldman, "Prostitution and Virtue in Nevada," in Irving L. Horowitz and Charles Nanry, eds., *Sociological Realities II* (New York: Harper & Row, 1975), pp. 352–57.

28. Louis A. Zurcher, Jr., and R. George Kirkpatrick, *Citizens for Decency: Antipornography Crusades as Status Defense* (Austin: University of Texas Press, 1976); Harrell R. Rodgers, "Prelude to Conflict: The Evolution of Censorship Campaigns," *Pacific Sociological Review* 18 (1975): 194–205.

29. Roy Wallis and Richard Bland, "Purity in Danger: A Survey of Participants in a Moral Crusade Rally," *British Journal of Sociology* 30 (1979): 188–205.

30. McWilliams, *Witch Hunt*, p. 3.

31. Boyer and Nissenbaum, *Salem Possessed*.

32. Scarlett Epstein, "A Sociological Analysis of Witch Beliefs in a Mysore Village," in John Middleton, ed., *Magic, Witchcraft, and Curing* (Garden City, N.Y.: Natural History Press, 1967), pp. 135–54.

33. George L. Mosse, *Germans and Jews* (New York: Howard Fertig, 1970) pp. 34–76.

34. Jerome H. Skolnick, *The Politics of Protest* (New York: Simon and Schuster, 1969), pp. 218–24.

35. Cohn, *Warrant for Genocide*, p. 53.

36. Harris, *Cows, Pigs, Wars and Witches*, p. 236.

37. Morton Grodzins, *Americans Betrayed: Politics and the Japanese Evacuation;* Edward H. Spicer et al., *Impounded People: Japanese-Americans in Relocation Centers* (Tucson: University of Arizona Press, 1969); Roger Daniels, *Concentration Camps, U.S.A.: Japanese-Americans and World War II* (New York: Holt, Rinehart and Winston, 1971).

38. Herbert Hill, "Anti-Oriental Agitation and the Rise of Working Class Racism," in Horowitz and Nanry, *Sociological Realities II*, pp. 396–404; Roger Daniels and Spencer C. Olin, eds., *Racism in California* (New York: Macmillan, 1972, pp. 55–180.

39. Parkes, *Antisemitism*, pp. 35, 43, 87.

40. Levin, *Political Hysteria in America*, pp. 94, 95.

41. John Higham, *Strangers in the Land: Patterns of American Nativism, 1860–1925* (New Brunswick, N.J.: Rutgers University Press, 1955), p. 223.

42. Schneir and Schneir, *Invitation to an Inquest*, pp. 70, 71.

43. Talcott Parsons, "Social Strains in America," in Daniel Bell, ed., *The Radical Right* (Garden City, N.Y.: Doubleday, 1964), pp. 209–29.

44. Edward A. Shils, *The Torment of Secrecy: The Background and Consequences of American Security Policies* (Glencoe, Ill.: Free Press, 1956), pp. 62, 63.

45. Cook, *Nightmare Decade*, pp. 209–38; Latham, *The Communist Controversy in Washington*, pp. 219–316.

46. William R. Locklear, "The Anti-Chinese Movement in Los Angeles," in Daniels and Olin, *Racism in California*, pp. 92–104.

47. Rudwick, *Race Riot at East St. Louis*, pp. 217, 218, summarizing population trends for East. St. Louis, Chicago, and Detroit.

48. Lee and Humphrey, *Race Riot*, p. 93.

49. Rudwick, *Race Riot at East St. Louis*, chap. 3 and pp. 218, 219.

50. Glass, *London's Newcomers*, p. 174.

51. Critics of the Rosenberg trial have developed evidence that the prosecutors in the case were well aware that the "secret" allegedly passed by the Rosenbergs was scientifically useless information. Gerald E. Markowitz and Michael Meeropol, "The Crime of the Century Revisited: David Greenglass' Scientific Evidence in the Rosenberg Case," *Science and Society* 44 (1980): 1-26.

52. Richard Hofstadter, *The Paranoid Style in American Politics and Other Essays* (New York: Alfred A. Knopf, 1966), pp. 3-40.

53. Shils, *Torment of Secrecy*, p. 78.

54. Grodzins, *Americans Betrayed*, pp. 20-179.

55. Rudwick, *Race Riot at East St. Louis*, pp. 7-15.

56. Cook, *Nightmare Decade*, chap. 7, 8.

57. Grosser and Halperin, *Causes and Effects of Anti-Semitism*, pp. 126-33.

58. Midelfort, *Witch Hunting in Southwestern Germany*, pp. 122-25.

59. Tuttle, *Race Riot*, pp. 216-22.

60. Waskow, *From Race Riot to Sit-In*, pp. 16-20, 121-74.

61. The moral outrage of the crusader may be supplemented by the threat that the persecution victims pose to the status of the crusaders. Thus the antiprostitution campaigns in frontier Nevada are described as partly the result of the fact that some prostitutes became prominent in charitable activity in western towns, depriving "respectable" married women of one of the few outlets for personal status striving. Goldman, "Prostitution and Virtue in Neveda."

62. Isidoro Aizenberg, "'Die or Leave': An Anti-Jewish Riot in Nineteenth Century Venezuela," *American Jewish History* 49 (1980): 478-87.

63. Midelfort, *Witch Hunting in Southwestern Germany*, pp. 17-19.

64. There is evidence, however, that the *popular* conception of the danger from witchcraft was almost totally confined to the conception of the witch as troublemaker and not the focus on the witch as an enemy of religion, which was the almost exclusive concern of church officials. Richard A. Horsley, "Who Were the Witches?: The Social Roles of the Accused in European Witch Trials," *Journal of Interdisciplinary History* 9 (1979): 689-715.

65. Midelfort, *Witch Hunting in Southwestern Germany*, pp. 75, 76.

66. Cohn, Europe's *Inner Demons*, pp. 164-205. For a similar analysis, see Edward Peters, *The Magician, the Witch and the Law* (Philadelphia: University of Pennsylvania Press, 1978).

67. Arnold Forster and Benjamin R. Epstein, *Danger on the Right* (New York: Random House, 1964), pp. 11-46.

68. Cohn, *Warrant for Genocide.*

69. Leo P. Ribuffo, "Henry Ford and *The International Jew,*" *American Jewish History* 49 (1980): 437–77.

70. Levin, *Political Hysteria in America*, p. 69.

71. Hofstadter, *The Paranoid Style,* p. 37.

72. Levin, *Political Hysteria in America*, p. 68.

73. For an 1882 episode in Hungary of such an accusation, see Parkes *Antisemitism*, pp. 31, 32.

74. For some contemporary artistic depictions of witches' sabbats, see the plates following p. 126 of Midelfort, *Witch Hunting in Southwestern Germany*; also those following p. 256 of Cohn, *Europe's Inner Demons.*

75. Hofstadter, *The Paranoid Style*, p. 22.

76. Turner and Surace, "Zoot-Suiters and Mexicans."

77. Brzezinksi, *The Permanent Purge*, p. 45.

78. See the several illustrations of Protocol covers in the plates following p. 144 of Cohn, *Warrant for Genocide.*

79. Levin, *Political Hysteria in America*, chap. 4.

80. Cook, *Nightmare Decade*, p. 204.

81. Rudwick, *Race Riot at East St. Louis*, pp. 86–89.

82. Waskow, *From Race Riot to Sit-In*; Dahlke, "Race and Minority Riots."

83. Waskow, *From Race Riot to Sit-In*, pp. 12–16.

84. Murray, *Red Scare*, p. 211.

85. Caute, *The Great Fear,* pp. 414–18.

86. Schneir and Schneir, *Invitation to an Inquest*, p. 119.

87. Dick Anthony, Thomas Robbins, and Jim McCarthy, "Legitimating Repression," *Society* 17 (March–April 1980), p. 40.

88. Cohn, *Europe's Inner Demons,* pp. 23–31.

89. Midelfort, *Witch Hunting in Southwestern Germany,* pp. 18–21.

90. Notestein, *History of Witchcraft* in England, pp. 164–205; Hole, *Witchcraft in England*, pp. 79–82.

91. Caute, *The Great Fear*, p. 94.

92. Cohn, *Europe's Inner Demons*, pp. 160, 161.

93. Caute, *The Great Fear*, pp. 133–38.

94. Kieckhofer, *European Witch Trials*, pp. 88, 89.

95. Leites and Bernaut, *Ritual of Liquidation*, p. 22.

96. Schneir and Schneir, *Invitation to an Inquest*, p. 422.

97. Midelfort, *Witch Hunting in Southwestern Germany*, pp. 69, 70.

98. Turner and Surace, "Zoot-Suiters and Mexicans."

  99. Murray, *Red Scare*, pp. 58–66.

100. In sentencing the Rosenbergs, Judge Kaufman articulated these alleged consequences of their treason. Schneir and Schneir, *Invitation to an Inquest*, p. 170.

101. Anthony Oberschall, *Social Conflict and Social Movements* (Englewood Cliffs, N.J.: Prentice-Hall, 1973), pp. 108–13.

102. Seymor M. Lipset, *Political Man* (Garden City, N.Y.: Doubleday, 1960), pp. 88–90.

103. For some of the profound differences of social attitude among different Protestant denominations, see Charles Y. Glock and Rodney Stark, "Is There an American Protestantism?" in Horowitz and Nanry, *Sociological Realities II*, pp. 421–28.

104. Zurcher and Kirkpatrick, *Citizens for Decency*.

105. Rodgers, *Prelude to Conflict*.

106. Zurcher and Kirkpatrick, *Citizens for Decency*, p. 150

107. Cook, *Nightmare Decade*, pp. 363, 364.

108. Murray, *Red Scare*, pp. 87–90.

109. Cohn, *Warrant for Genocide*, p. 110.

110. Forster and Epstein, *Danger on the Right*.

111. Glass, *London's Newcomers*, pp. 171–92.

112. Shupe, Spielmann, and Stigall, "Cults of Anti-Cultism."

113. Tuttle, *Race Riot*, pp. 32, 33.

114. The nearest approach to such persecutor counting seems to be the effort in some cases to indicate the size of a "mob" engaged in a riotous persecution. These estimates are subject to all the biases of crowd estimation, as indicated in the previous chapter.

115. Gusfield, *Symbolic Crusade*.

116. Zurcher and Kirkpatrick, *Citizens for Decency*.

117. Boyer and Nissenbaum, *Salem Possessed*.

118. C. Wright Mills, *White Collar* (New York: Oxford, 1951).

119. Rudolf Heberle, *From Democracy to Nazism* (Baton Rouge: Louisiana State University Press, 1945).

120. Daniel Bell, "The Dispossessed," in Bell *The Radical Right*, p. 1–45.On the "small business" side of support for McCarthy, see Martin Trow, "Small Business, Political Tolerance, and Support for McCarthy," *American Journal of Sociology* 44 (1958): 270–81.

121. Hans Gerth, "The Nazi Party: Its Leadership and Composition," *American Journal of Sociology* 44 (1940): 517–41.

122. Michael P. Rogin, *The Intellectuals and McCarthy: The Radical Specter* (Cambridge: M.I.T. Press, 1967), pp. 59–103.

123. For similar findings, see Nelson W. Polsby, "Towards an Explanation of McCarthyism," *Political Studies* 8 (1960): 76–80

124. Skolnick, *Politics of Protest*, p. 236.

125. Wallis and Bland, "Purity in Danger."

126. Midelfort, *Witch Hunting in Southwestern Germany*, p. 110.

127. Rudwick, *Race Riot in East St. Louis*, pp. 38–40.

128. Waskow, *From Race Riot to Sit-In*, pp. 105–20.

129. Tuttle, *Race Riot*, pp. 3–10; Lee and Humphrey, *Race Riot*, pp. 20–26.

130. Glass, *London's Newcomers*, pp. 130–35.

131. Levin, *Political Hysteria in America*, chap. 2.

132. Cook, *Nightmare Decade*, pp. 68, 69.

133. Louis Greenberg, *The Jews in Russia*, vol. 2 (New Haven: Yale University Press, 1951), p. 76.

134. Gary T. Marx, "Thoughts on a Neglected Category of Social Movement Participant: The *Agent Provocateur* and Informant," *American Journal of Sociology* 80 (1974): 402–42.

135. Morais, *A Short History of Anti-Semitism*, p. 208.

136. Levin, *Political Hysteria in America*, pp. 30, 31.

137. Cook, *Nightmare Decade*.

138. Tuttle, *Race Riot*, p. 29.

139. Waskow, *From Race Riot to Sit-In*, p. 25.

140. Tuttle, *Race Riot*, p. 8; Lee and Humphrey, *Race Riot*, p. 27.

141. See, for example, Agnes Sampson's insistence on "proving" herself a witch when personally examined by King James I in 1590 after the king began to believe that Sampson and her alleged co-conspirators "were all extreme liars." Hole, *Witchcraft in England*, p. 15.

142. Midelfort, *Witch Hunting in Southwestern Germany*, p. 108.

143. Leites and Bernaut, *Ritual of Liquidation*.

144. Levin, *Political Hysteria in America*, pp. 52, 53.

145. Caute, *The Great Fear*, p. 495.

146. *Washington Post*, 25 August 1980, p. 1.

147. Murray, *Red Scare*, pp. 64, 65, 105–21.

148. Cook, *Nightmare Decade*, p. 167.

149. McWilliams, *Witch Hunt*, pp. 102–213.

150. "What the university (of California) feared was a demagogic manipulation of the fear of communism." McWilliams, *Witch Hunt*, p. 104.

151. Caute, *The Great Fear*, pp. 26–29.

152. Cook, *Nightmare Decade*, p. 18.

153. Caute, *The Great Fear*, pp. 498–500; McWilliams, *Witch Hunt*, pp. 80, 81.

154. McWilliams, *Witch Hunt,* p. 112.

155. Caute, *The Great Fear*, pp. 506–14; Victor S. Navasky, *Naming Names* (New York: Viking, 1980).

156. Sanford J. Fox, *Science and Justice: The Massachusetts Witchcraft Trials* (Baltimore: Johns Hopkins University Press, 1968), pp. 84–86.

157. Brzezinski, *The Permanent Purge*, p. 127.

158. Cook, *Nightmare Decade*, pp. 520–40.

159. Levin, *Political Hysteria in America*, pp. 75, 76, 86.

160. Midelfort, *Witch Hunting in Southwestern Germany.*

161. Levin, *What Happened at Salem?*, pp. 117–26.

162. Murray, *Red Scare*, pp. 243, 244.

163. Levin, *Political Hysteria in America*, p. 78. For Post's own version of this episode, see Louis F. Post, *The Deportations Delirium of Nineteen-Twenty: A Personal Narrative of an Historic Official Experience* (New York: De Capo Press, 1970).

164. Cook, *Nightmare Decade*, pp. 261–63.

165. Zurcher and Kirkpatrick, *Citizens for Decency*, p. 174.

166. *New York Times*, 8 May 1978, IV, p. 8.

167. Especially in East St. Louis; in the aftermath of that riot, a Military Board of Inquiry heard many complaints against the antiblack bias of the Illinois National Guard. Rudwick, *Riot at East St. Louis*, pp. 74–94.

168. Midelfort, *Witch Hunting in Southwestern Germany*, p. 75.

169. Levin, *Political Hysteria in America*, pp. 87–90.

170. On such activity in New York state, see Lawrence H. Chamberlain, *Loyalty and Legislative Action* (Ithaca: Cornell University Press, 1951).

171. Higham, *Strangers in the Land.*

172. Levin, *Political Hysteria in America*, p. 90.

173. Neil R. McMillen, *The Citizens Council: Organized Resistance to the Second Reconstruction, 1954–1964* (Urbana: University of Illinois Press, 1971).

174. Forster and Epstein, *Danger on the Right;* Brooks R. Walker, *The Christian Fright Peddlers* (Garden City, N.Y.: Doubleday, 1964).

175. Cook, *Nightmare Decade*, pp. 571–79.

176. Waskow, *From Race Riot to Sit-In*, pp. 175–208.

177. Tuttle, *Race Riot*, pp. 209–16.

178. Waskow, *From Race Riot to Sit-In*, pp. 143–74.

179. Preston, *Aliens and Dissenters*, p. 143.

180. Glass, *London's Newcomers*, pp. 171–200, showing that the "Keep Britain White" groups were countered by "Keep Britain Tolerant" groups.

181. Benjamin W. Heineman, Jr., *The Politics of the Powerless: A Study of the Campaign Against Racial Discrimination* (London: Oxford, 1972).

182. Midelfort, *Witch Hunting in Southwestern Germany*, pp. 34–56.

183. Boyer and Nissenbaum, *Salem Possessed*, pp. 217–20.

184. Levin, *What Happened at Salem?* pp. 139–41; Hansen, *Witchcraft at Salem*, pp. 215–19.

185. Robert K. Merton, "The Unanticipated Consequences of Purposive Social Action," *American Sociological Review* 1 (1936): 894–904.

186. Parkes, *Antisemitism*, p. 119. Fein observes that during the Holocaust, Jewish communities undergoing persecution experienced enhanced solidarity only where they were able to develop collective defense mechanisms to combat their victimization. Otherwise, "when people are isolated, the threat of victimization does not unite them as a collectivity, but forces them to compete against each other for ways out." Fein, *Accounting for Genocide*, p. 322.

187. Nancy O, Lurie, "An American Indian Renaissance," in Stuart Levine and Nancy O. Lurie (eds.) *The American Indian Today* (Baltimore: Penguin, 1970) pp. 295–327.

188. Tuttle, *Race Riot*, pp. 208–41.

189. Sknolnick, *The Politics of Protest*.

190. Spicer et al., *Impounded People*, pp. 277–85.

191. William Caudill and George De Vos, "Achievement, Culture and Personality: The Case of the Japanese Americans," *American Anthropologist* 58 (1956): 1102–1126.

192. William Petersen, *Japanese Americans* (New York: Random House, 1971).

Chapter 5

Renewals

INTRODUCTION

HUMAN SOCIAL SYSTEMS OPERATE on the assumption of a certain level of commitment or enthusiasm of the people who are members of those systems. Team, community, or national "spirit" is related to the ability of these systems to win games or wars or to deal effectively with their outstanding problems. As with the other functional imperatives reviewed in earlier chapters of this book, there are routine mechanisms to engender the necessary commitments from members. Schools hold scheduled pep rallies and organize cheering sections at sports contests to promote the desired school spirit. Organized churches schedule regular "inspirational" worship services to renew the enthusiasm of the faithful. The rallies held during a political campaign often seem more a device to reinvigorate the efforts of campaigners than to convert new supporters. When protest and/or persecution develops to the level of organized social systems devoted to these efforts, Nuremberg rallies and Marches on Washington serve similar renewing functions. And of course the leaders of most nations have discovered that a "spirit of patriotism"[1] among citizens is indispensable to national survivals: and there are the well-scheduled rituals of Independence Day, Canada Day, May Day, Bastille Day, and so on.

In this chapter we consider *episodes* of renewal—outbreaks of such activity at extraordinary levels of intensity. The hallmark of such behavior is the unusually *enthusiastic* action of the participants. In everyday life in every social system people are encouraged to "keep their cool" in a number of respects. There is, one might suggest, a certain ambiguity in our socialization of social system members. Authoritative persons try, in some of the ways suggested above, to whip up enthusiasm for various social causes. At the same time, if the targets of socialization take these efforts too seriously and try to act out some of the inculcated ideals, they may find themselves condemned as "radicals," as threats to law and order, as fit targets of repressive persecutory action. Thus certain radical Christian sects (e.g,, Quakers, Diggers, Ranters) in seventeenth-century England were condemned and persecuted precisely for their religious "enthusiasm."[2] The repression of these enthusiasts is typical of the experience of those who take religious and other ideals too seriously. Since these episodes of renewal are so often *protests* against the alleged corruption and indifference of people in authority, they will furnish many occasions in the following analysis to relate this topic to protest as well as to persecution. Finally, we shall be noting that *disaster* may be one of the major provocative agents of renewal episodes, so that the full circle of our four types of collective behavior will appear in this as in the concluding chapter.

SOME FORMS OF RENEWAL EPISODES

As with other types of collective behavior, so with renewals: the range of episodes classifiable as renewals seems well-nigh overwhelming. If history is a "graveyard of revolutions," as is often asserted, it is a graveyard as well of countless renewal episodes. Along with the mélange of gravestones in this infinite cemetery, there remain as well the mark of renewal after-effects on virtually all *living* phenomena. In the face of this diversity, we shall try to isolate a few large subtypes by way of illustrating the range of the phenomenon and the type of material to which we return to raise our sociological questions. The hallmark of *all* these forms, despite their wide diversity of approaches to the problem, is that they treat as problematic the pattern maintenance/tension management mechanisms of social functioning. The moral and/or psychological state of persons is treated as a problem requiring drastic action to "renew" the human energies on which human social activity depends. We turn now to various manifestations of this renewal concern.

REVIVALS

One large category of renewal phenomena deals with episodes of "awakened" enthusiasm for commitments that had lapsed into relative indifference. There was a so-called Great Awakening of religious activity in the American colonies around 1740, associated both with "settled" revivalists such as Jonathan Edwards in Massachusetts and with the various "itinerant" preachers such as George Whitefield, an import from Britain, and Gilbert Tennant, the first great made-in-America itinerant.[3]

A Second Awakening occurred in about the years 1800–1830. Much of this revival activity centered on the frontier regions of Kentucky and western New York, among others areas.[4] There were several forces involved in this awakening. Partly it resulted from the "missionary" activities of Presbyterian and Congregational churches in New England, especially in New York, which was populated so heavily by New Englanders.[5] Would-be missionaries saw, with some exaggeration, the frontier regions (e.g., Niagara county, New York) as a "moral waste" requiring their missionary attention.[6] However the frontier regions themselves spawned revivalists in the itinerant tradition of the first awakening. The most celebrated evangelist of the era, Charles G. Finney, nominally a Presbyterian, began a career of renegade revivalism in upstate New York that carried him finally to Philadelphia and New York.[7] Finney employed such "new measures" as the "anxious seat" in front of the pulpit at which sinners were given special fire-and-brimstone treatment,[8] and his unorthodox measures engendered anxiety as well in his more staid New England ministerial colleagues, who tried with more or less success to restrain him.[9] A final element of the Second Awakening on the frontier was the spectacular success of a less "respectable" denomination, the Methodists, in gaining converts. Part of this success lay in the Methodist practice of standardizing itinerant evangelistic activity in the form of the "circuit rider," a zealous preacher who made a regular round of missionary activity on horseback.[10]

A less familiar aspect of the Second Awakening was the fervor with which adherents of "moral control" attacked the evils of the American city.[11] The American Bible Society, devoted to distributing free or cheap bibles for the moral edification of city dwellers, was founded in New York in 1816. At about the same time, the American Tract Society was founded to distribute written sermons on religious themes, and "bulk shipments went to Sunday schools, poorhouses, prisons, orphanages and immigration depots."[12] It was also the era in which churches established "Sunday schools" with rigid instructional curricula and strict codes of conduct for students and teachers. These rigidities were related to the movement's perception of the urban masses' need of moral discipline, directing their attention to "the vulnerability of 'wandering, ignorant' children amid the 'moral darkness of the city.'"[13]

Later celebrated revivals and revivalists are far less clearly examples of intense religious "enthusiasm." Three later revivalists of note are Dwight Moody, Billy Sunday, and Billy Graham.[14] Moody was a YMCA organizer in Chicago in the 1860s with a talent for organizing mass revivals with heavy support from the business community, perhaps because he avoided any of the "social consciousness" that was beginning to emerge in church circles.[15] Billy Sunday in 1908 gave up a career as a baseball player to become a lay preacher for the YMCA and went on to organize giant revivalist rallies in American cities in giant wooden "tabernacles" especially built for the purpose.[16] In recent years Billy Graham has similarly carried the organization of revivals to a fine point of efficiency as his "crusades" are carried out in Yankee Stadiums rather than Sunday-style tabernacles. McLoughlin dismisses Moody, Sunday, and Graham as major figures in the religious "awakenings" since the Civil War. In McLouglin's view, it was really the "social gospel" movement toward church concern with social problems that was the heart of the "Third Great Awakening of 1890-1920,"[17] He also claims that the "countercultural" rebellion against science and technology is really the core of the "Fourth Great Awakening of 1960-90."[18] We shall return below to social gospel and countercultural types of renewals.

MILLENARIAN MOVEMENTS

Some of the most "enthusiastic" of religious renewals involve episodes in which participants anticipate a sudden and radical

transformation of the world. Such episodes are often called millenarian, following the Christian belief, derived from the Biblical books of
Daniel and Revelation, that there will be a "second coming" of
Christ, who will rule over a perfected world for a thousand years until
the final apocalypse in which the world will end.[19] The further view
that there must be a confrontation on earth between Christ and an An-
tichrist during this period had some fateful consequences for the
persecution of individuals or groups believed to embody this An-
tichrist: the Jews, the Moslem infidels, and even the Pope in some versions.[20]

The concept of millenialism has been extended to cover other
episodes without the thousand-year idea of the classic Christian version. In fact *any* episode in which people give up their routine social activities in anticipation of an end of the world or the coming of a totally
different social order is a millenarian episode in this broader sense.
The hallmark is radical discontinuity between previous behavior and
that in the present and the anticipated future.[21]

The literature on millenialism in this broader sense covers a vast
territory of sociological, anthropological, and historical research.[22]
Cohn's classic work deals with the crusades of the eleventh to four-
teenth centuries, a dramatic instance of masses of poor people abandoning homes and properties to follow millenial visions of a perfected
life in a mysterious Jerusalem.[23] Another flurry of millenialist activity
was associated, on the European continent, with Anabaptism, Protestant sects that took Luther's criticisms of the church quite literally and
maintained radically different lifestyles in immediate anticipation of
the Second Coming.[24] Nineteenth-century remnants of millenarianism
in rural Italy are described in the studies of Hobsbawm.[25] In England
there were a great many millenarian sects that rose, and for the most
part fell, at the time of the Puritan revolution of the 1640s and 1650s;
Quakers, Ranters, Diggers, Fifth Monarchy Men, and so on.[26]

While the Christian origin of much millenarianism is rightly emphasized, there are many non-Christian or primitive peoples among
whom episodes of similar behavior have occurred. The messiah who
will save the people from reigning evil may not be Christ but some
cultural hero of traditional mythology, or some charismatic figure who
emerges specifically to carry out the necessary transformation. At the
time of the sepoy (natives in the British army) revolt against British
colonialism in 1857, the revolters turned to the traditional Hindu and
Moslem royalties, which had been deposed by British colonial rule, in

the mistaken belief that they could lead the people to a restoration of their traditional native culture.[27] This "nativism" or "revitalization" theme pervades much of the anthropological study of millenarian activity among primitive peoples.[28] Such notably enthusiastic movements among American Indians as the Ghost Dance,[29] the peyote cult,[30] and the Longhouse religion of the Iroquois[31] have all been related to Indian rejection of white ways and a revitalization of traditional Indian life. The cargo cults of the South Pacific similarly involve a combination of rejection of European influence and the expectation of an immediate total redemption in nativist activities.[32] Cargo cultists believe in the imminent return of their dead ancestors in ships or airplanes laden with European-style consumer goods; they have often ceased ordinary productive activity to build storage facilities for the fantasied cargo arrivals.

Millenarianism has sometimes taken the form of people gathered around end-of-the-world prophets engaged in activities designed to prepare themselves for this end. One of the most spectacular episodes of this kind occurred in 1844 when William Miller, a New York state Baptist preacher, climaxing more than a decade of warnings, convinced a large number of followers to divest themselves of all worldly involvements in anticipation of an Advent that never came.[33] A prophesied end of the world for 1967 generated slight support for a group later to be known as the Unification Church; the failure of the 1967 prophecy resulted in a readjustment of the apocalyptic timetable.[34] A small cult of such believers was studied by a team of social scientists.[35] A suburban housewife received messages from an extraterrestrial world of impending destruction from which only herself and her followers would be saved. This sturdy band of true believers waited vainly, as did the Millerites, for the prophecies to be fulfilled at a given time and place.

REFORM

Another direction of social renewal is represented in the actions of people who believe that they can somehow remake or reform the world without its existing imperfections. Revivalists, millenarians, and reformers have rather different programs of remedy of the world's ills. Whereas the revivalist expects to produce change through the reawakened faith of individuals, the millenarian urges indifference to worldly matters in happy anticipation of the coming millennium. The reformer, in contrast, shares neither the extreme individualism of the revivalist nor the extreme optimism of the millenarian. The reformer's mind is focused on *this* world and, often, on a strong sense of personal responsibility for promoting improvement in it.

This portrait of the zealous reformer strongly suggests the religious connections of reform, though we shall later observe some secular variants of this mentality. A this-worldly sense of personal responsibility is the essence of the "Protestant ethic" that Weber attributes to the Calvinist and that he argues was so essential to the historical origin of capitalism.[36] But this ethic may be conducive as well to the spirit of the crusading reformer or, as Walzer terms it, "radical politics."[37] The "mission" of the saint is not that of mystical contemplation or prophecy; it is the mission, as Weber had said, of seeing that "God's work" is accomplished on earth by human beings.

Reform in the missionary sense shows the fluctuation of intensity characteristic of all forms of collective behavior. There are "ages of reform" as there are religious awakenings and seasons of millenarian excitement. We may, to illustrate, note two such concentrations of reform activity, in Europe in the early part of the nineteenth century, and in the United States shortly before and after the turn of the twentieth century.

The years between the French revolution of 1789 and the socialist revolutions of 1848 were an interval of intensive reform activity of various sorts in Europe. It was a period, as Talmon describes it, of "socialist messianism,"[38] most notably of the optimistic socialism of Saint-Simon, who saw modern industrialism as the ultimate perfection of human society, requiring as reform only the elimination of the aristocratic and clerical elements of preindustrial order. It was an era too, of massive utopian community experiments. Such communitarian thinkers as Fourier and Considerant in France[39] influenced practical applications in, for example, the utopian communities of Robert Owen in England and in New Harmony, Indiana,[40] as well as in the somewhat later community established at Oneida, New York, by John Humphrey Noyes.[41] These communitarians saw themselves as engaged in experiments which, if successful, would serve as example and inspiration for the whole world. They thus rejected the other-worldly concerns of the millenarian approach, as when Robert Owen declares:

> What ideas individuals may attach to the term Millennium, I know not; but I know that society may be formed so as to exist without crime, without poverty, with health greatly improved, with little, if any, misery, and with intelligence and happiness increased an

hundred-fold; and no obstacle whatsoever intervenes at this moment, except ignorance, to prevent such a state of society from being universal.[42]

There have been several reform eras in American political history; that between about 1884 and 1920 was one of the most intense.[43] The year 1884 produced an episode in which a group of prominent Republicans, called Mugwumps, bolted their party, to support the Democratic nominee for president, Grover Cleveland, on the issue of civil service reform as opposed to the spoils system of government.[44] The Mugwumps quickly faded into historical obscurity, but they were replaced with much more potent political reform tendencies: the influence of William Jennings Bryan and the "free silver" issue on the Democrats, and the rise of the Progressive and Bull Moose parties of Robert LaFollette and Theodore Roosevelt from liberal Republican origins. On the level of local politics, it was an era of vigorous efforts to reform municipal administration, often by attempting to institute political nonpartisanship in city administration. As Holli shows, the urban reform movement never quite reconciled the demands for political purity and efficiency with those for the extension of welfare services.[45] By 1920, at any rate, the pressures of World War I and perhaps exhaustion from several decades of reform produced the period of political reaction or "normalcy" that separated early progressives from New Deal reformers.

The political reforms of the American age of reform were accompanied by efforts to make not only government but religion and education more relevant to what reformers saw as the need of the times. John Dewey and other educational reformers inaugurated a drive toward progressive education, the aim of which was to make the school a vital force in the "reconstruction" of human society.[46] The interest in educational reform sometimes combined with utopian community effort; thus a group of "anarchists" from New York City in 1915 opened an experimental school and colony near New Brunswick, New Jersey, and operated it with more or less success for many years.[47] We referred above to the "social gospel" movement in the churches that took hold during this era.[48] This movement "rejected individual salvation as the beginning and end of Christ's message and . . . argued that men must come to God not as discrete, atomistic individuals, pure only in and of themselves, but as parts of the brotherhood of man, in which each is spiritually and ethically united to his neighbor."[49] With such socialized motives to the fore, it is not surprising that a religious basis for the development of communes appeared in this era nor that some of these communes adopted pacifistic Oriental religious ideas. Thus the so-called Vedanta movement in America drew inspiration from a Brahman leader in establishing many communes in the United States around 1900.[50]

COUNTERCULTURES

A prominent form of social renewal for about the last twenty years is the social movement often referred to as the counterculture. McLouglin argues, in fact, that the counterculture is the spearhead of a "fourth great awakening," continuing in a more secularized form the more strictly religious awakenings of earlier American history.[51] The essence of the activity of counterculture adherents is their rejection of certain prevailing cultural values and the effort of these rejectors to fashion a life for themselves that provides a more satisfying "alternative" to the established culture. Counterculturalists have been described as "cultural radicals," by way of distinguishing them from the *political* radicalism of revolutionaries, militant protesters, and other political activists.[52]

Contemporary countercultural activities are not, of course, the first historical appearances of such episodes. A bohemian or counter-cultural lifestyle is one of those several "subterranean" cultural traditions with a long history and considerable continuity of ideas and cultural heroes.[53] These usually submerged currents of cultural radicalism sometimes surface in intense outbreaks in the collective behavioral style. One such period of countercultural intensification was the first half of the nineteenth century, that renewal-oriented period of the Second Awakening in America and of socialist and other utopian development in both Europe and America. It was an age of literary romanticism, most notably in Britain[54] and Germany,[55] and such writers as Shelley, Coleridge, and Fichte glorified intensive emotional experience over the rational calculation embodied in the emerging scientific-industrial order. These ideas, especially when combined with the nationalistic fervor of the period, were not without their behavioral effects, especially in Germany. There, in 1817, the Wartburg Festival celebrated a new German student organization and brought together thousand of students in the first great countercultural rally.[56]

The countercultures of recent years have been the subject of much description and analysis.[57] The development of alternative lifestyles is inspired by a body of popular writing sharply critical of the dehumanizing effects of modern "technocracy," its reduction of people to the level of "one dimensional man."[58] The aim of the movement is nothing less than the reconstruction of human life on the basis of a new form of thought, called Consciousness III, through which "the individual frees himself from automatic acceptance of the imperatives of society and the false consciousness which society imposes."[59]

The drive to reject "automatic acceptance" of societal imperatives takes a number of forms. One direction is toward the establishment of "communes" in which those with a shared set of values establish communities whose lifestyles will hopefully embody their countercultural values.[60] The small size and short life spans of most of these communes indicate some problems with this form of countercultural expression.

Another direction of the countercultural movement is the attempt to develop "alternative" styles of cultural expression in specific types of human activity. Religion, education, medicine, sexual relations, music, foods—in these and many more areas counterculturalists have attempted to substitute revitalized forms for what they see as the dehumanized forms that currently prevail. The monogamous family, which isolates husband, wife, and children in nuclear families, is challenged by new forms of sexual and parent-child interaction, including the increasingly popular practice of couples living together without "benefit" of marriage.[61] In higher education, disillusionment with university curricula led to the establishment of "experimental" colleges and "free" universities with such alternative practices as student determination of curricula.[62] An underground or alternative press flourishes in America and Britain to satisfy the suspicion that the news that is "fit to print" by established newspapers does not do justice to countercultural realities. Medical people with counter-cultural values have established "free clinics" to conduct medical practice without, presumably, the intrusion of commercial considerations,[63] and social workers disillusioned with the welfare bureaucracy have joined their clients in "welfare rights" movements on their clients' behalf.[64] Health food and folk music devotees have viewed their activities as involving the promotion of "alternative" foods and music. Even such archtechnocratic activities as that of city planning have seen expression given to an alternative approach that would allow cities to develop organically rather than by the planner's design.[65]

An extremely active area of such countercultural development of alternatives has been in the area of religion. Established churches have found themselves competing, sometimes rather unsuccessfully, with "new religions" that are less formal and more attuned to counter-cultural styles: the Children of God, Hare Krishna, the adherents of the Guru Maharaj Ji, the Unification Church, the Reverend Timothy Leary's League for Spiritual Discovery (LSD), the Peoples' Temple of the Reverend Jim Jones, and so on.[66] The challenge of these alter-native religious styles is reflected in changes of religious practice *within* established churches. The Roman Catholic church, for example, has given some approval to a Pentecostal, or charismatic, movement among its clergy and lay members.[67] The informalizing of religious worship among the established churches gives force to the early obser-vation of Davis that we may "someday" *all* be hippies.[68]

REVELS

A final type of episode of human behavior involves the *tension management* side of the renewal process: the idea that social systems must provide periodic releases from the tensions of everyday social ac-tivity. The concept of recreation is a recognition of the functional significance of play activity in the moral economy of society. Simmel's essay on sociability emphasizes the relation between serious and playful human interaction, as each serious form of interaction (e.g., sexual seduction) has its corresponding play form (e.g., flirtation).[69] The prevalence throughout human history of a "play element in culture" supports the view of the functional significance of playful behavior.[70]

As always, then, we must recognize that a type of collective behavior is an intensified or episodic form of more routine social behavior. Playful or fun-making behavior occurs in outbreaks that might be called *revels*. Some of these are in the nature of celebrations of success or victory in some uncertain undertaking: victory in war, in sports contests, in political campaigns. Such celebrations may result in violent destructiveness not easily distinguishable from that in protest riots.[71] It was observed, for example, that in 1768 a crowd in London went on a two-day rampage of destructiveness upon the election (not the defeat) of their hero, John Wilkes, as a member of Parliament.[72]

College campuses have, of course, been the sites of revels that go well beyond the routine "blasts" at local bars and other fun spots. The panty raids in which male students "invaded" women's dormitories demanding that unmentionables be turned over as trophies of the raid occurred on many American campuses in 1950s. In 1974 there were mass "streaks" of groups of unclothed people across many American campuses (as well as off-campus and around the world).[73] Some campuses experienced more idiosyncratic episodes, as when in 1964 the students at a large midwestern American state university, somewhat angered by local police enforcement of an ordinance against jaywalking, engaged in a mass jaywalk on a major city street that tied up traffic for a number of hours.[74]

College students have also been active participants in revels that occur off campus, particularly during school vacations. Resort beaches in Florida and elsewhere have experienced such revelrous episodes of vacationing students. The potential for revelrous behavior seems to exist wherever masses of people descend on a particular locale to indulge their interest in, for example, jazz or rock music, motorcycle racing, surfing, and so on.[75] Sometimes destructive riots are an element of these revels, and local officals may take heavy precautions to contain the destructive potential of such gatherings.[76] The most massive such convergence on a local community occurred near Woodstock, New York, in 1969, when a rock music festival attracted around a half million participants.[77] Although the gathering was notably peaceable in spite of its "fornication among the cows" atmosphere and near-disaster physical conditions, the local community in 1979 refused to allow a tenth-anniversary celebration of the famous event to be conducted in the area.[78]

BACKGROUND

The preceding section has shown that a type of collective behavior—renewals—actually breaks down into a number of rather different subtypes: revivals, millenarianism, reform, countercultures, revels. With most of these subtypes divisible into further subtypes, the problem now of pulling back from this analysis and offering *general* explanations of renewal episodes is obviously not easy to solve. There exist what seem to be general theories for explaining revivalism, reformism, millenarianism, and so on, but since the broader category of renewals has not been formulated, we must work with these narrower explanations and hope to inch our way toward more general ones.

The explanation of millenarian outbreaks will serve as a starting point. Barkun's study suggests three necessary conditions for millenarian movements.[79] These movements arise when: (1) there occurs a multitude of disasters that destroy the unity and coherence of a traditional lifestyle; (2) there is in the thought system of a people a set of millenarian ideas that can be mobilized into the promotion of millenarian action; and (3) there are charismatic leaders to prophesy the coming millennium and to organize people to prepare themselves for the new world. These conditions, with appropriate qualifications and adjustments to cover other kinds of renewal, along with a fourth factor, official responsiveness, not mentioned by Barkun, will now be discussed.

CULTURAL DISASTERS

If one adopts a sufficiently generous view of *disaster*—certainly broader than our view of that phenomenon in Chapter 2—one might indeed say that disaster is an essential condition in the production of renewal outbreaks. La Barre's concept of "crisis cults" is a terminological indication of the massive misfortune in the background of many renewal outbreaks.[80] Each of the four great "awakenings" in American religion discussed by McLoughlin occurred in a period of severe cultural crisis,[81] and these crises are worth reviewing here.

The great religious revival of 1730–60 occurred in a period of cultural uncertainty accompanying rapid frontier expansion and the growth of a commercial-industrial economy (the same tensions that, as we saw in the last chapter, contributed to a witchcraft persecution in Salem in 1692). Aggravating this cultural disorientation was the institutional rigidity of the established churches, their inability to respond to social tensions as effectively as such revivalists as Jonathan Edwards and the itinerant preachers.

The second period of mass revivalism, 1800–1830—also a major period for utopian community development—was an era in America of "enormous growth, when it was beset by the centrifugal forces of sectionalism and individualism."[82] The "missions" of New England Congregationalists and Presbyterians to the "moral waste" of western New York[83] and the organizational success of the circuit-riding

Methodist preachers suggest both the nature of the period's crisis and its renewal solution. There was a massive problem of *organization* of social life in an expanding and individualistic country, and the proliferation of religious associations in the period was part of the solution. Likewise, the promotion of Sunday schools and other religious activities in the cities reflected the rapid *urbanization* of the period: between 1790 and 1830, for example, Philadelphia tripled in size and New York experienced a sixfold increase.[84]

The "third awakening" of 1890–1920 we have described above as an "age of reform." It is certainly possible to argue that American social life had suffered the unmitigated disaster of twenty-five years of a vindictive post–Civil War reconstruction followed by the rise of the robber barons and the scarcely concealed plutocratic domination of politics at all levels, from the local courthouse to the White House. The "social gospel" development in religion discussed by McLoughlin was simply the religious side of a broad reform or progressive era.

Finally, we have the most recent awakening, which began at about the time of John F. Kennedy's election in 1960 and which, McLoughlin indicates, with a question mark, may extend to the year 1990. We have suggested above some of the diagnostics of contemporary cultural crisis in such ideologues of the countercultural movement as Marcuse, Roszak, and Reich. Richard Flacks speaks for the views of all when he notes that by mid-twentieth century "technology had created a superabundant economy in which the traditional virtues of thrift, self-denial and living by the sweat of one's brow seemed not only absurd, but actually dangerous to prosperity." In the resulting confusion, "cultural breakdown has reached the point of no return when the process of socialization no longer provides the new generation with coherent reasons to be enthusiastic about becoming adult members of the society."[85] If one postulates a human need for some object of "enthusiasm," it is hardly mysterious in the situation that the young (and not-so-young) become enthusiasts of Eastern religions, LSD, communal living, born-again religion, or any of the other numerous enthusiasms of the counterculture.

Our review of American "awakenings" may leave the reader with the feeling that the cultural "crises" of the indicated periods may have been exaggerated to fit the cultural crisis-disaster hypothesis. Does not every era in human history have its share of crisis? Why did awakenings occur in these and not in other crisis periods? One useful suggestion is Barkun's point, mentioned above, that *multiple* disasters rather than single ones (however massive individual disasters might be) are the major determinants of renewal tendency. Perhaps no single event preceding the reform era at the turn of this century distinguished that from earlier or later periods. But the 1880s, for example, involved an accumulation of crises, some of which were mentioned above, to which could be added such crises as the severe boom-and-bust economic cycles of the period and the beginning of a massive immigration of people who were not Anglo Saxon Protestants. The theory that multiple rather than single crises produce renewal activity can explain the remarkable lack of awakening activity during any of the country's major wars. Whereas the Revolutionary War, the Civil War, and the two world wars were certainly periods of great stress, there was a single mindedness about the source of that stress and the morale enhancement of concentration on the demands of a "war effort." Nor was the moral exhaustion that *followed* each of these wars favorable to renewal activity, however much it was conducive to some of the persecution episodes discussed in the last chapter.

Our examples so far of cultural crisis have concerned American and/or contemporary Western renewal phenomena. Consideration of renewal movements in other times and places will broaden the scope of our consideration. The well-known millenarianism of the medieval and early modern periods of European history certainly occurred in a context of various disasters, natural and man-made. The crusades occurred in years in which European peasants were suffering greatly from disease or famine.[86] The Protestant Reformation, itself created out of the crisis of the growing corruption and irrelevance of the established church, generated new turmoils. The religious wars and the continual religious conflicts of the period helped to produce millenarian activity both on the Continent and in Britain.[87]

Studies of renewal movements among primitive peoples have likewise emphasized their disaster or crisis origins. In a so-called colonial hypothesis,[88] it is asserted that European colonization had severely disorganizing consequences for the native peoples whom the colonizers met and subordinated. In the first place, sheer physical contact between Europeans and natives introduced the latter to diseases—like influenza—to which they had had no previous exposure and hence no immunity. It has been said in grim humor that what the European took to the natives was above all syphilization. The results, when combined with the near-genocidal wars of the colonists against the natives, was the catastrophe of rapid depopulation.[89]

The attempted spread of European values and civilization also had its crisis consequences for natives. In one version, European settlement deprived natives of the ecological basis for the maintenance of traditional lifestyles. The confinement of natives to reservations in the United States and to native reserves in South Africa restricts people to areas in which traditional ways are difficult if not impossible to maintain. The spread of the millenarian Ghost Dance among American Indians in the nineteenth-century illustrates this kind of crisis. The Ghost Dance phenomenon occurred in two waves, both originating in Nevada but, in the 1870s, spreading along the Pacific coast and, in the 1890s, into the midwestern plains states.[90] This may be explained by the fact that it was in these decades that white settlement first intruded heavily on Indian territorial control in the respective regions (the California gold rush prior to the 1870s, the western settlement in the plains with the coming of the railroads). The peyote religion spread among the Navaho when the stock-reduction program of the United States government had devastating effects in depriving Indians of lands required for livestock grazing.[91]

Some studies of native renewal movements have suggested the applicability of the "relative deprivation" concept to the cultural crisis underlying renewal movements.[92] When natives compare their present situation with that of an earlier "Golden Age" that preceded colonization, they may feel deprived. Likewise, natives in some instances compare their condition with that of colonizers and feel shame and resentment at the gap between themselves and the colonizers. The exotic cargo cults of natives seem more comprehensible when viewed in these terms. Peoples in the South Pacific were well impressed with the technological marvels introduced by colonizers along with missionary Christianity. They also saw very clearly that they, the natives, were not enjoying these goods and, believing that European colonizers received these goods from their god, they accused the missionaries of keeping the "secret" of how god was made to produce these consumer goods for them.[93] These resentments were intensified in many instances by the disdainful attitudes of Europeans toward natives. Traditional status-conscious Melanesian societies honor their "big men" (bigness being measured by their capacity to give away food in huge feasts) and look down on those they call "rubbish men"; and their complaint against European government officials was that they treated even native big men as rubbish men.[94] Confusion and embitterment may be intensified if ambitious natives, anxious to be respected by

Europeans, adopt European ways only to find themselves still rejected because of their native origins; such acculturated and disillusioned natives represent the leadership of many native movements.[95] Explosive outbreaks of nativism have sometimes followed real or imagined insults to natives and their way of life by Europeans. Native Indian soldiers in the British Army in 1857 nourished long-standing hostilities against the haughty and superior attitudes of their British officers. In a day in which bullets had to have the shells bitten off them before use, an apparently false rumor spread that the bullets had been treated with a mixture of pork and beef oils, making "biting the bullet" a gross affront to both Hindus and Moslems. The greasy-bullet rumor helped precipitate the sepoy revolt of 1857.[96]

A theoretical interpretation of all these instances of cultural confusion, breakdown, distortion, or threat is offered in an influential essay by Wallace.[97] Human behavior occurs in a "mazeway" of almost infinite possibilities of direction. Like the hapless unconditioned rat in the mazeway of a psychological experiment, we literally do not know which way to go without some guidance. Culture does for human beings what conditioning does for rats: produces a pathway—in the human case, a set of culturally approved norms of behavior that, if followed, will lead to culturally approved goals. People without such cultural guides are in a state of *anomie,*[98] a general term for the kind of cultural distortion or breakdown we are here considering. In anomic times, people are lost or adrift in a mazeway of alternatives without sure guides for the selection among alternatives. One asks how one should raise one's children or how one should treat one's spouse; one's best friend says one thing, Doctor Spock or Ann Landers says something else; but who is to say what is the *real* way? Renewals—or what Wallace calls revitalizations—are simply "resyntheses" of new ways for people to follow; a leader such as Christ proclaims "I am the way" and gathers followers along a new pathway. Such renewals hypothetically only occur when old ways have lost their meaningfulness and their authority. Some revitalizations recognize very directly this "mazeway resynthesis" nature of their origins. Thus the Black Muslims are formally known as the Lost-Found Nation of Islam in the Wilderness of North America.[99] The Muslims simply make explicit in their name and mythology what is implicit in the teaching of virtually all renewal activists: they are "born again" or saved from a previous state of sin, and their reforms are being made on a thoroughly corrupted world. People "find" themselves in renewals because they have previously been "lost," and it is of great sociological importance to know under what circumstances people have these lost feelings about themselves.

IDEOLOGY

Like grievances in relation to protest or threat in relation to persecutions, cultural disorientation is a necessary but not sufficient condition of renewal episodes. As in the case of protest and persecution, additional *mobilizing* factors must be present if the renewal potential is to be activated. Barkun's second and third factors—ideology and charismatic leadership—are examples of such essential mobilizing factors.

Most established social orders contain *ideologies* which, in Mannheim's sense of the term, provide justification for the existing social order.[100] Religious ideologies, for example, tend to provide a "theodicy of suffering" whereby human misfortunes can be explained away without resort to radical alterations in the existing social structure.[101] Commenting on one situation of massive misfortune *without* a millenarian outbreak, the Irish potato famine of the 1840s, Barkun observes that "an unusually strong church may have provided an explanatory framework which even a catastrophe of this magnitude could not erode."[102] By contrast, the very weak ideological hold of Christian "missions" on Oceanic natives[103] may have contributed to the intense millenarianism in that region.

The *absence* of an "explanatory framework" of an ideological nature may be important; but the *presence* of alternative idea systems to justify cultural revolution is also essential. Mannheim called such revolutionary idea systems *utopias*, a term still used in some analyses.[104] In the following, we attempt to define the character of the ideas whose development seems essential to renewal episodes.

In the first place, renewal episodes depend on ideas *critical* of the established social order. The contemporary commune movement is based on a "countercultural tradition" of literary criticism of the inhumane character of modern technological society.[105] "Muckraking" exposés of corruption in big business and big government were a vital factor in the development of the wave of reform in the progressive era in the United States.[106] Sometimes, critical ideas are not crystallized in any body of literature but simply take the form of a popular *mood* of resentment against elements of the established order. Thus the folk saying in South Africa that reflected the resentment of natives against white settlers and their Christian religion: "At first we had the land and you had the Bible. Now we have the Bible and you have the land."[107]

Second, the critical thought in question must contain an element of optimistic outlook for a new social order. Otherwise, social criticism takes the "cataclysmic" form of such American thinkers as Brooks Adams and Jack London; a style of thought conducive to the regressive populist movement marked more by persecution-propensity than by strong commitment to social reform.[108] This optimism about the future is epitomized, of course, in the millenial tradition in Christian thought: the belief in a Second Advent of Christ to establish a perfected social order. This theme of the capacity of a "savior" to correct present abuses undergoes many adaptations in societies in which Christianity has been more recently grafted onto native religious tradition. Thus natives in the *sertao* (inland) sections of Brazil and elsewhere have believed in the imminent return of a deceased King Sebastian,[109] and likewise African natives as late as the 1950s believed in the return of a John Chilembwe who had led an abortive native revolt against British colonial control in 1915.[110]

Third, few renewal movements could subsist on the idea of a *coming* millenium, at least not one whose fulfillment was long delayed. Weber's description of the torment of Calvinists, condemned to uncertainty about the ultimate salvation or damnation of their souls,[111] provides a model for the psychology that lies behind religious ethics—that is, those ideological prescriptions for *everyday* life, indicating what the faithful are to do "until the Messiah comes." "Enthusiastic" religions must necessarily operate with ethics that encourage more mysticism or emotionalism than in the "worldly asceticism" of the Calvinists, more vivid "signs" of one's religious status than the Calvinist's worldly success. John Wesley thus encouraged the interpretation of the jumping and jerking behavior of his audiences as signs of the "work of the heart" that true religion must be.[112] The revivalists of the Great Awakenings similarly promoted the idea that ecstatic behaviors were signs of the "the work" of God on the spirit of the sinner.[113] The Irvingites of eighteenth-century England were among those whose glossolalia (speaking in tongues) was taken as a sign of divine inspiration.[114] Snake-handling sects and other Pentecostal sects have also included glossolalia among the signs of "Holy Ghost" inspiration of their members.[115] These signs may entail the belief that behavior is of divine inspiration that shocks the moral sensibilities of nonbelievers. Thus is explained some of the pre-1974 "streaks" among European religious enthusiasts: public displays of nudity that were treated by the faithful as signs of their religious inspiration.[116]

Fourth, and partly because their "enthusiastic" behavior often elicits the possibility of official repression, enthusiasts will be encouraged by beliefs in their invincibility to this repression. The Ghost Dancers among the Sioux Indians were convinced that their "ghost shirts" would protect them from U.S. Army bullets, a belief tragically disconfirmed at Wounded Knee.[117] A fanatic cult of French Huguenots, the Camisards, were ordered by French troops in 1689 to disperse; assured by their leader that they were impervious to Royal weapons, they were fired upon in this defenseless posture.[118] Whether this degree of protection fantasy is always necessary, it may be true, as Rosen suggests, that "groups that wish to revitalize their societies and to create a more satisfying world . . . all require a belief and conviction that they are under some sovereign guidance and protection which will enable them to attain their heart's desire."[119]

LEADERSHIP

We now consider Barkun's assertion that charismatic leadership is an essential element in renewal episodes. The basis of such an assertion should be fairly clear. All the essential ideology of renewal outbreaks, reviewed above, involves ideas that somehow contravene those ideas supporting the existing social order. Renewal-oriented ideas are by definition extraordinary ideas in the given social context, and it would seem that these must be the products of thought and influence of extraordinary individuals. Peter the Hermit, who led one of the first crusades, had no *formal* authority to do this; he had only his personal say-so that "Christ had appeared to him and given him a letter commissioning him to summon the crusade." He had only his "commanding presence and great eloquence," his "irresistible fascination to the masses" as the basis for leading a crusade.[120] This is the general formula for the source of charismatic leaders' authority: they are "holders of specific gifts of the body and spirit; and these gifts have been believed to be supernatural, not accessible to everybody."[121] The "gift" is often in the form of a revelation: the hallucinatory vision of Handsome Lake, the founder of the Longhouse religion of the Iroquois,[122] the "face to face" conversation of Swedenborg with the angels in heaven,[123] the visit of an angel to Joseph Smith in 1823 with instructions on location of the "golden plates" from which the Book of Mormon was transcribed,[124] the American housewife "Mrs. Keech" with her mysterious voices from another realm.[125] These revelations almost invariably involve *prophecies* that command behavior at variance with established behavioral norms; the prophet proclaims, "It is written, but I say unto you."[126]

The charismatic prophet, in addition to basing this authority on a "gift of grace," is characterized by Weber as developing a lifestyle in which "the master as well as his disciples and followers, must stand outside the ties of this world, outside of routine occupations, as well as outside the routine obligations of family life."[127] This "standing outside" may take the libertarian or antinomian form of behavior of the Brethren of the Free Spirit that so scandalized fifteenth-century European respectables.[128] Alternatively, charismatic leaders and disciples may put aside worldly involvements with vows of poverty, celibacy, obedience, and even silence. In fact, Coser suggests, the celibacy of the Jesuits and the "free love" libertarianism of Leninists are functional equivalents for radical social movements: both practices serve to separate their leadership from distracting "routine obligations of family life."[129]

This view of the relation of charisma and prophetic leadership to renewal episodes has been challenged on several grounds, especially by students of "cargo cults." First, these movements' "ability to produce a second wave of leadership when the first wave were imprisoned or discredited, show that the movements were not dominated by individuals with rare gifts."[130] Similar to this observation is the fact that some movements are "dominated" by such long-absent personages as King Sebastian or John Chilembwe or by the continued influence of such jailed leaders as Birsa, the prophet of a messianic movement among the Munda in the state of Bihar, India.[131] Second, the leaders of many cargo cults are in fact the same "big men" who enjoyed authority in established traditional society—for example, the Ndugumoi who was an hereditary priest on Fiji and who became the prophet of the Tuka cult.[132] Similarly, many revivalists were not the enemies of established religious authority that the charismatic image suggests. John Wesley, for example, never intended a secession of his Methodist "societies" from the Church of England.[133] The "itinerant" preachers of the Great Awakenings saw themselves as agents of extension of influence of the established Congregationalist and Presbyterian churches.[134] Far from being charismatic individuals who "stood outside" established society, the Mogul emperors of traditional Indian society were *forced* by mutinous soldiers to assume leadership of their nativist revolts.[135]

A third critical point, addressed to the usual assumption that a renewal episode is led by a *single* charismatic leader, is the observation on cargo cults that "there may be not one but several prophets" and that "often each village or other social unit has its leader, and a 'federal' form of organization develops rather than a centralized movement united by loyalty to a particular leader."[136] This situation seems typical of virtually every kind of renewal outbreak we have discussed. Barkun thus comments on the extreme *localism* in all kinds of millenarian movements, even in the Pan-Indian Ghost Dance, in which each tribe had its local prophets.[137] Similarly, although the "commune movement" in Britain is recognized with a name and a magazine, it is at most a very loose confederation of a few of the communes in a movement characterized by decentralization.[138]

Finally, Worsley found a distinction in many cargo cults between the prophet and the organizer as leadership types—the prophet being the visionary who often sees himself as the passive vessel of divine inspiration, the organizer being the harder-headed pragmatist who welds an effective revolutionary organization.[139] This is a familiar distinction in sociological analysis—in Pareto's distinction, for example, between Lion and Fox forms of political leadership.[140] The complementary talents of George Whitefield and John Wesley as cofounders of the Methodist movement may illustrate the prophet-organizer distinction in leadership styles. Whitefield's charisma is described by Wesley himself as deriving from "the cheerful vitality and unabashed emotionalism of the lower orders from which he sprang."[141] On the other hand, Knox devotes five pages to the question "was Wesley an enthusiast?" with the basic conclusion that, while Wesley was a sympathizer and promoter of enthusiastic religion, he was not strongly endowed with a charismatic "gift of grace."[142] He was, however, a devoted organizer, and he nourished with great care the numerous Methodist "societies" established in various British towns.

OFFICIAL RESPONSIVENESS

In addition to the background factors discussed by Barkun, a fourth factor should perhaps be introduced: the disposition of authorities in the established social order to respond in certain ways to "enthusiastic" tendencies in social behavior. In some situations, it appears, authorities are tolerant or at least encouraging of these tendencies, at least as long as they are appropriately limited. Early itinerant preachers such as George Whitefield and Charles G. Finney were encouraged in their activities by some of the established churches of the time, although the issue of "itinerancy" tended in some cases to split authorities, as between the "Old Lights" and the "New Lights" in the Presbyterian church.[143] Such later revivalists as Dwight Moody, Billy Sunday, and Billy Graham were all vigorously "sponsored" by the established churches of the communities in which they operated.[144] The Sebastianic preaching in the Brazilian *sertao* by the charismatic Antonio Conselheiro, although ultimately savagely suppressed, was welcomed by many local priests who observed that an increase in their revenues for baptisms, confessions, etc. always followed a visit by Conselheiro.[145]

On the other hand, some authoritative regimes are highly suppressive of any outbreaks of enthusiastic behavior. The millenarianism that flourished in Europe in the first half of the seventeenth century was vigorously suppressed almost everywhere in the second half of that century. In Germany, for example, it was observed that the people there were "now and then troubled with men of like principles, but they soon shut them up, that they may not seduce others."[146] Burridge observes that cargo cults tend to thrive where there is a "regime which is either not powerful enough to suppress the activities or which for a variety of reasons is inhibited from deploying the power at its disposal."[147] Burridge goes on to suggest that the relation of colonial powers with colonized peoples tends to epitomize such tolerant "regimes." British colonies—well known for their "indirect rule" policy of minimal interference with "native" social practices[148]—may be especially productive of nativistic social movements. The indifferent attitude of authorities toward native rebellion may be illustrated in an observation about the behavior of officials of European mission churches in South Africa in the face of the schismatic activities of "Bantu prophets." Sundkler observes that "one has rather the impression that nowadays, there is more often a sigh of relief at the 'solution' to a nuisance than the agony of [earlier missionaries] who made the utmost efforts to avoid what to them appeared a calamity and catastrophe."[149]

PARTICIPATION

With renewal episodes, as with other kinds of collective behavioral episodes, (1) there are varying degrees of participation, from casual attendance at the religious revival to the uprooting of oneself from family, home, and job to join a crusade or to wait for the fulfillment of an end-of-the-world prophecy, and (2) there is a dual sociological interest in both the *numbers* of and the (sociological) *types* of people who participate in these episodes. In the following we consider the problem of *number* of renewal participants, and then that of their *types,* keeping in mind the distinction between the more intense and the more casual levels of involvement.

NUMBERS

Proponents and opponents of renewal episodes, like their counterparts in protest outbreaks, are likely to give very different estimates of the numbers of those who participate in these episodes. Revivalist preachers at Cane Ridge, Kentucky, during the Second Awakening in 1801 made "fantastic" estimates of as high as 25,000 persons at a given camp meeting, though one person actually counted only 21 wagons, the main source of conveyance of the congregation.[150] Similarly, John Wesley claimed that there were 20,000 to 30,000 persons at one of his open-air preaching sessions, based on the unlikely assumption that there were five persons for every square yard of available space.[151] Leaders of the Unification Church were making public claims of an American membership of around 30,000 in 1972, though their internal planning documents referred to no more than

2000 American members.[152] Opponents may also make exaggerated estimates to emphasize the "threat" that requires persecutory action. They may also give such estimates in the aftermath of an episode to exaggerate their achievement in having "saved" the people from a dire threat. Thus, George Fox, founder of the Quaker movement, quoted with approval the statement of an English Justice that the Quakers had saved England from being engulfed by Ranters, actually a relatively numerically insignificant English adaptation of the Anabaptist-style "free spirits" whose libertarian reputations so outraged English respectables.[153]

Underestimation of numbers may also be motivated by the self-interest of either opponents or proponents. To counter the right of the itinerant preacher Samuel Davies to maintain meeting houses in places with 15 or 20 families as communicants, a Presbyterian Church official in Virginia in 1752 complained that "there was no justification for every family or two to have a licensed meeting house solely 'that they may remain a little vacant congregation, to invite an occasional ministrator to give them a lecture, when he happens to come their way.'" [154] Some groups of cultural radicals, out of fear of repression if their real numbers are known, may take on the characteristics of the "secret society," keeping secret, among other things, the real number of their members.[155]

More disinterested estimates of the number of renewal participants seem most often to suggest that such participation is less frequent than the public notoriety of these episodes would suggest. In a study, for example, of the San Francisco–Oakland metropolitan area, Wuthnow questions a sample of 1000 residents on their involvement with the "new religions" in the area.[156] This is an area with a strong reputation for the strength of countercultural movements of all sorts.[157] Yet, in this population, when questioned about thirteen different new religious groups, subjects mostly indicated low degrees of knowledge, interest, or personal involvement with any of these groups. From 51 percent to 94 percent of subjects said they "know nothing" about a particular group; for those who did know about a given group, from 46 to 90 percent said they were either "turned off" or felt "nothing either way" about the group in question; and no more than 8 percent of the sample had ever taken part in the activities of any one of these groups.[158] In the Bay Area, there is apparently much *tolerance* for renewal forms of religion; many were at least "mildly attracted" to some of these religions,[159] and the majority of the subjects reported having had (or wishing that they had had) religiously ecstatic or "peak experiences" at some time in their lives.[160] Only in this very attenuated sense of new religious "participation" can it be said that most subjects had any involvement with the new religions. In a similar way, various surveys of student attitudes in the United States and Britain during the 1960s decade of "student radicalism" found that only 10 to 15 percent of students in these countries could be counted among the culturally "alienated."[161]

In some instances, the claims of proponents of renewal movements of massive participation are objectively documented. The Great Awakening on the American frontier did produce great increases in membership of the Methodist and Baptist churches.[162] The separatist church movements in South Africa between 1882 and 1967 had produced some 3 million adherents by the latter year.[163] Whether such massive participation in renewal episodes produces massive social impacts is a matter to be considered at the end of this chapter.

TYPES

What kinds of people (in terms of such sociological categories as age, sex, and social class) are most likely to participate in renewal episodes? The evidence is complex and contradictory. It may help to reduce these difficulties by distinguishing two rather different varieties of renewal activities, a distinction that roughly, but not exactly, divides the forms of renewal activity introduced at the beginning of this chapter. These two varieties resemble "A" and "B" varieties of countercultural attitudes developed by Musgrove in his British study.[164] Based on factor analyses of subjects' responses to eighty statements of values drawn from the countercultural literature, Musgrove found a clustering of responses on an expressive-passive dimension and on an anarchist-activist dimension. These orientations will here be slightly restyled and related to the foregoing types of renewal episodes:

CLUSTER 1: an *ecstatic* form of renewal, emphasizing extraordinary and emotionally "enthusiastic" behavior; embracing most of the millenarian, revivalist, and revelrous episodes described above; and

CLUSTER 2: a *culturally radical* form of renewal, emphasizing hopes for improvement if not perfection in the human social condition; embracing most of the reformist and countercultural episodes discussed above.

For each of these clusters, we shall articulate a sociological profile of the typical participant, indicating some crucial points of discrepancy between empirical fact and this ideal-typical portrait.

1. *Ecstatic renewal participation (cluster 1).* Millenarianism has been characterized as the "religion of the oppressed,"[165] and this may serve as a very provisional formula for defining the types of people attracted to "cluster 1" renewals. The "oppressed" would include the poor, the less educated, the marginally employed (i.e., the lower social classes), and any other minority groups, such as racial or religious minorities, who experience severe discrimination. We shall review some empirical evidence of cluster 1 participation among such groups, and then indicate some difficulties or exceptions to this formulation.

Medieval millenarianism was overwhelmingly supported by "the poor," especially by landless peasants. Cohn describes the extreme poverty of groups of people in the first crusade who set out to make their fortunes in a mysterious Jerusalem, some under the direction of a beggar king, King Tafur.[166] The economic desperation of this group was indicated by the savagery with which they "lived off the land"—plundering from the unfortunates who fell into their path. The Peasants' War that inflamed Europe in 1524 and 1525, though to some extent a *protest* demand for peasants' rights, was stimulated by doomsday prophecies and the influence of such visionary preachers as Thomas Münster.[167] The revivalism on the American frontier attracted people whose social condition has been described as follows: "to paraphrase Hobbes, life for members of such groups is poor, miserable, nasty, short and above all insecure."[168] This condition would approximately describe as well such groups as the impoverished black followers of Father Divine in American cities[169] or of the Reverend Jim Jones' People's Temple;[170] the snake-handling Pentecostal group in West Virginia,[171] and the followers of Antonio Conselheiro in Brazil, whom a local official described with slight exaggeration as a multitude of "the credulous and the ignorant."[172] Finally, for the revelrous episode of the "dance frenzy" in fifteenth-century Europe, it is said that "for the most part, lower social groups were involved. While people of all social classes and occupations were among the dancers, wealthy individuals and clerics were few. The majority comprised peasants, artisans such as tailors and shoemakers, servants, housewives, unmarried women, young people of both sexes, beggars, and idlers."[173]

There are various interpretations of the relation between "oppression" and ecstatic religious participation. In one version, emotional experience and ecstatic behavior furnish a compensation for the earthly miseries of the oppressed. The very *excitement* associated with enthusiastic episodes may be an important consideration. The sparseness of settlement of the Appalachian region at the time of the revivals meant that "there were few sources of recreation to relieve the monotony of daily life."[174] Over a hundred years later, studying in the same area, Liston Pope quotes a millworker in North Carolina who says about local revivals, "These prayer meetings are about the only entertainment we have."[175]

A rather different interpretation of ecstatic movements among the oppressed has been suggested by other writers. These emphasize the sense of personal unworthiness generated by the relative deprivation of the oppressed in the presence of the more privileged. New Guinea natives who first saw a European aircraft were said to have seen "a deployment and demonstration of capacities and power which they had to absorb and explain to themselves if they were to retain their integrity as men."[176] African natives, degraded by the assumptions of Europeans that God was a white who would exclude blacks from heaven, were amenable to the idea of native prophets of a "reverse colour bar" by which *whites* would be excluded from heaven.[177] The appeal of sectarian churches to the poor is indicated in Pope's observation that "members of the newer religions do not belong anywhere and so they belong, wholeheartedly, to the one type of institution which deigns to notice them."[178] Lower-caste people in India similarly find "integrity as men" by participating in a millenarian movement: "Persons of low social status are thrilled because they find themselves treated with a respect in their new communities such as they have never before experienced."[179]

Some apparent exceptions to the concentration of cluster 1 participation among the "oppressed" must now be noted. It should be observed, in the first place, that millenarian activity among the socially prominent is by no means unknown. The "Fifth Monarchy Men" of seventeeth-century England were made up mostly of higher-class persons, including even Oliver Cromwell himself as a "fellow traveller" of the movement.[180] The Irvingite speakers-in-tongues who appeared in England in 1830 were influenced by Edward Irving, "the fashionable preacher in whose Presbyterian congregation you might find Peel and Coleridge among your fellow worshippers."[181] Contemporary "scientology," with its essentially fantastic or science fictional explanations of phenomena, has attracted a following of people with at least some pretension to higher educational status. As Wallis says about the adherents of one cult in the general scientology mold, "an essential prerequisite is sufficient education to cope with the extensive occult literature and its abstruse terminology, but insufficient to penetrate its tortured logic and their thin veneer of 'science.'"[182] Nor are all intellectuals who support contemporary renewals of this "pseudo-intellectual" variety. Much support for evangelical or charismatic movements in religion is found among a so-called "new class" of "knowledge workers" who often combine political liberalism with theological conservatism.[183] Finally, some involvement of nonintellectual segments of the middle classes are reported for some ecstatic movements: the "shopkeepers" who predominated in the Rochester revivals in the Second Awakening,[184] the Full Gospel Business Men's Fellowship International, which provides support for Pentecostalism from quite respectable middle-class adherents.[185]

Another difficulty in the "oppressed" formulation is that many ecstatic movements appeal especially to *young* people, a group which may or may not experience oppression in the classic sense of deprived living conditions. Cohn thus describes the pathetic band of children who set off on a crusading venture in 1212, with the usual outcome: death along the way for most.[186] We observed above that students have been major participants in such revelrous episodes as streaks and public disorders in resort areas. And, of course, young people have been heavily involved in such "new religion" groups as the Jesus People, Children of God and Hare Krishna, all of which involve more or less "ecstatic" religious practices.[187]

It is possible to assimilate these last findings to an "oppression" model of cluster 1 participation, provided we are willing to recognize a concept of oppression in other than strictly economic terms. Many prominent and many young people feel oppressed by the impersonality of the bureaucratic or overorganized "system" in which they live. A young Californian thus complains, "Like you've been pressured to conform and take on middle-class neuroses, private property, and alienated labor, and all this shit shoved . . . down your throat until just, you're throwing it up, man."[188] It might be added that oppressively "boring" social conditions are not limited to Kentucky frontiersmen; the same feelings are rumored to have been engendered while sitting in a classroom or before a typewriter.

2. *Culturally radical renewal participation (cluster 2):* In contrast with ecstatic renewal episodes, reformist ones appear to draw their par-

ticipants from relatively higher status groups. Some exceptions will again be noted after we establish the pattern.

Utopian reformist schemes of a "technocratic" nature have, almost by definition, been dominated by scientists and other intellectuals. The followers of Saint-Simon in France in the 1820s and 1830s were intellectuals; indeed it was said that "the intellectual character of the dogma makes it inevitable that only a very small class . . . only the 'small number' of those who devote their lives to the investigation of the social sciences will be able to analyze the dogma scientifically."[189] Likewise, the "backwoods utopians" of the era, with their attempt to show the way to the world with their "experimental communities," tended toward social elitism in their membership and social attitudes. Though such a community as Robert Owen's New Harmony, Indiana emphasized manual labor, leaders sometimes complained of a lack of "skillful and steady hands" in the community.[190] Such hands as *were* available tended to elicit the repugnance of other members. The sharp class differentiation between communitarians and Great Awakening participants of the period is expressed in the objection to persons in the community who were described as "native backwoodsmen, strongly tinctured with methodism."[191] Communitarians of a century later in Stelton, New Jersey, were urban intellectual refugees from New York City (many fleeing from Attorney General Palmer's "enemy alien" raids). Though one of their leaders said that "most radicals would like to live in the country and many of them dream of the time when they can settle there permanently,"[192] the Stelton residents quickly established noncountry ways in their colony. Founded in 1915, "by the summer of 1918 lectures were being held every Saturday evening on some phase of politics, history or the arts, often combined with violin and piano recitals, and always followed by free-for-all discussions."[193] Visiting a contemporary commune in Rockridge, New Mexico, Vesey was struck with "how many of its members come from well-off families."[194]

The "new left" movement among students throughout the world, with its combination of political and cultural radicalism, was likewise dominated both in its membership and in its leadership by "members from well-off families." Flacks documents the middle-class—and especially intellectual—family backgrounds of student activists, noting only that these parents tended to be "old left" socialist and other strictly political radicals.[195] This movement also took much of its direction from the ideas of such intellectuals as C. Wright Mills, Paul

Goodman, and Herbert Marcuse.[196] The lack of involvement of *minority* youth in this movement is widely noted and is thus interpreted by Keniston:

> Most blacks, chicanos, and working-class youth . . . view the counterculture with mistrust and hatred. The youth revolt recruits only that minority of the young who are so solidly *in* technocratic society that they can afford to demand something more from life than security, affluence and the prospect of political power.[197]

Finally, the "age of reform" in America between 1884 and 1920 was largely the work of persons of relatively high social status. The Mugwumps who bolted the Republican Party in 1884 to support the reforms of Grover Cleveland were predominantly men in highly respected professions, many being prominent businessmen, though their ranks tended to be filled with men of "old" wealth and to exclude the "self-made" millionaires of the period like Andrew Carnegie.[198] The politically more productive successor to the Mugwumps, the Progressive movement, broadened its appeal to a wider cross-section of middle-class America. Rejecting the agrarian and working-class Populists as "wild anarchists,"[199] the Progressives were, as William Allen White said of the Bull Moose movement in 1912, "a movement of little businessmen, professional men, well-to-do farmers, skilled artisans from the upper brackets of organized labor."[200] The movement was widely supported in three professional groups: two of which (clergymen and lawyers) were beginning to see their traditional sources of respectability erode; and a third of which (professors, especially social scientists) was enjoying a recent great increase in respectability.[201] However, the Progressive movement appealed as well to many socially mobile lower-middle-class white-collar workers, newly sprung from working-class origins. Hofstadter thus comments on the contents of journals that contained muckraking exposés for their Progressive readers: "Simply by moving one's eye from left to right, from one column to the next, one could pass from the world in which the Beef Trust or Standard Oil was being exposed and denounced, to the world in which 'You Too Can Be a Certified Public Accountant.'"[202]

Exceptions to the pattern of reform participation among persons of higher status must now be noted. In the first place, we can note the influence on English commune development of the "only real proletarian mass movement of the nineteenth century, Chartism."[203]

Chartism was an early instance of a land reform movement, aimed at the establishment of a "peasant proprietary class" on the land.[204] Not only peasants but urban proletarians as well were able to obtain small plots of land in Chartist land colonies. Yet, while working-class people certainly predominated in such colonies, a paternalistic dominance by the relatively well-to-do is suggested by the fact that many were formed as wealthy people bought large estates to be subdivided among the "peasant" colonists. When, in an adaptation of the Chartist scheme, a prominent manufacturer relocated his factories in the countryside and built a utopian community for his workers, he expressed the middle-class view that "drink and lust" are at the bottom of social evils, and erected a sign at the town limit which read ALL BEER ABANDON YE THAT ENTER HERE.[205]

A more serious exception to the reformer participation profile is involved in the Populist movement in the United States. For all its involvements with persecution (antiforeign, anti-Semitic, anti-Catholic, etc.), Populism *was* a reform movement, and its adherents were likely to be marginal farmers and urban proletarians. "Hard-pressed" farmers in Kansas in 1890 donated bushels of wheat to support their movement and engaged in a "six-mile long" procession of wagons through the streets of Wichita to demonstrate their demands.[206] The proletarian section of the movement organized itself around the Knights of Labor in similar grassroots fashion; a strike of railroad workers in 1885 "began from below, with individual locals walking off the job at various points along the railroad line" to protest the firing of an employee who was a Knights activist.[207] Thus one cannot accurately characterize the Populist movement, like the Chartist land colonies, as subsisting on middle-class paternalism. What can be said, however, is that Populism was a reform movement of the *white* working classes, excluding minority participation in the same way as did the middle-class countercultural movement.[208]

PROCESS

The disparity between two theoretical approaches to the study of social process—the evolutionist and the interactionist—is nowhere better illustrated than in the sociological study of renewals. Thus, in the evolutionist mold, Wallace postulates, for revitalizations as for disasters, a "sequence of happenings," which he calls "behavioral units'' and sees as being ''based on generic human attributes, both physical and psychological.²⁰⁹ Similarly, students of *sects,* renewal-oriented religious groups, have proposed the existence of ''generic'' tendencies for sectarian religions to evolve into denominationalist forms.²¹⁰ On the other hand a contemporary interactionist, Robert Lauer, proposes that we must understand a social movement not in terms of ''fixed sequences'' but rather by ''viewing the movement as an interactive phenomenon vis-à-vis the larger society.''²¹¹

In this section an attempt will be made to synthesize evolutionist and interactionist perspectives. To be specific, we do attempt to construct an ideal-typical set of ''sequences'' or phases through which renewals tend to move. At the same time we remain very sensitive here (as in the case of protests and persecutions) to the causal importance of the interaction between collective behavior participants and persons more firmly entrenched in the routine social order. The interactionist perspective is perhaps best articulated in the idea that societal reaction ''amplifies'' tendencies in the renewal process. ²¹² The behavior of renewal participants precipitates wider societal response (encouragement, amusement, suppression, etc.), and these responses are seen as causal agents in the amplification (or deamplification) of the given behavior. If, as we suggest, there is a ''usual'' sequence in renewal episodes, it is probably because there is a ''usual'' sequence in the history of the relationship between a renewal movement and its wider social environment. When ''unusual'' sequences in this relationship occur, we have no problem at all in seeing how the ''usual'' course of renewal episodes changes direction.

One additional preliminary observation on the renewal phases here defined: the second and third phases almost coincide with the sectarian and denominationalist forms of religious organization mentioned above; and the first phase with Wallis'²¹³ view that a *cult* phase precedes the sectarian phases of some religious organizations. Since we do not confine our discussion of renewal to its religious forms, the cult-sect-denomination language would be a bit misleading. However, a great deal of what follows is informed by the research and discussion in this important area of the sociology of religion.

PHASE 1

An ideal-typical portrait of a renewal episode in its early stages would emphasize several characteristics. With great regularity, the appearance of a *charismatic* leadership (one or more persons) is a feature of the inauguration of a renewal episode. In Wallace's view, the intervals of "individual stress" and "cultural distortion" that precede the revitalization period lack any available course of action that has any "internally consistent structure." This structure is furnished by the prophet's personal inspiration or revelation, which is "abrupt and dramatic, usually occurring as a moment of insight, a brief period of realization of relationships and opportunities."[214] Kurt Back thus describes the "moment of insight" when a group of psychologists at a workshop, under the inspiration of Kurt Lewin, quite suddenly "discovered" the idea of sensitivity training.[215] Referring, like Wallace, to the "probings" that precede renewal outbreaks, Burridge observes that "until a prophet emerges to symbolize the new man by concentrating these probings in himself and giving them coherence, the activities remain inchoate and disorganized."[216]

We referred above to the assertion that many renewal episodes have more than one charismatic leader, and we can now suggest a second characteristic of this phase, its so-called *fissiparous* character.[217] Renewal episodes at their origin tend to have little central organization, especially if there is an ideology of "epistemological individualism"[218] in which all persons are believed to have access to the inspiration of the "Holy Ghost" or the revealed "truth." Gerlach and Hine, studying modern Pentecostalism, observe some practical value to renewal groups of their notoriously "polycephalous" (many-headed) character: the fact that decentralized groups with a variety of inspirations can appeal to a wide range of persons; and that in the case of failure by one segment of the movement, the whole movement cannot be found at fault.[219] It is perhaps partly for these reasons that the separatist church movement in Africa gained force with very little coordination or even awareness by people from one region that the movement was occurring in other regions.[220]

A third element in this cluster of characteristics follows somewhat from the first two. Groups involved in renewals at this stage are noted for being *open* to the coming and going of individual participants. A new religion such as Scientology operates in a "cultic milieu"[221] in which there is a wide variety of esoteric religions available to potential members; and many persons have very mobile careers as "seekers" who move quickly from involvement with one cult to involvement with others.[222]

Two additional characteristics refer to the interaction between renewal participants and persons and tendencies in the routine social world. One is the frequent syncretism by which cultural radicals combine novel ideas with ideas that are part of the culture supposedly being attacked. This syncretism is well illustrated in the case of the Oceanic cargo cults; for example, a New Zealand cult in 1862 was organized around the salvaged mast of a sunken English ship, the Christian symbols being adapted to the symbolism of the native culture.[223] Handsome Lake, the Seneca Indian whose visions in 1799 were the basis of a non-Christian religious movement among the Iroquois, received "Good Messages" that were heavily influenced by Christian thought, especially by that of the Quakers, who were locally prominent.[224]

A final characteristic of many early renewal episodes is the fact that they do not challenge the established social order. As we have noted, "itinerant" revivalists from George Whitefield to Billy Graham have been encouraged in their enthusiastic activity by established churches. Renewal prophets may use their positions in the established order to promote their renewal activities, as Timothy Leary was able for a time to enjoy the protection of his psychologist colleagues at Harvard for his experiments in hallucinogenic drugs, as well as to publish his findings in psychological journals.[225] Likewise, Scientology's founder, Ron Hubbard, was taken seriously enough by medical professionals that his healing techniques were tested and the reports (usually negative) appeared in medical journals.[226] At this stage, renewal movements may attract the support of "respectable" persons and agencies: witness the reputable publishing house that published the religious tracts of the Ranters,[227] and the Lady Huntingdon who provided an intellectual "salon" atmosphere for early Methodism to counter the "cruder" evangelism of Whitefield and Wesley.[228] One reason for the absence of challenge may be the recognition that radical rhetoric is just that: a matter of words that are impotent to generate any real change. Thus, early Progressive reformers such as Theodore Roosevelt could issue bellicose statements about the necessity for antitrust legislation, knowing full well that such legislation could not affect the real power of large corporations.[229]

PHASE 2

Many—probably most—episodes never go beyond the stage described above. To cite an example: most communes in the United States and Britain have been very small, very isolated from other communes, very "open" to members coming and going, essentially non-challenging to the existing social order—and their mortality rate has been exceedingly high.[230] The relatively few communes that *have* survived for more than a few years have some features that differentiate them from the short-lived ones.[231] These are groups that have, or develop, some of the following characteristics, many of which are involved in Wallis' conception of sectarianism.[232]

More complete and rigid *organization* is one of the features of renewal movements in this phase. The second religious awakening in America was in a sense a continuation of the earlier awakening, but it was marked by a high degree of development of missionary societies by the established New England churches, the well-organized "circuit-riding" system of the Methodists, and the development of "Sunday schools" with highly regimented structures.[233] The growth of Methodism in England was related to Wesley's aim to make of the Methodist societies "not merely a church within the Church but a nation within the nation; a sort of enclave not only in their piety but in daily life."[234] Longer-lived communes such as the Oneida community formed by John Humphrey Noyes were well-known for the minute planning of all aspects of common life.[235] This organization may, of course, have to be achieved by vigorous countering of the decentralizing tendency of phase 1. Originating as a loose confederation of highly localized and autonomous cults, the Divine Light Mission of the Guru Maharaj Ji attempted, with its Millennium Festival at the Houston Astro-Dome in 1973, to bring some degree of central control to this movement.[236] When Ron Hubbard attempted to impose his authority on the Scientology movement, he had to dissolve a "dianetics" movement with too many independent practitioners of "black dianetics" (i.e, anything Hubbard opposed), and to institute a heresy hunt for Subversive Persons.[237] At this point the renewal-organizing process can easily become involved with the process of persecution.

This organizing process may take either of two directions.[238] One direction is that of the mass movement—the collective behavioral equivalent of the "mass society" background condition discussed in Chapter 3. The Watch Tower Bible and Tract Society disseminates "literature" from its New York headquarters, and Jehovah's Witnesses throughout the world follow instructions and disseminate information with very little "mediation" of local Witness organizations. By contrast, the Unification Church employs the organizational method of "community intensity," in which devotees live in communes or

Unified Families. For these people, "participation in an international movement is highly developed but not formally signified."[239] The later fate of a renewal episode may be influenced by the organizational direction taken.

As renewal movements become more organized, they also tend to become more closed, or exclusionary, in their relationship to the outside world. This exclusiveness may appear in the form of membership becoming more difficult to attain, as renewal enthusiasts set up "tests" of the would-be joiner's qualification for membership. In some communes, a major focus of group discussion and, sometimes, a major source of intragroup tensions, is the question of whether to admit new applicants for membership.[240] Some sectarian religions (e.g., Hare Krishna, Maharaj Ji) recognize "two levels" of membership,[241] and neophytes must spend more or less time as probationers while they are arriving at the revelatory "truth" of the religion. Thus Scientologists (adopting the idea of a "clear" key on a computer to their notion that the clearing away of past life elements is necessary preparation for the new life) distinguish between their "pre-clears," who have not yet been successfully "audited" to achieve this state, and "clears," who have been so audited.[242] As groups become more difficult to join, they may make it more difficult for members to leave. The apparent refusal of the Reverend Jim Jones to allow would-be defectors to leave his People's Temple compound in Guyana was a factor in the outside investigations that led to mass suicides there in 1978.[243]

The more closed, or exclusionist, character of phase 2 renewals is also reflected in the intensification of the ideology that tends to separate members from nonmembers. When Jones' personal charisma was challenged in Jonestown, he followed a common adjustive strategy: "to modify or strengthen the ideology which justifies the group's existence, its goals and its strategies."[244] As Ron Hubbard was faced with the proliferation of subprophets, he abolished the whole precursor dianetics movement and founded the Scientology movement, based on a new revelation and a more esoteric set of ideas and techniques.[245] As Timothy Leary was faced with the negative societal response to his "deviant" experiments with hallucinogens, he founded his League for Spiritual Discovery (LSD) and began to play the "messiah game."[246] Even without such negative societal response, the escalation of ideological distinctiveness may stem from the desire of a given renewal organization to compete successfully with competitors in the cultic milieu. The Synanon movement originated simply as one

among many volunteer programs of drug rehabilitation. As competition among these groups intensified, the Synanon movement came to
be represented to potential followers as "the growing tip of humanity,
and living in Synanon was like living in the twenty-first century."[247]

With growing organizational rigidity, increased exclusiveness, and
intensified ideology, renewal participants are typically subjected to an
increased demand for personal commitment to the renewal cause. We
may refer here to Becker's view of commitment (e.g., to an occupational career) as the process by which persons make "side bets" on
their social involvements.[248] When one has invested time, money, and
energy into preparation for a career or the establishment of a marriage, these side bets may sustain one across periods of doubt about the
given involvement. The problem of renewal participants, especially in
this phase, is that their involvement with "deviant" activities subjects
them to all the usual social controls against deviant involvement. In
fact one's very commitment to routine social involvements—job or
spouse, for example—may mean that one is subject to pressures to
avoid deviant commitments, lest they endanger these social statuses.

Renewal-oriented groups use several basic devices for generating
member commitment. One is to project a "higher" commitment than
those of the routine social world. Communes with strong religious
ideologies have tended to be the most enduring ones.[249] They can appeal to the example of Christ, who taught that a disciple's career as a
"fisher of men" was more important than a mundane occupation, that
a woman who worshipped with him was not to be chastised for ignoring domestic chores. Renewal commitment is also engendered by "intensive interaction," by surrounding the participant with co-par-
ticipants who reinforce the rightness of the "deviant" commitment.[250]
This effect is intensified when renewal adherents are encouraged to
give "testimony" of their religious experience to an assembled
faithful.[251] Some renewal organizations require "bridge burning" acts
of their members: a public "speaking in tongues," for example, that
stabilizes a "deviant" identification and decisively separates the
speakers from nonrenewal commitments.[252] These acts may take the
form of requiring some "atrocity," such as the Mau Mau requirement
of the killing of an enemy as a condition of full membership.[253] Finally,
it has been suggested that such "new religions" as Hare Krishna and
the Unification Church have been able to solve at once some of their
financial and membership-commitment problems through their programs of street solicitation of funds: "In the Unification Church, for

example, the fund-raising situation provides each individual with a crucible for testing and developing one's spiritual strength."[254]

PHASE 3

The final, or "termination," phase of renewal episodes will now be considered. The definition of an endpoint for a renewal episode is probably more difficult than for any other collective behavior type we have discussed. The revivals, for example, that occurred in waves were followed by a continuing tradition of revivals within the established churches, and the obvious problem is that of determining when a wave becomes a ripple. We can, nevertheless, attempt to delineate some forces in the decline of intensity of renewals.

Three different models of the decline process will now be discussed. The distinction between them is only analytic, since specific renewals probably decline as a result of a combination of these and other forces.

The *routinization* model is the great contribution of the sect-to-denomination idea in the sociology of religion. In this view, the charisma that galvanized the renewal in the first phase (and, as the above suggests, survives and may even be intensified in the second) declines in favor of more impersonal social forms. Weber's discussion of the "routinization of charisma" is influential on the model.[255] The prophet has a highly personalized form of revelation and inspiration, and renewal movements thus face the problem of "succession" of leadership when the charismatic leader (or leaders) pass on. About the Shakers it was said that, around 1800, "Ann Lee's charismatic legacy was routinized" by successive leaders by whom "full communitarianism was established as the fundamental organizational principle of the Shaker Church."[256] How far this "principle" failed in replacing the charismatic inspiration of Ann Lee is indicated in the observation that, after the Civil War, "the few converts who joined the sect were predominantly mature or elderly women, many of whom appear to have been motivated as much by a desire for tranquillity and economic security as by religious conviction."[257]

Even apart from such "succession crises," renewal movements may experience routinization simply as a result of the increasing organizational work associated with the growth in membership of the movement. Both Jehovah's Witnesses and Seventh-Day Adventists in Cuba were shown to change as they grew in membership, decreasing their demands on members' commitments.[258] The Transcendental Meditation movement, originating in heavy Oriental mysticism, lost much of this sectarian eccentricity as TM was "marketed" to a mass audience.[259]

A routinized renewal movement may produce a deflection of members' involvement from the original "enthusiasm" in favor of other motives. Visiting the United States as a tourist around 1900, Weber remarked on the vitality of sectarian religion in terms of membership, but also noted that people were apparently using their affiliations with these churches as sources of "certification" of their moral qualities in order to promote their worldly success. About a Baptist banker in North Carolina whose baptism was witnessed by Weber, it was said that "once being baptised he will get the patronage of the whole region and he will outcompete everybody."[260] This concern with moral certification is also suggested in a study of sectarian Marxist and Maoist groups in Canada whose members appear less interested in promoting the "revolution" than in reassuring themselves of the rightness of their own moral stance.[261] Likewise, a study of people's involvement in a "church of magic"[262] suggests that many participants use their membership in that church in the same way that, according to Herberg, Americans generally use their religious affiliations: to provide themselves a recognizable social identity in a "mass society."[263]

Another possible result of routinization is that people may begin to treat playfully a type of activity that had originated with very serious intent. Thus, although there are still satanic cults in the United States whose members are very serious about black magic,[264] the recent "occult revival" (the interest in astrology, exorcism, etc.) is, according to Truzzi, an indication of a decline in serious belief in the occult: "It is precisely because we no longer believe in the fearsome aspects of the occult that we are willing to experiment with them."[265] All this may throw more light on Simmel's notion of the "play-forms" of serious social life.[266] He emphasizes a positive function of these forms for serious activity; but it may be suggested as well that play forms may survive as the formal shells of human activites that have lost their serious content.

A second model of renewal decline emphasizes the process of *attrition* or loss of membership of renewal organizations over a period of time. Weber suggests a possible explanation of this sort in the observation that charismatic leaders demand the *total* commitment of their followers, and a frequent condition of this commitment is the promise that the fulfillment of the prophecies is imminent.[267] People will leave families and jobs in anticipation of an immediate arrival of cargo or the Second Advent, but what happens "when prophecy fails"?[268] What often happens, of course, is that prophets say they made a "miscalculation" and that, as Millerites said, the end of the world would come sometime in 1844 rather than the original specific date in 1843.[269] Prophets may maintain credibility by blaming nonfulfillment of prophecies on the failure of people to follow the prophet's instructions for preparation. The nonarrival of a prophesied cargo in the Cook Islands in 1947 was blamed on one man who refused baptism and supposedly offended the gods.[270] Disconfirmed prophecies may lead to redoubled efforts, especially at recruiting more membership.[271] Ultimately, however, the disillusionment of nonfulfillment will take its toll.

Attrition tendencies resulting from the organizational discipline typically imposed at phase 2 may also be noted. In "mass movement" kinds of renewal organizations such as Jehovah's Witnesses (as mentioned above), members find themselves judged solely in terms of headquarters-imposed production quotas (amount of literature distributed) and many defect if they cannot fulfill these quotas.[272] Those organizations based on "community intensity," such as the Unification Church, are quite vulnerable to crises in these communities. In some communes, the whole enterprise is abandoned or severely curtailed when some issue arises that can only be resolved by the withdrawal or expulsion of members.[273]

Finally, we consider a *suppression* model of renewal decline. The hostility in the established social world toward "heretics" of all sorts was documented in Chapter 4. Cohn shows, for example, how a great many heretical sects—most of the them of the millenarian variety—were persecuted and suppressed by Church and State in Europe.[274] The rise of enthusiastic movements thus frequently results in "moral panics" of the crusader variety.[275] The fate of the Ranters in England is typical. State and church officials and the popular press vied with one another to exaggerate the evils of this group of "free spirits."[276] We should not overlook, of course, the observation that heretics may *thrive* on opposition to some extent, but in these as in most cases the *ultimate* power of official suppression is likely to prevail. Timothy Leary, whose movement did benefit at some stages from the opposition to it, finally announced after much suppression in 1968 that he would

go "underground," a position from which his movement has not
flourished.[277] Hubbard's Scientology movement was forced to make
gestures of adaptation, at least in softening the heretic hunts that
followed an F.D.A. raid and a publicizing of Scientological practices in
1963.[278] Even quite recently, however, the Church of Scientology has
largely continued its sectarian stance of belligerence toward its
"enemies," especially toward apostates like the two former Scientologists against whom the Church filed a large defamation suit.[279]

CONSEQUENCES

We turn finally to the question of the consequences of renewal
episodes, especially to the impact of these episodes on long-term social
change. At least three different positions on this question have been
argued: (1) the nonconsequences of renewal episodes; (2) their liberal
or revolutionary consequences; and (3) their conservative or reactionary consequences.

RENEWALS AS NONCONSEQUENTIAL

It is arguable, first, that renewal episodes are among those "sound
and fury" human events that really signify very little as causal agents
in long-term social change. Episodes are said to have an "expressive"
function of allowing people an opportunity to gratify their personal
needs without much implication for "instrumental" effects on social
change.[280] The socially isolated victims of "mass society" find a sense
of belonging in sectarian activity, a home away from the homes they
have lost in modern societies.[281] Thus in one interpretation of the
"new religions," their emphasis on rituals of purification, meditation,
and so on furnishes the devotee with "armor" to protect himself or
herself against a sense of personal worthlessness.[282] While these activities may reflect very fundamental consequences for the individuals
involved, their *social* consequences are somewhat dubious.
One interpretation along this line is that while enthusiastic
religious activity may have been socially consequential in primitive
social structures, in modern societies with their impersonal bureaucratic structures, enthusiastic movements are quite irrelevant. Bryan

Wilson, for example, interprets the "new religions" as a manifestation of the long-term secularization tendency; these movements express precisely "the extent to which religion has become inconsequential for modern society."[283] In modern society, "enthusiasm" can exist "only in the interstices between institutional orders, in the narrow social space that remains for collective behavior, spontaneous faith, and unconstrained obedience and adulation."[284] In this view, new religions have all the social nonsignificance of such faddish behavior as the "pop religion" interest in the occult, or those springtime revels of 1974, the streaks. Wilson's view of new religions as reflecting religious secularization is given some empirical support in Wuthnow's study in the San Francisco area, although the study shows a broader pattern of connection between disillusionment with religion and involvement in the countercultural activities of the 1960s.[285]

RENEWALS AS HAVING REVOLUTIONARY OR LIBERALIZING EFFECTS

Other interpreters of the significance of renewals have argued, in contrast, that these episodes have had profound effects in the direction of altered social orders. The worldwide revolt of native people against the colonial domination of European powers has been especially related to the influence of millenarian ideas that represent a syncretism of native and European sources. The actual demonstration of the role of native revitalization movements in anticolonial revolts is rarely undertaken. The messianic or millenarian ideas behind the sepoy revolt in India,[286] the Taiping rebellion in China,[287] and the Mau Mau revolt in Kenya[288] are among the revolutionary movements that have been studied in this way.

Less-than-revolutionary consequences have been claimed for some renewal episodes; almost every type we have studied here has been shown to have effects in the direction of encouraging longer-term social changes. The Second Awakening in America in the first half of the nineteenth-century was shown, in its challenge to ecclesiastical authority, to have contributed strongly to Jacksonian and later versions of popular democracy.[289] The northern abolitionist reformers of the era were often influenced by the revivalist preachers of the day: for example, the abolitionist Theodore Weld was moved by the preaching of Charles G. Finney.[290] The Progressive reform era of 1884–1920 produced some enduring political reforms.[291] It seems to have produced some delayed-reaction effects as well. As we noted above, the antitrust agitation of around 1910 was more verbal bluster than actual accomplishment; it would not be until the New Deal era, when there was no popular antitrust agitation but when there was a professionalization of antitrust prosecution in the Justice Department, that this earlier reform effort would bear fruit.[292]

During the upsurge of countercultural activity among college youth, established churches recognized the futility of a "ministry" to youth by established forms and instituted "campus ministries" whose practices and ideologies have diverged rather sharply from those of the sponsoring churches.[293] Another adaptation of established churches to the movement was a deliberate "encounter" with the counterculture in the form of modification of church practice—the incorporation of folk music, body contact, and other innovations into church worship. A study of the "encounters" of three churches in the San Francisco area is interesting in revealing conditions that retard or promote such modifications.[294] One church changed greatly because it was endowed by outside sources that could resist local conservatism; another because it had a strong leader who was so disposed and a white middle-class congregation that did not feel threatened by the local counterculture. A third, a downtown church with flower children literally on its doorstep but with a conservative congregation, was little affected by its "encounter." By all accounts, the "charismatic" movement among Catholics is being carried out with considerable acceptance by the church, charismatic practice being accepted as simply an alternative "faith style."[295]

RENEWALS AS HAVING REACTIONARY OR CONSERVATIVE EFFECTS

We consider, finally, the possibility that renewal episodes may retard social change or even promote a return to an earlier social condition. Religious revivals are often asserted to have this effect. The established community's promotion of Billy Sunday and Dwight Moody revivals was clearly related to such observations as contained in a small-town newspaper headline: "W. A. Sunday Ushers in Big Clean-up. Fiery Evangelist in Opening Sermon Tells of Good He Will Accomplish in Ridding Ottumwa of Crime."[296] Bible belt towns were notorious prey to reformers who would bring the milennium "right here in River City" by bringing the word of God, a boy's band, or whatever. The Second Awakening, with its democratizing and reform-promoting effects in the North, is described as having contributed to the reactionary "mind of the South"; the Baptist and Methodist revivalists, by their great stress on personal piety, engendered profound indifference to slave or any other "social" questions.[297] Revivalists in Appalachia were credited with having generated a sober work force for the cotton mills that moved into the area,[298] and Jehovah's Witnesses, a strong religious force in many African countries, are shown to encourage the same qualities of sobriety and efficiency required for participation in a modernizing society.[299]

Even outside the South and especially in cities, revivalism has been associated with the effort to tame asocial "passions."[300] The view has also been developed that the "rhetoric" of gospel hymns suggests a major concern with generating a "community of feeling" among believers—a development that could be used to justify closing ranks against those (Catholics, Jews, and perhaps communists more recently) who fall outside the pale of that communion of the faithful.[301]

Finally, the "new religions" of the 1970s have been interpreted by several sociologists as having a fundamentally conservative or "integrative" social function.[302] The "freak" ethos of the counterculture of the 1960s was one of "dropping out" of conventional society, with its traditional concepts of work, discipline, deferred gratification, and so on.[303] As the young (and near-young) experienced disillusionment with drugs, commune living, subsistence on welfare, and other counterculture trends, they were, in this interpretation, seeking ways to "drop in" to the conventional culture they had left.[304] The idea, for example, of the "Jesus freak" was ideally suited to this purpose. Without totally abandoning their side bet commitment to the counterculture, ex-hippies could discover a new "high" or "trip" that would allow them their ecstatic experience without the accompanying removal from conventional society. Thus, according to Adams and Fox, the Jesus people "welcome the Jesus trip as an expedient means of returning to middle-class virtues while retaining peer approval."[305] It is interesting to speculate whether we may reach the situation in which being one of the Jesus people or a Hare Krishna is a "certificate" of moral worth that can be used to promote worldly success in the same way that Max Weber observed that being a southern Baptist in 1900 provided such a certification.

Notes

1. Ruth A. Wallace, "The Secular Ethic and the Spirit of Patriotism," *Sociological Analysis* 34 (1973): 3–11.

2. W. H. G. Armytage, *Heavens Below: Utopian Experiments in England 1560–1960* (London: Routledge and Kegan Paul, 1961).

3. Alan Heimert and Perry Miller, eds., *The Great Awakening: Documents Illustrating the Crisis and Its Consequences* (Indianapolis: Bobbs-Merrills, 1967); Edwin E. Gaustad, *The Great Awakening in New England* (New York: Harper, 1957); Wesley W. Gewehr, *The Great Awakening in Virginia, 1740–1790* (Durham, N.C.: Duke University Press, 1930); Charles H. Maxson, *The Great Awakening in the Middle Colonies* (Gloucester, Mass: Peter Smith, 1958); William G. McLoughlin, *Revivals, Awakenings and Reform: An Essay on Social Change in America, 1607–1977* (Chicago: University of Chicago Press, 1978), pp. 47–97; Bernard A. Weisberger, *They Gathered at the River: The Story of the Great Revivalists and Their Impact upon Religion in America* (Boston: Little, Brown, 1958), pp. 54–59.

4. McLoughlin, *Revivals, Awakenings and Reform,* pp. 98–140; Weisberger, *They Gathered at the River,* pp. 3–159; John B. Boles, *The Great Revival, 1787–1805* (Lexington: Universtiy of Kentucky Press, 1972); Whitney R. Cross, *The Burned-over District: The Social and Intellectual History of Enthusiastic Religion in Western New York, 1800–1850* (Ithaca, N.Y.: Cornell Universtiy Press, 1950); Paul E. Johnson, *A Shopkeeper's Millennium: Society and Revivals in Rochester, New York, 1815–1837* (New York: Hill & Wang, 1978).

5. Cross, *Burned-over District,* pp. 14–29.

6. Ibid., p. 48.

7. Weisberger, *They Gathered at the River,* pp. 87–126; Cross, *Burned-over District,* pp. 151–69; McLoughlin, *Revivals, Awakenings and Reform,* pp. 122–131.

8. McLoughlin, *Revivals, Awakenings and Reform,* p. 124.

9. Weisberger, *They Gathered at the River,* pp. 109–21.

10. Ibid., pp. 42–50.

11. Paul Boyer, *Urban Masses and Moral Order in America, 1820–1920* (Cambridge: Harvard University Press, 1978).

12. Ibid., p. 27.

13. Ibid., p. 37.

14. McLoughlin, *Revivals, Awakenings and Reform,* pp. 141–50; Weisberger, *They Gathered at the River,* pp. 175–265; William G. McLoughlin, *Billy*

Sunday Was His Real Name (Chicago: University of Chicago Press, 1955); Kurt Lang and Gladys E. Lang, "Decisions for Christ: Billy Graham in New York City," in Maurice R. Stein, Arthur J. Vidich, and David M. White, eds., *Identity and Anxiety* (Glencoe, Ill.: Free Press, 1960), pp. 415–27; Ronald C. Wimberley, Thomas C. Hood, C. M. Lipsey, Donald Clelland, and Marguerite Hay, "Conversion in a Billy Graham Crusade: Spontaneous Event or Ritual Performance?" *Sociological Quarterly* 16 (1975): 162–70.

15. McLouglin, *Revivals, Awakenings and Reform,* p. 142.

16. See the photographs of Sunday's tabernacles preceding p. 115 of Weisberger, *They Gathered at the River.*

17. McLoughlin, *Revivals, Awakenings and Reform,* pp. 162–78.

18. Ibid., pp. 179–216.

19. The ideological sources of Christian millenial thought are reviewed in Norman Cohn, *The Pursuit of the Millennium: Revolutionary Millenarians and Mystical Anarchists of the Middle Ages* (New York: Oxford University Press, 1970), pp. 19–36.

20. Ibid., pp. 75–81.

21. This type of *action* consequence of millenarian thought is emphasized in a useful compilation in Sylvia Thrupp, ed., *Millenial Dreams in Action* (The Hague: Mouton, 1962).

22. See the lengthy bibliography in the important essay by Weston La Barre, "Materials for a History of Studies of Crisis Cults: A Bibliographic Essay," *Current Anthropology* 12 (1971): 3–44.

23. Cohn, *Pursuit of the Millennium,* pp. 61–107. For a dramatic narrative of the crusades in a similar vein, see Charles Mackay, *Extraordinary Delusions and the Madness of Crowds* (Boston: L. C. Page, 1932).

24. Cohn, *Pursuit of the Millennium,* pp. 235–80; George H. Williams, *The Radical Reformation* (Philadelphia: Westminister, 1972).

25. E. J. Hobsbawm, *Primitive Rebels: Studies in Archaic Forms of Social Movement in the 19th and 20th Centuries* (New York: Praeger, 1963), pp. 65–107.

26. Armytage, *Heavens Below;* A. L. Morton, *The World of the Ranters: Religious Radicalism and the English Revolution* (London: Lawrence and Wishart, 1970); B. S. Capp, *The Fifth Monarchy Men: A Study in Seventeenth-Century English Millenarianism* (London: Faber and Faber, 1972).

27. Harold Gould, "The Utopian Side of the Indian Uprising," in David W. Plath, ed., *Aware of Utopia* (Urbana: University of Illinois Press, 1971), pp. 86–116. On the messianic theme in earlier Indian history, see Stephen Fuchs, *Rebellious Prophets: A Study of Messianic Movements in Indian Religions* (New York: Asia Publishing House, 1965).

28. Ralph Linton, "Nativistic Movements," *American Anthropologist* 45 (1943): 230–40; Anthony F. C. Wallace, "Revitalization Movements," *American Anthropologist* 58 (1956): 264–81; La Barre, "Materials for a History of Studies of Crisis Cults."

29. Bernard Barber, "Acculturation and Messianic Movements," *American Sociological Review* 6 (1941): 663–69; Weston La Barre, *The Ghost Dance* (New York: Doubleday, 1970); Michael P. Carroll, "Revitalization Movements and Social Structure: Some Quantitative Tests," *American Sociological Review* 40 (1975): 389–401.

30. David F. Aberle, *The Peyote Cult Among the Navoho* (Chicago: Aldine, 1966).

31. Anthony F. C. Wallace, *The Death and Rebirth of the Seneca* (New York: Alfred A. Knopf, 1970).

32. Peter Worsley, *The Trumpet Shall Sound: A Study of 'Cargo Cults' in Melanesia* (London: Paladin, 1970); Peter Lawrence, *Road Belong Cargo: A Study of the Cargo Movement in the Southern Madang District New Guinea* (Manchester: Manchester University Press, 1964); Kenelm Burridge, *New Heaven New Earth: A Study of Millenarian Activities* (New York: Schocken, 1969); Mircea Eliade, "Cargo-cults and Cosmic Regeneration," in Thrupp, *Millenial Dreams in Action,* pp. 139–43.

33. Frances D. Nichol, *The Midnight Cry* (Washington, D.C.: Review and Herald Publishing Company, 1944); Cross, *The Burned-over District,* pp. 287–321.

34. John Lofland, *Doomsday Cult: A Study of Conversion, Proselytization and Maintenance of Faith,* enl. ed. (New York: Irvington, 1977).

35. Leon Festinger, Henry W. Riecken, and Stanley Schachter, *When Prophecy Fails* (New York: Harper Torchbooks, 1956).

36. Max Weber, *The Protestant Ethic and the Spirit of Capitalism,* trans. Talcott Parsons (New York: Scribner's, 1930).

37. Michael Walzer, *The Revolution of the Saints: A Study in the Origins of Radical Politics* (Cambridge: Harvard University Press, 1965).

38. J. L. Talmon, *Political Messianism: The Romantic Phase* (New York: Praeger, 1960), pp. 35–225.

39. Talmon, *Political Messianism,* pp. 125–56.

40. Armytage, *Heavens Below,* pp. 77–167; Arthur E. Bestor Jr., *Backwoods Utopias* (Philadelphia: University of Pennsylvania Press, 1950).

41. Cross, *Burned-over District,* pp. 238–51; Maren Lockwood Carden, "The Experimental Utopia in America," *Daedalus* (1965): 403–18. Rosabeth M. Kanter, *Commitment and Community: Communes and Utopias in Sociological Perspective* (Cambridge: Harvard University Press, 1972), pp. 9–18.

42. Quoted in Armytage, *Heavens Below,* p. 77.

43. Richard Hofstadter, *The Age of Reform: From Bryan to FDR* (New York: Vintage, 1955); Lewis L. Gould, ed., *The Progressive Era* (Syracuse: Syracuse University Press, 1974).

44. Gerald W. McFarland, *Mugwumps, Morals and Politics, 1884–1920* (Amherst: University of Massachusetts Press, 1975).

45. Melvin G. Holli, "Urban Reform in the Progressive Era," in Gould, *The Progressive Era,* pp. 133–51.

46. Lawrence A. Cremin, *The Transformation of the School: Progressivism in American Education, 1876–1957* (New York: Alfred A. Knopf, 1961).

47. Laurence Veysey, *The Communal Experience: Anarchist and Mystical Counter-Cultures in America* (New York: Harper & Row, 1973), pp. 77–203.

48. McLoughlin, *Revivals, Awakenings and Reform,* pp. 162–78; Allen F. Davis, *Spearheads for Reform* (New York: Oxford University Press, 1967).

49. McLoughlin, *Revivals, Awakenings and Reform,* pp. 171, 172.

50. Vesey, *The Communal Experience,* pp. 207–78.

51. McLoughlin, *Revivals, Awakenings and Reform,* pp. 179–216.

52. Vesey, *The Communal Experience,* p. 52.

53. David Matza, "Subterranean Traditions of Youth," *Annals of the American Academy of Political and Social Science* 338 (1961): 102–18.

54. Frank Musgrove, *Ecstasy and Holiness: Counter Culture and the Open Society* (Bloomington: University of Indiana Press, 1974), pp. 65–80.

55. Talmon, *Political Messianism,* pp. 177–201.

56. Lewis S. Feuer, *The Conflict of Generations: The Character and Significance of Student Movements* (New York: Basic Books, 1969), pp. 54–62.

57. See, for example, Musgrove, *Ecstasy and Holiness;* Lawrence Lipton, *The Holy Barbarians* (New York: Messner, 1959); Kenneth Kenniston, *The Uncommitted* (New York: Harcourt Brace, 1960); Jack Newfield, *A Prophetic Minority* (New York: New American Library, 1966); Keith Melville, *Communes in the Counter Culture* (New York: William Morrow, 1972).

58. Theodore Roszak, *The Making of a Counter-Culture* (Garden City, N.Y.: Doubleday, 1969): Charles Reich, *The Greening of America* (New York: Random House, 1970); Herbert Marcuse, *One Dimensional Man* (Boston: Beacon, 1964); Philip Slater, *The Pursuit of Loneliness* (Boston: Beacon, 1970); and Jacques Ellul, *The Technological Society* (New York: Vintage, 1967).

59. Reich, *The Greening of America,* p. 225.

60. On American communes, see Melville, *Communes in the Counter Culture;*

Veysey, *The Communal Experience;* Kanter, *Commitment and Conformity,* pp. 165–212. On British communes, see Philip Abrams and Andrew McCulloch, *Communes, Sociology and Society* (Cambridge: Cambridge University Press, 1976); and Andrew Rigby, *Alternative Realities: A Study of Communes and Their Members* (London: Routledge and Kegan Paul, 1974).

61. Judith T. Lyness, Milton E. Lipetz, and Keith R. Davis, "Living Together: An Alternative to Marriage," *Journal of Marriage and the Family* 34 (1972): 305–11. See also Charles Palson and Rebecca Palson, "Swinging in Wedlock," *Trans-action* 9 (February 1972): 28–37. On the general phenomenon of alternative family forms, see Lucille Duberman, *Marriage and Its Alternatives* (New York: Praeger, 1975).

62. See, for example, Joseph Berke, "The Free University of New York," in Joseph Berke, ed., *Counter Culture: The Creation of an Alternative Society* (London: Peter Owen, 1969), pp. 212–22.

63. Herbert J. Freudenberger, ed., "The Free Clinic Handbook," *Journal of Social Issues* 30 (1974): 1–208.

64. Richard A. Cloward and Richard M. Elman, "Advocacy in the Ghetto," *Trans-action* 4 (December 1966): 27–35.

65. Richard Sennett, *The Uses of Disorder* (New York: Alfred A. Knopf, 1970).

66. Robert Wuthnow, *Experimentation in American Religion: The New Mysticisms* (Berkeley: University of California Press, 1978); Thomas Robbins, Dick Anthony, and James Richardson, "Theory and Research on Today's New Religion," *Sociological Analysis* 39 (1978): 95–122; Jacob Needleman and George Baker, eds., *Understanding the New Religions* (New York: Seabury, 1978); Bryan Wilson, *Contemporary Transformations of Religion* (London: Oxford University Press, 1976). Charles Y. Glock and Robert N. Bellah, eds., *The New Religious Consciousness* (Berkeley: University of California Press, 1976). On Leary's movement see Robert H. Lauer, "Social Movements: An Interactionist Analysis," *Sociological Quarterly* 13 (1972): 315–28. On the People's Temple, see James T. Richardson, "People's Temple and Jonestown: A Corrective Comparison and Critique," *Journal for the Scientific Study of Religion* 19 (1980): 239–55; and Doyle P. Johnson, "Dilemmas of Charismatic Leadership: The Case of the People's Temple," *Sociological Analysis* 40 (1979): 315–23.

67. C. Lincoln Weigart and Andrew J. Weigart, "An Emerging Faith Style: A Research Note on the Catholic Charismatic Renewal," *Sociological Analysis* 39 (1978): 165–72; Michael T. Harrison, "The Maintenance of Enthusiasm: Involvement in a New Religious Movement" *Sociological Analysis* 36 (1975): 150–60; Joseph Fichter, *The Catholic Cult of the Paraclete* (New York: Sheed and Ward, 1975).

68. Fred Davis, "Why All of Us May be Hippies Someday," *Trans-action* 5 (December 1967): 10–18.

69. Georg Simmel, "The Sociology of Sociability," *American Journal of Sociology* 55 (1949): 254–61.

70. Johan Huizinga, *Homo Ludens: A Study of the Play Element in Culture* (Boston: Beacon, 1955).

71. Gary Marx, "Issueless Riots," in James E. Short, Jr. and Marvin E. Wolfgang, eds. *Collective Violence* (Chicago: Aldine-Atherton, 1972), pp. 47–59. We have already observed "Roman holiday" stages of protest riots; and also the "euphoric" behavior in the aftermath of some disasters; demonstrating the connection of celebrations to other kinds of collective behavior.

72. George Rude, *The Crowd in History* (New York: Wiley, 1964), p. 58.

73. Robert R. Evans and Jerry L. L. Miller, "Barely an End in Sight," in Robert R. Evans, ed., *Readings in Collective Behavior,* 2d ed. (Chicago: Rand McNally, 1975), pp. 401–17.

74. E. L. Quarantelli and James R. Hundley Jr., "A Test of Some Propositions About Crowd Formation and Behavior," in Evans, *Readings in Collective Behavior,* pp. 370–86.

75. On surfing, see John Irwin, "Surfing: The Natural History of an Urban Scene," *Urban Life and Culture* 2 (1973): 131–60.

76. See the description of police action in anticipation of a motorcycle rally in Maryland in Robert Shellow and Derek V. Roemer, "The Riot That Didn't Happen," *Social Problems* 14 (1966): 221–33.

77. H. L. Nieburg, "Agonistics: Rituals of Conflict," in Short and Wolfgang, *Collective Violence,* pp. 89, 90.

78. *New York Times,* 22 July 1969, X, p. 1.

79. Michael Barkun, *Disaster and the Millennium* (New Haven: Yale University Press, 1974), pp. 34–90.

80. La Barre, "Materials for a History of Studies of Crisis Cults."

81. McLoughlin, *Revivals, Awakenings and Reform.*

82. Ibid., p. 104.

83. Cross, *Burned-over District.*

84. Boyer, *Urban Masses and Moral Order,* pp. 3, 4.

85. Richard Flacks, *Youth and Social Change* (Chicago: Markham, 1971), p. 22.

86. Cohn, *Pursuit of the Millennium,* pp. 53–59.

87. Williams, *The Radical Reformation.*

88. Barkun, *Disaster and the Millennium,* p. 34.

89. A. Grenfell Price, *White Settlers and Native Peoples* (Melbourne: Georgian House, 1950). The effects of such demographic disaster on native

234 OUTBREAKS: THE SOCIOLOGY OF COLLECTIVE BEHAVIOR

Americans is demonstrated in Russell Thornton, "Demographic Antecedents to a Revitalization Movement: Population Change, Population Size and the 1890 Ghost Dance," *American Sociological Review* 46 (1981): 88–96.

90. Barber, "Acculturation and Messianic Movements."

91. Aberle, *The Peyote Cult.*

92. David F. Aberle, "A Note on Relative Deprivation as Applied to Millenarian and Other Cult Movements," in Thrupp, *Millennial Dreams in Action,* pp. 209–14.

93. Burridge, *New Heaven New Earth,* pp. 64–69.

94. Cochrane, *Big Men and Cargo Cults.*

95. Philip Mason, *Patterns of Dominance* (New York: Oxford University Press, 1970), chap. 3.

96. Gould, "The Utopian Side of the Indian Uprising."

97. Wallace, "Revitalization Movements." Anthony F. C. Wallace, "Mazeway Re-synthesis: A Bio-cultural Theory of Religious Inspiration," *Transactions of the New York Academy of Sciences,* 2d ser. 18 (1956): 626–38.

98. Emile Durkheim, *Suicide,* trans. John A. Spaulding and George Simpson (Glencoe, Ill.: Free Press, 1951); Robert K. Merton, *Social Theory and Social Structure* (Glencoe, Ill.: Free Press, 1956), pp. 132–39.

99. E. Eric Lincoln, *The Black Muslims in America* (Boston: Beacon, 1961).

100. Karl Mannheim, *Ideology and Utopia,* trans Edward A. Shils and Louis Wirth (New York: Harcourt Brace, 1936).

101. Max Weber, "The Social Psychology of the World Religions," in H. H. Gerth and C. Wright Mills, eds., *From Max Weber: Essays in Sociology* (New York: Osford University Press, 1958), p. 275.

102. Barkun, *Disaster and the Millennium,* p. 64. It should be noted, however, that there *was* a massive emigration from Ireland to the United States and elsewhere during this period, indicating that, while the Church may have immunized the Irish to millenarianism, it certainly did not prevent their seeking other forms of relief of their misfortune.

103. Burridge, *New Heaven New Earth,* pp. 37, 38.

104. Plath, *Aware of Utopia;* Bestor, *Backwoods Utopias.*

105. Vesey, *The Communal Experience;* on recent criticism see above, note 58.

106. R. Laurence Moore, "Directions of Thought in Progressive America," in Gould, *The Progressive Era,* pp. 35–53.

107. Bengt G. M. Sundkler, *Bantu Prophets in South Africa,* 2d ed. (London: Oxford University Press, 1961), p. 33; see also Burridge, *New Heaven New Earth,* p. 22.

108. Frederic C. Jaher, *Doubters and Dissenters: Cataclysmic Thought in America, 1885–1918* (New York: Free Press of Glencoe, 1964).

109. Rene Ribiero, "Brazilian Messianic Movements," in Thrupp, *Millennial Dreams in Action,* p. 66.

110. George Shepperson, "Nyasaland and the Millennium," in Thrupp, *Millennial Dreams in Action,* pp. 145, 146.

111. Weber, *The Protestant Ethic and the Spirit of Capitalism.*

112. R. A. Knox, *Enthusiasm: A Chapter in the History of Religion* (London: Oxford University Press, 1931), pp. 529–35.

113. Weisberger, *They Gathered at the River,* pp. 99, 100.

114. Knox, *Enthusiasm,* pp. 550–58.

115. Weston La Barre, *They Shall Take Up Serpents* (New York: Schocken, 1969); Luther P. Gerlach and Virginia H. Hine, *People, Power, Change* (Indianapolis: Bobbs-Merrill, 1970).

116. George Rosen, "Psychic Epidemics in Europe and the United States," in George Rosen, *Madness in Society* (Chicago: University of Chicago Press, 1968), p. 209.

117. La Barre, *The Ghost Dance,* pp. 230–32.

118. Knox, *Enthusiasm,* p. 362.

119. Rosen, "Psychic Epidemics," p. 211.

120. Cohn, *Pursuit of the Millennium,* p. 62.

121. Max Weber, "The Sociology of Charismatic Authority," in Gerth and Mills, *From Max Weber,* p. 245.

122. Wallace, *Death and Rebirth of the Seneca.*

123. Armytage, *Heavens Below,* pp. 58, 59.

124. Leonard J. Arrington and Davis Bitton, *The Mormon Experience: A History of the Latter-Day Saints* (New York: Alfred A. Knopf, 1979), p. 8.

125. Festinger et al., *When Prophecy Fails.*

126. Weber, "Sociology of Charismatic Authority," p. 250.

127. Ibid., p. 248.

128. Howard Kaminsky, "The Free Spirit in the Hussite Revolution," in Thrupp, *Millennial Dreams in Action,* pp. 166–86.

129. Lewis A. Coser, *Greedy Institutions* (New York: Free Press, 1974).

130. Cochrane, *Big Men and Cargo Cults,* p. 147.

131. Fuchs, *Rebellious Prophets,* p. 31.

132. Worsley, *The Trumpet Shall Sound,* p. 30.

133. Knox, *Enthusiasm,* p. 506.

134. Cross, *The Burned-over District.*

135. Gould, "Utopian Side of the Indian Uprising."

136. Worsley, *The Trumpet Shall Sound,* p. 279.
137. Barkun, *Disaster and the Millennium,* p. 92.
138. Rigby, *Alternative Realities.*
139. Worsley, *The Trumpet Shall Sound,* p. 279.
140. Vilfredo Pareto, *The Mind and Society* (New York: Harcourt Brace, 1935).
141. Quoted in Knox, *Enthusiasm,* p. 490.
142. Knox, *Enthusiasm,* pp. 449–54.
143. Gewehr, *The Great Awakening in Virginia,* p. 13.
144. McLoughlin, *Revivals, Awakenings and Reform.*
145. Euclides da Cunha, *Rebellion in the Backlands* (Chicago: University of Chicago Press, 1944), p. 137.
146. Capp, *The Fifth Monarchy Men,* p. 237.
147. Burridge, *New Heaven New Earth,* p. 34.
148. E. Franklin Frazier, *Race and Culture Contacts in the Modern World* (New York: Alfred A. Knopf, 1957), pp. 191–202.
149. Sundkler, *Bantu Prophets,* p. 61.
150. Weisberger, *They Gathered at the River,* p. 31.
151. Knox, *Enthusiasm,* p. 460.
152. Lofland, *Doomsday Cult,* p. 347.
153. Morton, *The World of the Ranters,* pp. 110, 111.
154. Gewehr, *The Great Awakening in Virginia,* p. 78.
155. Kurt Wolff, *The Sociology of Georg Simmel* (Glencoe, Ill.: Free Press, 1950), pp. 345–376.
156. Wuthnow, *Experimentation in American Religion;* Robert Wuthnow, "The New Religions in Social Context," in Glock and Bellah, *The New Religious Consciousness,* pp. 267–93.
157. For a description of some sources of the tolerance for nonconformity in San Francisco, see Howard S. Becker and Irving L. Horowitz, "The Culture of Civility," *Trans-action* 7 (April 1970): 12–19.
158. Wuthnow, "The New Religions in Social Context," pp. 270, 271.
159. Ibid., p. 271.
160. Wuthnow, *Experimentation in American Religion,* p. 101.
161. Cited in Musgrove, *Ecstasy and Holiness,* pp. 97, 98.
162. Weisberger, *They Gathered at the River,* pp. 13, 14; Cross, *The Burned-over District,* pp. 252–54.
163. David B. Barrett, *Schism and Renewal in Africa* (Nairobi: Oxford University Press, 1968), p. 78.
164. Musgrove, *Ecstasy and Holiness,* pp. 84–100. The following distinction

can also be related to Vesey's distinction between "anarchist" and "mystical" types of communes in the United States (Vesey, *The Communal Experience).*

165. Vittorio Lantaneri, *The Religions of the Oppressed: A Study of Modern Messianic Cults* (New York; Mentor, 1965).

166. Cohn, *Pursuit of the Millennium,* pp. 61–70.

167. Williams, *The Radical Reformation,* pp. 64–84.

168. Rosen, "Psychic Epidemics," p. 217. On the lack of sympathy for the Kentucky revival among "members of society," see Boles, *The Great Revival,* p. 58.

169. Hadley Cantril, *The Psychology of Social Movements* (New York: John Wiley, 1941), pp. 123–43.

170. Richardson, "People's Temple and Jonestown."

171. La Barre, *They Shall Take Up Serpents.*

172. Da Cunha, *Rebellion in the Backlands,* p. 138.

173. Rosen, "Psychic Epidemics," p. 197.

174. Ibid., p. 217.

175. Liston Pope, *Millhands and Preachers,* (New Haven: Yale University Press, 1942), p. 89.

176. Burridge, *New Heaven New Earth,* p. 35.

177. Sundkler, *Bantu Prophets,* pp. 290, 291.

178. Pope, *Millhands and Preachers,* pp. 136, 137.

179. Fuchs, *Rebellious Prophets,* p. 288.

180. Capp, *The Fifth Monarchy Men.*

181. Knox, *Enthusiasm,* pp. 551, 552.

182. Roy Wallis, "The Aetherius Society: A Case Study in the Formation of a Mystagogic Congregation," in Roy Wallis, ed., *Sectarianism* (New York: Wiley, 1975), p. 29.

183. James D. Hunter, "The New Class and the Young Evangelicals," *Review of Religious Research* 22 (1980): 155–69. See also Colin Campbell, "The Secret Religion of the Educated Classes," *Sociological Analysis* 39 (1978): 146–56.

184. Johnson, *A Shopkeeper's Millennium.*

185. David E. Harrell, *All Things Are Possible: The Healing And Charismatic Revivals in Modern America* (Bloomington: University of Indiana Press, 1975), pp. 146–49.

186. Cohn, *Pursuit of the Millennium,* pp. 89, 90.

187. On the age composition of those involved in new religion groups in the Bay Area, see Wuthnow, "The New Religions in Social Context," pp. 285–91.

188. D. Lawrence Wieder and Don H. Zimmerman, "Generational Experience and the Development of Freak Culture," *Journal of Social Issues* 30 (1974): 143.

189. Talmon, *Political Messianism,* p. 86.

190. Bestor, *Backwoods Utopias,* p. 163.

191. Ibid., p. 176.

192. Vesey, *The Communal Experience,* p. 110.

193. Ibid, p. 124.

194. Ibid, p. 196.

195. Flacks, *Youth and Social Change.*

196. Vesey, *The Communal Experience,* pp. 37–41; Feuer, *The Conflict of Generations,* pp. 389, 390, 525, 526.

197. Kenneth Kenniston, *Youth and Dissent* (New York: Harcourt Brace Jovanovich, 1971), p. 341.

198. McFarland, *Mugwumps, Morals and Politics,* pp. 11–34. As a near-contemporary of the Mugwumps, Walter Weyl, said, "once wealth is sanctified by hoary age . . . it tends to turn quite naturally against new and evil ways of wealth getting, the expedients of social climbers." Quoted in Hofstadter, *The Age of Reform,* p. 146.

199. Hofstadter, *The Age of Reform,* p. 131.

200. Quoted in ibid., p. 132.

201. Ibid., pp. 148–64.

202. Ibid., p. 219.

203. Talmon, *Political Messianism,* p. 30.

204. Armytage, *Heavens Below,* p. 225.

205. Ibid., p. 254.

206. Lawrence Goodwyn, *Democratic Promise: The Populist Moment in America* (New York: Oxford University Press, 1976), pp. 194, 195.

207. Goodwyn, *Democratic Promise,* p. 52.

208. On the largely unsuccessful attempt to forge an alliance of white and black populists, see Goodwyn, *Democratic Promise,* chap. 10.

209. Wallace, "Revitalization Movements," p. 201.

210. H. Richard Niebuhr, *The Social Sources of Denominationalism* (New York: Holt, Rinehart, 1954); Bryan R. Wilson, "An Analysis of Sect Development," *American Sociological Review* 24 (1959), 3–15; John A. Coleman, "Church-Sect Typology and Organizational Precariousness," *Sociological Analysis* 29 (1969): 55–66.

211. Robert H. Lauer, "Social Movements: An Interactionist Analysis," *Sociological Quarterly* 13 (1972): 315–28.

212. Roy Wallis, "Societal Reaction to Scientology," in Wallis, *Sectarianism,* pp. 86–116.

213. Roy Wallis, "The Cult and Its Transformation," in Wallis, *Sectarianism*, pp. 35–49.
214. Wallace, "Revitalization Movements," p. 268.
215. Kurt W. Back, *Beyond Words: The Story of Sensitivity Training and the Encounter Movement* (New York: Russell Sage, 1972), pp. 6–9.
216. Burridge, *New Heaven New Earth*, p. 111.
217. Worsley, *The Trumpet Shall Sound*, pp. 78, 79.
218. Roy Wallis, *The Road to Total Freedom: A Sociological Analysis of Scientology* (New York: Columbia University Press, 1977), p. 76.
219. Gerlach and Hine, *People, Power, Change*, chap. 3.
220. Barrett, *Schism and Renewal in Africa*, p. 276.
221. Wallis, "The Cult and Its Transformation," p. 41.
222. Lofland, *Doomsday Cult;* T. Taylor Buckner, "The Flying Saucerians: An Open Door Cult," in Marcello Truzzi, ed., *Sociology and Everyday Life* (Englewood Cliffs N. J.: Prentice-Hall, 1968), pp. 223–30.
223. Burridge, *New Heaven New Earth*, pp. 16, 17.
224. Lantenari, *Religions of the Oppressed*, pp. 115–20.
225. Lauer, "Social Movements."
226. Wallis, *Road to Total Freedom*, pp. 71–73.
227. Morton, *World of the Ranters*.
228. Knox, *Enthusiasm*, pp. 487–89.
229. Hofstadter, *The Age of Reform*, pp. 246, 247.
230. Vesey, *The Communal Experience*, pp. 178–203.
231. Kanter, *Commitment and Conformity*.
232. Wallis, *Sectarianism*.
233. Boyer, *Urban Masses and Moral Order*.
234. Knox, *Enthusiasm*, p. 448.
235. Kanter, *Commitment and Conformity*, pp. 9–18.
236. Thomas Pilarzyk, "Origin, Development and Decline of a Youth Culture Religion: An Application of Sectarianization Theory," *Review of Religious Research* 20 (1978): 23–42.
237. Wallis, *The Road to Total Freedom*, chap. 3.
238. James Beckford, "Two Contrasting Types of Sectarian Organization," in Wallis, *Sectarianism*, pp. 70–85.
239. Ibid., p. 77.
240. Vesey, *The Communal Experience*, pp. 185–90.
241. Robbins, Anthony, and Richardson, "Theory and Research in Today's New Religions."
242. William S. Bainbridge and Rodney Stark, "Scientology: To Be Perfectly Clear," *Sociological Analysis* 41 (1980): 128–36.

243. While Jonestown was "not a prison camp," it was certainly difficult for persons to enter or leave the compound. Richardson, "People's Temple and Jonestown."

244. Johnson, "Dilemmas of Religious Leadership," p. 318.

245. Wallis, *Road to Total Freedom.*

246. Lauer, "Social Movements."

247. Richard Ofshe, "The Social Development of the Synanon Cult: The Managerial Strategy of Organizational Transformation," *Sociological Analysis* 41 (1980): 109-27.

248. Howard Becker, "Notes on the Concept of Commitment," *American Journal of Sociology* 66 (1960): 32-40.

249. Karen H. Stephan and G. Edward Stephan, "Religion and the Survival of Utopian Communities," *Journal for the Scientific Study of Religion* 12 (1973): 89-100.

250. Lofland, *Doomsday Cult;* J. L. Simmons, "On Maintaining Deviant Belief Systems: A Case Study," *Social Problems* 11 (1964): 250-56.

251. Meredith McGuire, "Testimony as a Commitment Mechanism in Catholic Pentecostal Groups," *Journal for the Scientific Study of Religion* 16 (1977): 165-68.

252. Virginia H. Hine, "Bridge Burners: Commitment and Participation in a Religious Movement," *Sociological Analysis* 31 (1970): 61-66.

253. Donald L. Barrett and Karai Njama, *Mau Mau from Within* (London: Monthly Review Press, 1966).

254. David G. Bromley and Anson D. Shupe, "Financing the New Religions" *Journal for the Scientific Study of Religion* 19 (1980): 227-39.

255. Weber, "The Sociology of Charismatic Authority," pp. 248-50.

256. John M. Whitworth, "Communitarian Groups and the World," in Wallis, *Sectarianism,* p. 123.

257. Ibid., pp. 126, 127. See also the discussion of "communes for mutual support" in Rigby, *Alternative Realities,* pp. 115-19.

258. B. E. Aguirre and Jon P. Alston, "Organizational Change and Religious Commitment: Jehovah's Witnesses and Seventh-Day Adventists in Cuba, 1938-1965," *Pacific Sociological Review* 23 (1980): 171-98.

259. Hank Johnston, "The Marketed Social Movement: A Case Study of the Rapid Growth of TM," *Pacific Sociological Review* 23 (1980): 333-54.

260. Max Weber, "The Protestant Sects and the Spirit of Capitalism," in Gerth and Mills, *From Max Weber,* pp. 305.

261. Roger O'Toole, "Sectarianism in Politics," in Wallis, *Sectarianism,* pp. 162-89.

262. Frederick R. Lynch, "'Occult Establishment' or 'Deviant Religion'?: The Rise and Fall of a Modern Church of Magic," *Journal for the Scientific Study of Religion* 18 (1979): 281-98.

263. Will Herberg, *Protestant-Catholic-Jew* (Garden City, N.Y.: Doubleday, 1955). See also Martin Marty, "The Occult Establishment," *Sociological Review* 39 (1970): 212–30.

264. Randall H. Alfred, "The Church of Satan," in Glock and Bellah, *The New Religious Consciousness*, pp. 180–202; Edward J. Moody, "Urban Witches," in Jeffrey E. Nash and James P. Spradley, eds., *Sociology: A Descriptive Approach* (Chicago: Rand McNally, 1976), pp. 442–53; William S. Bainbridge, *Satan's Power: A Deviant Psychotherapy Cult* (Berkeley: University of California Press, 1978).

265. Marcello Truzzi, "The Occult Revival as Popular Culture: Some Random Observations on the Old and the Nouveau Witch," *Sociological Quarterly* 13 (1972): 16–36.

266. Simmel, "The Sociology of Sociability."

267. Weber, "Sociology of Charismatic Authority."

268. Festinger et al., *When Prophecy Fails*.

269. Ibid., pp. 12–22.

270. Burridge, *New Heaven New Earth*

271. Festinger et al., *When Prophecy Fails*.

272. Beckford, "Two Contrasting Types of Sectarian Organizations."

273. See the discussion of such tension in the "Red Dawn" commune in Britain in Abrams and McCulloch, *Communes, Sociology and Society*, pp. 72–85.

274. Cohn, *Europe's Inner Demons*.

275. Stanley Cohen, *Folk Devils and Moral Panics* (London: MacGibbon and Kee, 1972).

276. Morton, *World of the Ranters*, chap. 4.

277. Lauer, "Social Movements."

278. Wallis, "The Societal Response to Scientology."

279. *New York Times*, 19 April 1980, p. 8.

280. For an interpretation of political sectarianism in these terms, see O'Toole, "Sectarianism in Politics."

281. Peter Berger, *Facing Up to Modernity* (New York: Basic Books, 1977).

282. Frederick Bird, "Charisma and Ritual in New Religious Movements," in Needleman and Baker, *Understanding the New Religions*, pp. 173–89.

283. Wilson, *Contemporary Transformations of Religion*, p. 96.

284. Bryan Wilson, *The Noble Savage: The Primitive Origins of Charisma* (Berkeley: University of California Press, 1975), p. 125.

285. Wuthnow, *Experimentalism in American Religion*, chap. 6.

286. Gould, "The Utopian Side of the Indian Uprising."

287. Eugene P. Boardman, "Military Aspects of the Taiping Rebellion (1851-64)," in Thrupp, *Millennial Dreams in Action*, pp. 70–79.

288. Barnett and Njama, *Mau Mau from Within.*

289. McLoughlin, *Revivals, Awakenings and Reform,* pp. 138-40; John L. Hammond, *The Politics of Benevolence: Revival Religion and American Voting Behavior* (Norwood, N.J.: Ablex, 1979).

290. David Donald, *Lincoln Reconsidered: Essays on the Civil War Era* (New York: Alfred A. Knopf, 1956), pp. 19-36.

291. Gould, *The Progressive Era.*

292. Richard Hofstadter, "What Happened to the Antitrust Movement?," in Richard Hofstadter, *The Paranoid Style in American Politics and Other Essays* (New York: Alfred A. Knopf, 1966), pp. 188-237.

293. Barbara Hargrove, "Church Student Ministries and the New Consciousness," in Glock and Bellah, *The New Religious Consciousness,* pp. 205-26.

294. James Wolfe, "Three Congregations," in Glock and Bellah, *The New Religious Consciousness,* pp. 227-44.

295. Weigart and Weigart, "An Emerging Faith Style."

296. McLouglin, *Revivals, Awakenings and Reform,* p. 147.

297. Boles, *The Great Revival,* pp. 183-203.

298. Pope, *Millhands and Preachers.*

299. Wilson, *Contemporary Transformations of Religion,* pp. 57-60.

300. Boyer, *Urban Masses and Moral Control.*

301. Sandra S. Sizer, *Gospel Hymns and Social Religion: The Rhetoric of Nineteenth-Century Revivalism* (Philadelphia: Temple University Press, 1978); Sandra S. Sizer, "Politics and Apolitical Religion: the Great Urban Revivals of the Late Nineteenth Century," *Church History* 48 (1979): 81-98.

302. Armand L. Mauss and Donald W. Petersen, "The Cross and the Commune: An Interpretation of the Jesus People," in Charles Y. Glock, ed., *Religion in Sociological Perspective* (Belmont, Cal.: Wadsworth, 1973); Thomas Robbins, Dick Anthony, and Thomas Curtis, "Youth Culture and Religious Movements: Evaluating the Integrative Hypothesis," *Sociological Quarterly* 16 (1975): 48-64.

303. Wieder and Zimmerman, "Generational Experience and the Development of Freak Culture."

304. In one description of "postmovement" religious groups of the 1970s, it is observed that they "advocated self-discipline, self-sacrifice, hard work, systematic and orderly living, and renunciation of the pleasures of the flesh." Daniel A. Foss and Ralph W. Larkin, "The Roar of the Lemming: Youth, Postmovement Groups, and the Life Construction Crisis," *Sociological Inquiry* 49 (1979): 264-85.

305. Robert L. Adams and Robert J. Fox, "Mainlining Jesus: The New Trip," *Society* 9 (February 1972): 50-56.

Chapter 6

Conclusions

IN THIS CHAPTER we attempt to develop some conclusions about the four dimensions of sociological concern in the study of collective behavior. Obviously the reference here is to the conclusions of one very wide-ranging and tentative study of the subject. Not only are there many questions in this field that have as yet no convincing answers; a major problem has been that the relevant questions have often not been asked. The questions proposed by this work may be a start on developing some relevant ones. In the following brief comments, we observe several answers that tend to dominate in each area of analysis and, when different answers seem both contradictory and fruitful, try to suggest some way of integrating them.

BACKGROUND

Like all human behavior, collective behavior occurs in terms of what Parsons calls a "situation," which, he says, is "analyzable into two elements: those over which the actor has no control, that which he cannot alter, or prevent from being altered, in conformity with his end, and those over which he has such control. The former may be termed the "conditions" of action, the latter the "means.""[1] The various background factors discussed in this book will likewise be "analyzable" as either conditions or means of collective behaviorial "action."

There seems to be an interesting tendency among students of collective behavior to take an either/or position about the background or causes of this kind of behavior. *Either* the attempt is made to define episode-generating conditions (e.g, relative deprivation, mass society), *or* it is argued that such conditional factors cannot explain variability in collective behavior and that one must avoid conditional in favor of "means" kinds of explanations.[2] Examination of the "background" sections on protest, persecutions, and renewals in this book will reveal a combination of conditions and means in collective behavior background; to ignore either factor is to ignore a vital aspect of the "situation" in which this kind of human behavior occurs.

CONDITIONS

Such terms as *deprivation, stress, threat,* and *crisis,* which appear throughout this study, are a reflection of the general fact that collective behavior appears under conditions of social dislocation. Durkheim's concept anomie will cover most such conditions, provided we are willing to apply it in both the ways he uses the term in his own work.

In *The Division of Labor in Society*, Durkheim was attempting to demonstrate the effect of occupational specialization in generating social solidarity.[3] He must admit, however, that there are some "abnormal" social conditions in which the division of labor produces not solidarity but social conflict. One of these abnormal forms he calls the anomic division of labor: a condition in which there are *no* clear normative guides to the interaction of, for example, workers and managers.[4] In this sense, *anomie* justifies its frequent English translation as *normlessness,* a situation of ambiguity or uncertainty about appropriate human behavior. This condition Durkheim sees as generated by rapid social change, in the course of which people have not had time to develop new social norms to govern novel social situations.

Anomie of this type is in the background of many collective behavioral episodes. With the frightening and uncertain events in Europe in 1938, it was quite understandable if "War of the Worlds" listeners felt that "anything can happen." When black Americans were being brutalized by the everyday condition of ghetto life, it must have seemed that there was no moral restraint against *any* kind of protest, as long as it was effective. When so many blacks in 1917 or 1943 were forgetting their "place" and so many "radicals" in 1919 were making inflammatory statements, white Americans experienced their social conditions as very insecure or threatening. The unsettled social conditions on the American frontier at the time of the religious awakenings and the great uncertainty introduced into native societies by European colonizers are further examples. In this view, collective behavior is basically a response to massive social change. Far from being a pathological manifestation of social disorganization in the old-fashioned view, collective behavior represents human attempts—however misguided they may be—to generate elements of order in disorganized situations.

Other elements of collective behavior-generating background emphasize the different conception of anomie developed in Durkheim's *Suicide*.[5] In this work, anomic suicide, unlike egoistic and altruistic suicides, is not related to social pathologies in normative integration. Rather, the lack of social regulation of people's aspirations or ambitions is the characteristic of anomie as now defined. High suicide rates in times of extreme prosperity are one example of anomic suicides; also, in an infrequently cited section on "conjugal anomie," Durkheim proposes to explain the high suicide rates of divorced persons in the same way. Divorced persons are perhaps those with unrealistic expectations of conjugal bliss; similarly, in boom economic periods people develop a "sky's the limit" mood of recognizing no limits on personal ambition.

Both the "relative deprivation" discussion in Chapter 3 and the discussion in Chapter 5 of native millenarianism arising from contacts with Europeans suggest this source of social discontent. The cargo cultist, for example, who develops a taste for European consumer goods but sees natives consistently denied these goods is a perfect example of this second meaning of anomie: a discrepancy between aspiration and expectation for achievement. So too was apparently the ghetto black of the 1960s, caught between the halfway measures being undertaken for black improvement and the rapidly escalated expectations generated by the civil rights movement.

The discussion of *disaster* background is admittedly not well integrated with these other background discussions, but it may nevertheless offer a needed corrective to these anomie explanations. The emphasis there is on "adjustment to hazard," the varied reasons why people avoid adequate protection from the destructiveness of potential disaster. Related factors could be noted with other types: conditions that suggest abnormal passivity or lack of activity rather than the hyperactivity suggested in much of the anomie imagery.[6] We noted, for example, that the sheer *boredom* of everyday life in frontier areas may make the residents susceptible to revivals as "entertainment"; that the *invisibility* of potentially protesting minorities to people in positions of power may generate protests to call attention to themselves. Assuming the absence of anomic conditions, would there be protest in utopias, rebels in Eden? Probably so, for the "hell" of doing something beyond the established routine, if for no other reason.

What is being suggested, in short, is that if collective behavior, by definition, involves *unusual* behavior, it should reflect conditions that violate *usual* social conditions. Social systems seem to operate *routinely* by a combination of forces that generate both excitement and the social regulation of extreme forms of excitement. There seems to be a "normal" balance between those forces that keep people "alive" at the lower level of activity but that prevents them going "off the wall" at the upper limit. Those social conditions that fall below the lower threshold (e.g., excessive boredom or indifference to dangers) or above the higher threshold (e.g., obsessive fear of an enemy, anger at some authority) will generate tendencies toward "unusual" behavior. The point should not, but probably does, need explicit statement that, in characterizing collective behavior as a response to unusual or abnormal conditions, we make no value judgments like the "pathological" view of collective behavior as undesirable human behavior. Explanations of behavior in terms of system *imbalance* take on this connotation only if one makes the judgment that "balance" is best.

MEANS

In recent years something like a "cult" of social scientists has developed around the proposition that we must develop the "means" side of explanation of collective behavioral episodes. Frequently referred to as the "resource mobilization" view of social movements, this approach addresses itself to the elements that movement adherents can "manipulate" in their situations.[7] Likewise this book has stressed the importance for a collective behavior episode of such necessary "resources" as an ideology to support or legitimate the action in question, a set of social organizations predisposed to engage in a line of action, the availability of prophets and organizers to articulate the ideology and coordinate the action.

While insisting that adequate attention must be given to the availability of such means of collective behavior action, the present work has certainly not urged the abandonment of "conditions" variables such as relative deprivation. Rather than adopting the either/or stance, it might be more appropriate to suggest the *limitation* of conditions explanations by citing Cloward's criticism of the anomie theory of deviance.[8] His view is that this theory makes the apparent assumption that, in explaining the *motivation* for deviance, we have adequately explained deviance itself. In fact, as Cloward argues, to understand deviance we must know the structure of illegitimate *opportunities*: in the words of our present analysis, the means that the would-be deviant commands or lacks to carry out the deviant motives. In the same way, as we have suggested many times in this book, deprivation, threat, cultural disorientation, and so on are perhaps necessary but certainly not sufficent factors in the outbreak of collective behavior. To the would-be organizer of a collective behavior episode, a structure of supporting organizations and a charismatic leader may be resources that are as vital as the would-be bank robber's possession of a gun and a floor plan of the bank. Our only argument with the adherents of the "resource mobilization" approach is to note that collective behavior requires motivation *as well as* resources, just as the gun and the floor plan of the bank cannot produce a bank robbery without the human actor who is so motivated to use these resources.

PARTICIPATION

The relationship between background and participation analysis is an especially close one. In fact, many of our inferences about the causation of collective behavior (the question of background) are based on evidence (for example), that millennarians tend to be the socially "oppressed," supporting the inference that "oppression" is a major cause of millennarianism.

The conditions/means discussion of background will thus translate directly into participation explanation. We take the cue from Merton's essay on the relationship between anomie and deviance.[9] He observes that, if anomie (in the sense of aspiration/achievement discrepancy) is a general condition in some societies (e.g., the United States), the force of the resultant "pressure" toward deviance falls with unequal weight upon people (e.g., lower-class people) who are deprived of *legitimate* opportunities to achieve. This is, of course, a "means" explanation of deviance participation. Likewise, our discussion, for example, of protest as the "politics of the powerless" and renewals as the "religions of the oppressed" emphasizes the view that collective behavior is often the behavior of people lacking favorable standing in the hierarchies of power in established social orders. However, this explanation does not account for the greater participation of higher-class persons in such episodes as disaster rescue, reporting other people's damages in pseudo disasters, the youth revolt, segments of the anticommunist persecutions, and the reformist type of renewal episode. We can deal with such facts in at least two ways.

First, we may reiterate Cloward's point on illegitimate opportunity structures. Collective behavior, like deviant behavior, is not simply the behavior of people deprived of ordinary means of expression of the special interests of their kind of people. Also like deviant behavior, collective behavior may have its own rewards in terms of anticipated outcomes, and those with more "resources" to attain these rewards are more likely to indulge in this behavior. Just as middle-class people are better situated to engage in "white-collar crime," the same people may have command of more of the means of collective behavioral action: membership in predisposed organizations, awareness of legitimating ideologies, adequate funds to support their "causes," and so on.

Second, focusing on conditions rather than means explanations, we may recognize that such variables as "power" and "oppression," as subjectively experienced, may be relative to the aspirations of the people who define their own conditions in these terms. While an "objective" observer might have difficulty equating the "oppression" of an unemployed black man with the "oppression" of a white-collar worker who is "sick and tired" of seeing his bureaucratic rivals promoted ahead of himself, the behavioral consequences of these "objectively" different oppressions may be quite similar. At any rate, given the relativity of deprivation to aspirations (and also the possibility of a "fraternal" deprivation felt on behalf of *others*), we should not be too surprised to find that collective behavior is by no means the monopoly of the downtrodden of the world.

PROCESS

Our studies of the process of various types of collective behavior have encountered several recurring views of the appropriate ways of studying this process. Three such approaches may be reviewed:

1. A "natural history" approach, which attempts to delineate the typical "stages" of a collective behavioral episode. Several such efforts to define collective behavioral stages have been examined as perhaps useful in bringing some order to the seeming chaos of events associated with episodes. The riot stages of the Lemberg Center or the sect-to-denomination theory (especially with a *cult* phase added) are perhaps excellent clotheslines on which to hang some tentative conclusions about "phases" in collective behavior episodes.

2. A "dialectic" approach that notes the self-limiting tendency of many collective behavior episodes: rioters elicit the activities of counterrioters, persecutors the opposition of powerful social forces when their attacks escalate to a certain level, and so forth.

3. An "interactionist" approach, which may deny the existence of preordained stages or of self-limiting tendencies and which sees the course of development of a collective behavior episode as *contingent* on whether certain factors favorable to that development happen to appear. Several explanations of this sort, such as studies of Ron Hubbard's Scientology movement or Timothy Leary's drug-use cult, emphasize variable "societal reactions" as the interactive factor that may either "amplify" or "deamplify" the intensity of a collective behavioral episode.

A full-fledged sociological perspective on collective behavior process should be able to accommodate all three of these insightful viewpoints. The natural history view contributes an important insight about human behavioral process: that people tend to program their behaviors in terms of what they see as a "natural" sequence of behaviors: it is natural for authorities to attempt to negotiate a nonviolent settlement with protesters before instituting a military siege against them, for people in disaster areas to engage in rescue effort in their immediate environments before extending this activity to the wider community, and so on. The major caution that should perhaps be mentioned in connection with this approach is the obvious point that what is "natural" behavior in one cultural context may be quite unnatural in another. Our studies of collective behavior still seem to be rather Western-culture centered, despite the useful contributions of anthropologists and other students of non-Western societies. More cross-cultural studies are needed to verify the universality of these "natural" stages, or else to make such modifications as these studies might suggest.

The dialectic view captures the insight that many human behavioral events involve sharp ambivalence among their participants. The mental reservations with which people enter marriages, business partnerships, or public office are probably matched in people's two-mindedness about their involvement in protests, persecutions, and so on—especially when, as so often happens, this participation involves violation of some important values held by these participants. We have seen, for example, that large majorities of Americans opposed protest demonstrations in the 1960s when these involved any degree of militancy. While protesters themselves may have had these values neutralized by protest ideologies in the heat of the protest episode, many must have awakened on the "morning after" to the pangs of conscience that these antiprotest values within themselves may have engendered. Perhaps when we are dealing with *unusual* behavior, we are entitled to the presumption, subject to change with available evidence, that this behavior will *not* continue far into the future.

Finally, the interactionist view best comes to grips with the insight that there is much that is contingent or accidental in human events. Certainly there is a "tragic" insight into human experience that emphasizes the mindless irrationality of the fates that befall individuals. Abandoning the assumption of inherent tendencies toward change of either the stage or dialectic variety, the interactionist attempts only to indicate that certain developments are more likely when favoring conditions occur.

Combinations of these three perspectives in the study of collective behavior process would perhaps move us toward an ideal theory of that process. Let us, by all means, search for any usable set of natural sequences through which collective behavioral episodes tend to proceed—for example, the phase 1, 2, and 3 stages of renewal defined in Chapter 5. It may well be, however, as the well-known sect-to-denomination theory suggests, that dialectic processes operate at each given stage and provide the dynamic for movement to the succeeding stage; the "contradiction," for example, in trying to sustain a social movement at the sectarian level generates the drive toward a denominational form. Finally, it may be noted that even when we are able to identify a set of stages that succeed one another in a dialectic process, we may still observe that there are many contingencies that influence at least the speed with which the stages are traversed, or that may even arrest or reverse the "natural" sequence. We have noted at many points that the response of social control agents such as police to collective behavior episodes seems to be such a contingency that may lead to one or another consequence in the collective behavioral process. Some protests, for example, escalate into all-out warfare against established authority because protesters elicit police brutality with its "radicalizing" effects on participants. It is always possible, of course, to treat police responses and other contingencies as occuring in a deterministic framework, perhaps as predictable behaviors taking place in a framework of "natural" stages. One's judgment on what variables are determined and determining in a situation is a function of one's perspective. The suggestion here is that if one chooses to emphasize that the collective behavior process follows a set of fixed stages, one may consider the interactionist's contingent factors as determining forces that introduce variations in the outcomes of these supposedly determined processes.

CONSEQUENCES

We consider finally the vital question of the social effects of collective behavior episodes. Two different issues concerning these effects seem to emerge from our discussion of the consequences of various types of collective behavior episodes.

First is the question of the effects of an outbreak of a type of collective behavior in terms of the likelihood of later repetitions of similar episodes. On the one hand, there are episodes that seem to have an "immunizing" effect, discouraging further episodes of the same sort: for instance, victims of a pseudo disaster are reluctant to be "fooled" again, and once a major riot has occurred in a city or a prison, such riots tend not to occur again in the same place. On the other hand, some episodes help to generate a "tradition" of that kind of behavior that encourages future repetitions: current counterculturalists drawing inspiration from a long tradition of countercultural thought and action, the "red scare" of 1919–20 providing a model for the later Mc-

Carthy era of how to subvert democracy in spirit without a formal violation. A third possibility, perhaps really an extension of the first, is that an outbreak of a particular sort may have as a consequence that it provides *background* for another type of collective behavior. We have noted, for example, that the consequences of disaster represent a background condition for renewal movements, that renewal movements spawn "heresies" that add to the insecurity in the background of persecutions which may, indeed, select just such renewal heretics as their victims.

There seems at this point to be no coherent theory from which we could deduce the likelihood of a given outbreak having one or another of these consequences. We have offered several ad hoc explanations for particular problems. For example, in explaining why the antiradical persecution of 1919–20 was followed by similar outbreaks for the next two decades while the violent antiblack race riots of the same era did not recur very frequently in this period, we pointed to the importance of militant organizations (e.g., the NAACP) supporting potential racial victims but *not* potential victims of antiradical persecutions. In explaining why disasters did *not* spawn millennarian renewals during the Irish potato famine, we pointed to the power of the Church in being able to furnish orthodox rationalizations for suffering. While these "explanations" of variability in outbreak outcomes may be more or less satisfactory for the problem at hand, the use of explanations at such low levels of abstraction seems to condemn us to resort to mental ingenuity in finding ad hoc answers to an infinite number of questions. A general theory of those forces productive of social change is clearly called for at this point, a task which this book has obviously not undertaken. Perhaps it will provide some material to aid in the inductive process by which such a theory would have to be developed.

A second issue concerns the consequences of episodes in terms of encouraging or discouraging broad social change—the familiar conservative-versus-progressive argument about the effects of an outbreak. We have again offered numerous examples of both such outcomes, especially in the discussion of renewal episodes. Also considered there is the prominent view that collective behavior is basically inconsequential one way or another in maintaining or attacking the social status quo. Obviously we are in the same need mentioned above of a general theory to explain the varied outcomes of different episodes. One generalization that seems to fit many cases is that many episodes seem to have a short-run consequence of a progressive nature: intensive efforts to address the grievances of protesters in the aftermath of a riot, and a period of enlightenment or relative tolerance in an immediate revulsion against the "excesses" of a witch hunt or a red scare. Over the longer term, the view of an outbreak as inconsequential for social change seems closer to the truth in many cases. Conditions on college campuses a few years after dramatic protests were very like they had been before the protests, and black ghettos were not radically altered after riots despite immediate intense efforts in that direction, to cite just two examples. In view of this apparent fact, Jefferson's statement about revolution—that one is needed every twenty years—might be applied to outbreaks by suggesting that, for these to have longer-range effects, we would need frequent repetitions of protests, renewals, and so on. The rather remarkable resistance of most social systems to radical and permanent change should be an ingredient in a "general theory" of social change.

The discerning reader will have discerned by now the general style of these conclusions. The tone is clearly eclectic, asking that we adopt insights from perspectives whose adherents have often engaged in polemic controversy. A scientific field advances by controversy, as adherents of different theoretical schools develop their alternative explanations and debate who has offered the "best" explanations. This contest conception of scientific perspectives may be justified on grounds similar to those used to justify the "advocacy" system in criminal justice procedures with prosecutors and defense attorneys making their "cases" in ways that clearly favor the side that each is advocating. A treatise on collective behavior from a functionalist or conflict or symbolic interactionist perspective would similarly be an exercise in social scientific advocacy. This book, however, is fundamentally a book for *students* (both professional and nonprofessional) of collective behavior. As students of this field we, like judge or jury in a criminal case, must reach our "verdicts" (i.e., our understanding of collective behavior) by examining the cases presented to us by these various theoretical advocates as well as by our own observations of the "evidence." As a fellow student of the reader, the author has tried to examine the evidence with the open mind that the judge instructs a jury to exercise. As a fellow human being, the author is subject to the biases of perception and judgment associated with his background, education, and past and present social situations. For all the flaws of the judicial system, justice is *sometimes* rendered in courtrooms, and *some* books contribute to a clearer understanding of a subject. That was the sole aim of this book.

Notes

1. Talcott Parsons, *The Structure of Social Action* (New York: McGraw-Hill, 1937), p. 44.
2. This is an arguable feature of the following: Clark McPhail, "Civil Disorder Participation: A Critical Examination of Recent Research," *American Sociological Review* 36 (1971): 1058–71, and Joe R. Feagin and Harlan Hahn, *Ghetto Revolts: The Politics of Violence in American Cities* (New York: Macmillan, 1973).
3. Émile Durkheim, *On the Division of Labor in Society*, trans. George Simpson (New York: Macmillan, 1933).
4. Durkheim, *Division of Labor in Society*, pp. 353–73.
5. Émile Durkheim, *Suicide*, trans. John A. Spaulding and George Simpson (Glencoe, Ill.: Free Press, 1951).
6. Herbert Blumer, "Collective Behavior," in A. M. Lee, ed., *New Outline of the Principles of Sociology* (New York: Barnes & Noble, 1946).
7. John McCarthy and Mayer N. Zald, "Resource Mobilization in Social Movement Organizations: A Partial Theory," *American Journal of Sociology* 82 (1977): 1212–39; Charles Tilly, *From Mobilization to Revolution* (Boston: Addison-Wesley, 1978). For an excellent recent study in the resource mobilization vein, see David G. Bromley and Anson D. Shupe, Jr., "'*Moonies*' in America: Cult, Church, and Crusade" (Beverly Hills, Cal.: Sage Publications, 1979).
8. Richard A. Cloward and Lloyd B. Ohlin, *Delinquency and Opportunity: A Theory of Delinquent Gangs* (New York: Free Press of Glencoe, 1960).
9. Robert K. Merton, *Social Theory and Social Structure*, rev. ed. (Glencoe, Ill.: Free Press, 1956), pp. 139–57.

Selected Bibliography

BARKUN, MICHAEL, *Disaster and the Millennium* (New Haven: Yale University Press, 1974). Demonstrates connection between natural disasters and the development of renewal movements.

BARTON, ALLEN H., *Communities in Disaster* (Garden City, N.Y.: Doubleday, 1969). Emphasizes the difficulty of communities in responding efficiently to disaster conditions.

BLUMER, HERBERT, "Collective Behavior," in A. M. Lee (ed.), *New Outline of the Principles of Sociology* (New York: Barnes and Noble, 1946). A systematic statement of the nature of collective behavior and its various forms in the traditional definition of the field.

BOYER, PAUL, *Urban Masses and Moral Order in America, 1820–1920* (Cambridge: Harvard University Press, 1978). Demonstrates the motives of moral reformers and promoters of biblical study in helping to contain the chaos that urban masses were thought to represent.

BOYER, PAUL AND STEPHEN NISSENBAUM, *Salem Possessed: The Social Origins of Witchcraft* (Cambridge: Harvard University Press, 1974). Interprets Salem witch trials as resulting from pre-existing community tensions.

BROMLEY, DAVID G. AND ANSON D. SHUPE JR., *"Moonies" in America: Cult, Church and Crusade* (Beverly Hills, Ca.: Sage Publications, 1979). Factors in growth of the Unification Church; also a description of repressive action against the Church.

255

CANTRIL, HADLEY, *The Invasion from Mars* (Princeton: Princeton University Press, 1940). Social psychologist's interviews with people affected by the fictitious radio broadcast.

CAUTE, DAVID, *The Great Fear: The Anti-Communist Purge Under Truman and Eisenhower* (New York: Simon and Schuster, 1978). Explores the various political motivations for the range of prosecutions of "un-American" activity in the 1940s and 1950s.

COHN, NORMAN, *Europe's Inner Demons* (New York: Basic Books, 1975). Describes the changes in official and popular conceptions of witchcraft leading up to the witch trials of the 15th–17th centuries.

COHN, NORMAN, *The Pursuit of the Millennium: Revolutionary Millennarians and Mystical Anarchists of the Middle Ages* (New York: Oxford University Press, 1970). Wide-ranging study of millenarian social movements, including the crusades and the various forms of European Anabaptism.

COUCH, CARL J., "Collective Behavior: An Examination of Some Stereotypes," *Social Problems* 15 (1968): 310–23. A critical look at the heritage of "crowd" conceptions of collective behavior as inherited from LeBon.

ERIKSON, KAI T., *Everything in Its Path: Destruction of Community in the Buffalo Creek Flood* (New York: Simon and Schuster, 1976). Sociologist's study of the aftermath of a flood in a coal mining community in West Virginia.

EVANS, ROBERT R., *Readings in Collective Behavior* 2d ed. (Chicago: Rand McNally, 1975). Collection of articles, featuring "classic" statements and articles on protest form of collective behavior.

FEAGIN, JOE R. AND HARLAN HAHN, *Ghetto Revolts: The Politics of Violence in American Cities* (New York: Macmillan, 1973). Review of research on the ghetto riots of the 1960s.

GARROW, DAVID J., *Protest at Selma: Martin Luther King Jr. and the Voting Rights Act of 1965* (New Haven: Yale University Press, 1978). Studies the relationship between various black protest activities in the 1960s and the civil rights acts of the same period.

GLOCK, CHARLES Y. AND ROBERT N. BELLAH (eds.), *The New Religious Consciousness* (Berkeley: University of California Press, 1976). Collection of articles reporting studies of different new religious groups.

HEIRICH, MAX, *The Spiral of Conflict* (New York: Columbia University Press, 1971). The process of protest development and decline is emphasized in this study of the Berkeley campus.

HOFSTADTER, RICHARD, *The Age of Reform: From Bryan to FDR* (New York: Knopf, 1955). Essays on the various reform movements of the period 1890–1920.

HOFSTADTER, RICHARD, *The Paranoid Style in American Politics and Other Essays* (New York: Alfred A. Knopf, 1966). Essays on persecutory episodes in earlier American history and "right wing radicalism" in contemporary America.

KNOX, R. A., *Enthusiasm: A Chapter in the History of Religion* (London: Oxford University Press, 1931). Description of various European expressions of religious radicalism, especially in sixteenth and seventeenth century England.

LEVIN, MURRAY B., *Political Hysteria in America: The Democratic Capacity for Repression* (New York: Basic Books, 1971). Analysis of the "red scare" of 1919–20 and its after-effects in encouraging later anticommunist persecutions.

LIPSKY, MICHAEL, *Protest in City Politics: Rent Strikes, Housing and the Power of the Poor* (Chicago: Rand McNally, 1969). Describes the use of disruptive tactics by poor people's movements.

LOFLAND, JOHN, *Doomsday Cult: A Study of Conversion, Proselytization and Maintenance of Faith*, enl. ed. (New York: Irvington, 1977). Study of the Unification Church (Moon religion) from its American origins to the present.

MCLOUGHLIN, WILLIAM G., *Revivals, Awakenings and Reform: An Essay on Social Change in America, 1607–1977* (Chicago: University of Chicago Press, 1978). Studies four religious "awakenings" in America and the implications of each for broader social change.

MARX, GARY T., "Civil Disorder and the Agents of Social Control," *Journal of Social Issues* 26 (1970): 19–57. Showing how the response of police and other officials to civil disorder may contribute to the escalation of protest episodes.

MASON, HENRY L., *Mass Demonstrations Against Foreign Regimes* (New Orleans: Tulane University Press, 1966). Describes, among others, the anti-Nazi revolts in Holland during World War II, the Hungarian revolt in 1956.

MIDELFORT, E. C. ERIK, *Witch Hunting in Southwestern Germany 1562–1684* (Stanford: Stanford University Press, 1972). Studies the process of build-up in large scale witch persecutions in German towns and cities.

National Advisory Commission on Civil Disorders, *Report* (Washington, D.C.: U.S. Government Printing Office, 1968). The "Kerner report" on the street riots in American cities in 1967.

New York State Special Commission on Attica, *Official Report* (New York: Praeger, 1972). An account of conditions leading to the riot at Attica prison and the behavior of rioters and officials during the riot.

PUGH, MEREDITH D., *Collective Behavior: A Source Book* (St. Paul: West Publishing, 1980). Collection of articles, including many on disaster and pseudo-disaster.

ROSEN, GEORGE, "Psychic Epidemics in Europe and the United States," in George Rosen, *Madness in Society* (Chicago: University of Chicago Press, 1968). The psychological factors involved in such episodes as the "dancing mania" and frontier revivalism.

SEARS, DAVID O. AND JOHN B. MCCONAHAY, *The Politics of Violence: The New Urban Blacks and the Watts Riot* (Boston: Houghton Mifflin, 1973). Study of motives and behavior of rioters in a Los Angeles ghetto in 1965.

SKOLNICK, JEROME, *The Politics of Protest* (New York: Simon and Schuster, 1969). Study of the varieties of protest (student, antiwar, civil rights) prominent at the time in the United States.

SMELSER, NEIL J., *Theory of Collective Behavior* (New York: Free Press, 1962). The nature and types of collective behavior, formulated in the framework of Parsons' "social action" theory.

TAYLOR, JAMES B., LOUIS A. ZURCHER AND WILLIAM H. KEY, *Tornado: A Community Responds to Disaster* (Seattle: University of Washington Press, 1970). Study of Topeka, Kansas tornado in 1966.

VEYSEY, LAURENCE, *The Communal Experience: Anarchist and Mystical Counter-Cultures in America* (New York: Harper and Row, 1973). Two strands of the counter-cultural tradition as reflected in historical and contemporary American communes.

WALLIS, ROY (ed.), *Sectarianism* (New York: Wiley, 1975). Articles that demonstrate how Scientology and other radical religious groups have moved from a *cult* to a *sect* form.

WASKOW, ARTHUR I., *From Race Riot to Sit-In: 1919 and the 1960s* (Garden City, N.Y.: Doubleday, 1966). Deals mainly with the repressive race riots around World War I, their development and the public response to them.

WEISBERGER, BERNARD, *They Gathered at the River: The Story of the Great Revivalists and Their Impact upon Religion* (Boston: Little, Brown, 1958). Describes careers of American revivalists from Jonathan Edwards to Billy Graham.

WHITE, GILBERT F. (ed.), *Natural Hazards: Local, National, Global* (New York: Oxford University Press, 1974). Articles by geographers on various "adjustments to hazard" leading people to remain in disaster-prone areas.

WORSLEY, PETER, *The Trumphet Shall Sound: A Study of "Cargo Cults" in*

Melanasia (London: Paladin, 1970). Anthropologist's study of native millennarianism in the South Pacific.

ZURCHER, LOUIS A. JR. AND R. GEORGE KIRKPATRICK, *Citizens for Decency: Antipornography Crusades as Status Defense* (Austin: University of Texas Press, 1976). Study of antipornography campaigns in two American communities.

Name Index

Subject Index

Virginia, Presbyterian church officials in, 205, 207
Volcanic eruptions, in Washington, 42
Volunteers:
  in disaster, 52, 66*n*
  in riot control, 111

Waco, Texas, tornado in, 52, 56–58
Warning in disaster, *see* Threat
War:
  panic in, 25, 28
  and persecution, 144, 145
  as protest stage, 104, 105
  and renewals, 197
Wartburg Festival, 191
Washington, D.C.:
  protest riot, 107, 108, 111, 123*n*
  riot of 1919, 163
Welfare bureaucracy and protest, 90
West Indians in Britain, 140, 157

West Virginia, snake-handlers in, 209
White Citizens Councils, 160
Wichita, Kansas, farm protest, 214
Winston-Salem, North Carolina, protest riot in, 110
Wisconsin, support for McCarthy, 160
Witches, persecution of, 138, 143, 144, 147, 153, 154, 159, 161, 163, 165, 166, 171
Withdrawal behavior, 50
Women's liberation movement, 78, 117, 122*n*
Woodstock festival, 194
Worcester, Massachusetts, tornado in, 41, 48, 57

Youth revolt, *see* Student protests; New left
Yuba City, California, flood in, 59